Fenelon.

FÉNELON

HIS FRIENDS AND HIS ENEMIES

1651-1715

BY

E. K. SANDERS

Mais nous ne trouverons le divin dans les autres qu'en leur montrant d'abord le divin dans nous-mêmes.
—MAETERLINCK.

WITH PORTRAIT

WIPF & STOCK · Eugene, Oregon

Wipf and Stock Publishers
199 W 8th Ave, Suite 3
Eugene, OR 97401

Fénelon
His Friends and His Enemies, 1615-1715
By Sanders, E. K.
Softcover ISBN-13: 978-1-6667-8210-3
Hardcover ISBN-13: 978-1-6667-8211-0
eBook ISBN-13: 978-1-6667-8212-7
Publication date 6/1/2023
Previously published by Longmans, Green, and Co., 1901

This edition is a scanned facsimile of the original edition published in 1901.

CONTENTS

PART I

FÉNELON AND THE CONTROVERSIES OF THE CHURCH

CHAP.		PAGE
I.	THE EARLY YEARS OF FÉNELON	3
II.	LOUIS, DUKE OF BURGUNDY	39
III.	MADAME DE MAINTENON	64
IV.	MADAME GUYON	91
V.	THE QUIETISM CONTROVERSY	122
VI.	BOSSUET AND "TÉLÉMAQUE"	154
VII.	FÉNELON AND THE JANSENISTS	179

PART II

FÉNELON IN EXILE

I.	THE FAMILIAR FRIENDS OF FÉNELON	215
II.	FÉNELON THE POLITICIAN	249
III.	FROM CAMBRAI TO VERSAILLES	293
IV.	FÉNELON THE ARCHBISHOP	321
V.	THE SPIRITUAL LETTERS	352
VI.	THE LAST YEARS OF EXILE	381
	APPENDIX	411
	INDEX	421

PART I

FÉNELON AND THE CONTROVERSIES
OF THE CHURCH

CHAPTER I

THE EARLY YEARS OF FÉNELON

In this endeavour to portray the figure of François de Fénelon, Archbishop of Cambrai, it has been my desire to discover and set forth the truth, and not to shroud and overwhelm him with the glories of a perfection to which he did not attain. There is no dimness or uncertainty to obscure his reputation. His name occurs in less or greater prominence in most of the innumerable memoirs and correspondence of the period; but he attained to that unenviable pitch of eminence which makes a character a party question, and the testimonies regarding it are therefore curiously conflicting. It is certain that he was ambitious, but he lacked the cool and wary temper that secures fulfilment of ambition. He was headstrong, and his self-confidence lured him to inconsistency. He could be jealous also, and, even when the passage of the years had purified and tempered many weaknesses, a little spark of malice, lying far below the surface, woke into flame. But though these stains, and others such as these, lie marked and defined upon the pages of his record, it does not cease to be a fair one, and every stage in the advance to closer knowledge of him establishes the conviction of his abiding purity of faith and conduct with greater clearness.

In spite of the many splendid qualities of which his earlier years gave proof, he was marked by destiny as one of those who may not come to full development save through the fire of suffering and humiliation. Great as was his celebrity, he was—as far as his own advantage was concerned—perpetually unsuccessful, and only the strenuous vitality of his temperament could have supported him against the pressure of misfortune. The courage thus aroused was a greater acquisition than the glory of success. If Fénelon had been unharmed by royal prejudice and tyranny, and impervious to dexterous slander, he might take a more prominent place in the annals of his country; but he would have missed his hold on the countless troubled human beings whom loneliness and sorrow taught him to encourage and direct.

Considering the strength of his loyalty to the Roman Catholic Church, it is curious that he should ever have strayed upon the borderland of heresy; but heresy, nevertheless, was the plea for the banishment that ruined his temporal prospects and reversed all the conditions of his life, and it would be impossible for the most ingenious apologist to prove him innocent of the charges brought against him. He was accused of being a mystic, and though the term has been so much misused that its meaning is difficult of definition, it would seem to be a fair description of him. If Mysticism be the true name for a realisation of God as transfused throughout the universe, as inspiring the prayers that link men to Him, as being immanent, in short, in material things and in mankind alike, then not only was Fénelon a mystic, but he shared his belief with the writer of St. John's Gospel and Epistles, and with those who have meditated most deeply on the secrets of existence. "What is God?" said Seneca; "the sum total of all thou seest and all thou canst not see." For he spent his life in seeking God, although it was not given to him to know the manifestation of divinity which was the highest reality of Fénelon's religion; and the long succession of such seekers are not divided by the difference in their faith; their common need and common labour after truth is a stronger link than any dogma, and it may be that the brotherhood of mystics should stand first in the ranks of those who have sought to benefit mankind. It was, therefore, only because of the trend of thought in the age of Louis XIV. that the name of mystic became one of reproach, and quietists and mystics were united as the objects of suspicion and contumely.

Fourteen years before Fénelon came to Court, Michel de Molinos, an obscure Spanish priest, published a book of original meditations called "The Spiritual Guide," which acquired extraordinary celebrity in the Catholic world. He was encouraged at the Vatican, and made welcome by the Pope himself. For six years his teaching and example animated his hearers to an endeavour after purer living, and he diffused a new spirit of piety through the society of Rome. But he taught that a man may aspire to personal intercourse with his God without the intervention of a priest. Such a theory assailed the whole system of authority, and meant ruin to the Jesuits. It must be regarded as a marvel that they suffered him so long. Louis XIV. upheld the

Jesuits—the strange fanaticism which was a part of his complex personality had delivered him into their hands; he was, moreover, by instinct, the champion of authority in any form. By a curious paradox it became possible for him to challenge the conduct of the Pope in support of papal infallibility; he was a stronger man than Innocent XII., and therefore Molinos was discovered to be a heretic, a monster of impiety, worthy of the extreme penalties of the Inquisition. His books were burnt, and he disappeared for ever into the dungeons of the Vatican, leaving behind him a new weapon to lovers of intrigue.

He was not, in fact, a leader among mystics. Jacob Boehme, Francis de Sales, and Joseph Hall, had, each in his native land, thought and preached much the same doctrine, had caught a glimpse of the reality of God, and, losing himself in that infinite revelation, forgotten to allow for the limitations of his hearers, so that his speech was esteemed extravagant and even blasphemous; but it was reserved for Molinos to make Mysticism synonymous with heresy—a name of terrible import, hardly to be whispered with impunity.

Having compassed the fall of Molinos, Louis XIV. felt himself established as the watch-dog of the Church, the prop of despotism in general. From the Roman mystics he turned to his own offending subjects, and allowed the errors of the Huguenots to occupy him for many years. The suppression of heresy was an exercise of his authority which acted also as a salve to his conscience. He welcomed every opportunity of displaying his zeal for orthodoxy, and it was necessary for those who desired favour to exhibit a similar disposition. To this

THE EARLY YEARS OF FÉNELON

fact may be traced the persecution of Mme. Guyon and the disgrace of Fénelon. Mme. Guyon professed to have originated opinions resembling those of Molinos. She clung to them with great tenacity, and braved the fate they brought upon her; and there was much in her writings that Fénelon approved, although he admitted that some of her theories were questionable, and might be dangerous to the majority. When a general outcry was raised against her he refused to join in it, and remained silent when required to condemn her publicly. Such, in brief, was the history of their connection. His fortune had raised him high enough to be a mark for jealousy, for he was the friend and confidant of Mme. de Maintenon. It was a period of perpetual intrigue and treachery, in which there were no adepts equal to the priests. The fall of Molinos provided them with a convenient missile to which Fénelon laid himself open; a charge of mysticism was hard to define, but harder to refute. He struggled desperately against overwhelming force; but his adversaries, among whom the King himself is numbered, allowed other and less exalted considerations to reinforce religious zeal, and thus the ruin of his career and his many years of exile were due in great measure to the promptings of jealousy.

A history of the life of Fénelon is not in any sense a history of the crowded stirring times in which he lived. He had many great contemporaries who rose to high place and power, and left their mark on the history of France; but they all centred round the figure of the King, the light of their achievements shed fresh glory upon him, and contact with the curious grandeur of his personality inspired them to renewed effort for their own advancement and for his. The bond between Louis XIV. and his favoured servants was so close that all that affected him affected them, and therefore their welfare was bound up in that of the State, and their history is the history of the period.

Fénelon stands apart: not by virtue of his priesthood, for holy orders were often proved the surest ladder to eminence, but because his world was not the world which bowed before the greatness of King Louis. His influence was individual; he left but little mark upon his age; yet among all the brilliant figures grouped about the throne there are few who can still be credited with a hold upon the minds of men, and that honour may be claimed for Fénelon. Here and there at rare intervals in the history of the world a name stands out as separated from the ordinary honours that men covet, and yet endowed with a lustre which the lapse of time cannot tarnish. No light of favour or success shone upon Fénelon; he lived many years in disgrace and exile, and died unpardoned; yet his reputation has a glory that personal honours and prosperity could not have given it, for he sought the truth undaunted by many errors and much discouragement, and forced his personal ambitions to take a second place.

He was a loyal servant of the Roman Church, and religion was the reason of his being. This is the primary fact, without which all understanding of his character would be impossible; but his faith was Catholic in the purer sense, rising above the forms and symbols consecrated by tradition, and, as the years passed, his deepening

THE EARLY YEARS OF FÉNELON 9

sympathy for all sorts and conditions of mankind widened his tolerance and brought the spirit of charity into his religion.

He lived in days when men saw their lives vividly, and suffered no side of life to grow stagnant from want of notice. To the Court the discoveries of science, the fresh suggestions of philosophy, the strange new theories of religion, might be only so many topics for brilliant dialogue, occasions for display of keen wit and shrewd argument, and, therefore, opportunities to catch the notice of the King. But to the thinkers such things as these are vital, and difficulties that seem, in retrospect, to be only mists of delusion arising from overfertile imaginations, rose dense and thick enough to cloud the destiny of such a man as Fénelon.

He was born in 1651, when the wonderful reign of Louis XIV. was at its zenith. He was a younger son by a second marriage of a Gascon noble, de Salignac de la Mothe Fénelon, and therefore began the world with no prospects but those resulting from high and honourable lineage. As a child he was very delicate; but his unusual talents were recognised by his family, and his uncle, the Marquis de Fénelon, who had lost his own son, took François under his especial protection. The marquis was a man of very independent character, austere in the conduct of his private life, and of deeply religious bias. The society which he gathered around him at his apartment in the Abbaye St. Germain was representative of the purer and more thoughtful of the Court; Bossuet, Bishop of Meaux and tutor to the Dauphin, M. de Beauvilliers, the friend of Madame de Maintenon, and Fleury, as yet an obscure priest, were among his constant guests. Nature seemed to have designed François de Fénelon for a scholar, and, according to the custom of the time, he was destined for the priesthood before he had come to an age to make the selection for himself. M. de Fénelon sent him to the College of Saint-Sulpice, which was then under the direction of M. Tronson, and in so doing gave the pious inclination of his mind the very fullest opportunity of development.

It is idle to speculate on the possible results of different treatment in the formation of a character, yet Fénelon throughout his life looked back with gratitude on the influence of his early days. M. Tronson was a high type of the Roman priest and confessor; living in personal obscurity, not joining in the race for preferment, nor coveting any external recognition, he was, nevertheless, the possessor of the highest form of ecclesiastical power, and, from his position as Superior of Saint-Sulpice, the responsibility of directing the minds of many of the coming generation of priests rested upon his shoulders.

Amidst the contention of the Jesuits and the faction of Port Royal the congregation of Saint-Sulpice succeeded in maintaining peacefully a distinct character for piety and erudition, joined to a certain liberty of thought, which disposed its members to consider the opinions of others before absolutely condemning them. M. Olier, a man celebrated for his saintly life, was appointed to the parish of Saint-Sulpice in 1642, when it had obtained considerable notoriety as the most depraved quarter of Paris. His labours for the reforming of his flock were unremitting, and the young priests and clerks who were associated with him in his task formed the nucleus of the seminary and community of Saint-Sulpice. M. Olier believed himself to be miraculously commissioned to organise this institution, and it became the chief object of his life. The necessary building—a square edifice capable of receiving a hundred inmates—was completed in 1652, and enabled him to put his theories into practice.

They were based on his high ideal of the sacerdotal character: he would not admit any who embraced the sacred calling from considerations of ambition or expediency; he considered that the priesthood should mix with other men, that they might learn the conditions of life, and so be able to remedy the evils they observed; but in their period of training and probation he subjected them to as sharp a test as the noviciate of a strict community. Whatever their birth or condition, they were required to perform the menial duties of the house, and to live on terms of absolute equality. The complete immolation of self was to be the aim of those who desired the tonsure. He was an ascetic himself, and he encouraged the practices of self-mortification. The vices of the world were very obvious and very terrible; he turned from them to the most literal interpretation of the teaching of his Master. He urged his pupils to study the Gospels till they could bring the Divine Life before them at any moment in a series of mental pictures, to keep themselves in such a disposition that meditation on that Life would never demand a violent revulsion, whatever their outward circumstances might be.

All the ceremonial of the Church was observed with the most minute exactness; obedience was more essential in the ecclesiastical than in any secular profession, as a necessity for the upholding of the Church and as an exercise in humility, and for both reasons it was enforced by M. Olier. He aimed at perfection, and, regardless of the cost, he required his pupils to renounce whatever most attracted them in the world outside. In the blankness and silence that succeeds the struggle of renunciation they would find Christ coming to them, a Christ who had borne all, and understood all, whose Presence with them was more worth having than the prizes they had missed; this was his assurance, often repeated, and it would seem that members of the community did indeed learn to forget ambition, so long, at any rate, as they remained within the walls of Saint-Sulpice.

His ideas of intellectual training were not especially enlightened; the students learned theology, but no secular studies were required of them. M. Olier believed piety to be more essential to a good priest than deep learning, and did not recognise the possible combination of the two; "*scientia inflat*" was a favourite maxim with him. Nevertheless, the self-discipline he inculcated and observed is as great an aid to learning as to piety, and the College of Saint-Sulpice has produced many eminent scholars in defiance of the desires of its founder.

So great was the personal affection and loyalty which he won, that there was a danger of the collapse of the institution when he was removed from the care

THE EARLY YEARS OF FÉNELON

of it; but his belief in the Divine blessing upon it was justified by the chance which gave him M. Tronson as successor—a man not only learned in theology, but capable to an unusual degree of imparting knowledge; not only religious himself, but disposed to continue the traditions of Saint-Sulpice according to the rules laid down by M. Olier.

It was to the personal influence of M. Tronson, and to the scheme of probation conceived by M. Olier, that Fénelon owed his training, and, in some degree, the purity of motive and uncalculating self-surrender which characterised the teaching and practice of his after-life; but the value of the system depended on personal intercourse and that nice discrimination which can perceive the salient qualities of an undeveloped character and nourish them towards their richest growth, rather than to any tabulated system. M. Tronson appears to have been one of the few for whom the riches and pleasures of this life have no attraction; he regarded the world from a standpoint of indifference, and thus was supremely competent to inculcate the true sacerdotal sense of isolation, wherein is rooted so much of the power of the Roman priesthood.

François de Fénelon was a favourite with M. Tronson. He was very young when he entered Saint-Sulpice, but the charm of manner so universally recognised in him was his in childhood, and his natural disposition promised a future character which would do honour to those who helped in its formation. In later years he was not wanting in strength of will, but he gave himself up unreservedly to the direction of his Superior; he laid his heart bare before him, accepted his decisions as absolutely final, and was as completely dominated for the time as any pupil of the Jesuits. He seems, indeed, to have revelled in the insidious joy of a confidence which claimed and received the perfection of sympathy.

"I desire passionately," he wrote to his uncle in a burst of gratitude, "to be able to tell you now some part of all that passes between M. Tronson and me, but, indeed, Monsieur, I know not how to do so."[1]

Undoubtedly in those early years he did make M. Tronson the keeper of his conscience. He merged his will completely in that of the Superior, and had no desire for freedom; but his native force of character was strong enough to survive the enervating effect of such conditions.

He was twenty-four when he received the tonsure, and for three years longer he worked as one of the community of priests of the parish of Saint-Sulpice, living still at the seminary, and labouring to spread the light of his own faith among the poor wherever he could reach them best, whether in prison, in the hospitals, or in their own quarters. Such an experience enlarged his sympathies and deepened his view of life at the outset of his career. It brought him also into touch with children, and taught him primary principles of training which applied to them in all ranks; no doubt the knowledge of them which was afterwards so valuable to him when the King's unruly grandsons were entrusted to his care was acquired among the ragged

[1] *Correspondance de Fénelon*, ii. 1.

THE EARLY YEARS OF FÉNELON

and hungry children of Saint-Sulpice. He had no vision then of future honours; he was content with present and obvious usefulness, serving God in the full conviction that he had chosen the only worthy service, finding courage and inspiration in forms of worship which to many were but empty ceremonial, and endeavouring to bring others to a knowledge and a share of his own happiness. The influence and example of M. Tronson were still near to him; and though he cannot have been unconscious of his own endowments, and life was only beginning, he was at that time ready to accept a humble lot, with no scope for ambitious dreams, upheld by the conviction that a life of devotion was sufficient to satisfy every craving of his heart.

But the King, in his many differing characters, had need of every order and degree of servant, and Fénelon's place was waiting for him. The clamour of the Court was but a distant murmur to the young priest at Saint-Sulpice, interesting in that it concerned a few to whom he was bound by ties of blood and affection, but of no personal import. It was a powerful factor in Louis's greatness that he could discern and utilise the qualities he needed even when their possessors did not seek his notice. He was bigoted in religious matters despite the vague morality which distinguished his personal conduct; and he is supposed to have believed that the forcible conversion of his heretic subjects would condone his private offences. The brilliant successes of his youth had made victory appear his natural heritage; no subsequent failure had power to disturb the impression, and he included the souls as well as the bodies of his subjects within the limits of his absolute sovereignty. The instincts of bigotry and despotism combined to inspire his treatment of the Huguenots; he was shrewd enough to know that persecution was impolitic; he must have foreseen some, at least, of the disastrous results of the revocation of the Edict of Nantes, and only his belief that he could thus cancel a record which disquieted his conscience, explains his conduct. But though he did not spare the heretics, and their blood was shed freely to buy him immunity from future punishment, if he could win them to the Church of Rome by gentler means, he was disposed to do so. For this purpose he encouraged and supported an institution known as the Nouvelles Catholiques, which had been founded early in his reign by De Gondi, the first Archbishop of Paris. Its object was the instruction and confirmation of ladies who were inclined towards the Roman faith; it was conducted by a community who did the work of sisters of charity outside its walls, and presided over by a priest selected by the Archbishop of Paris.

When Fénelon was working at Saint-Sulpice the Nouvelles Catholiques was prominent in the public notice; Turenne, lately a convert from Calvinism, gave largely to it, and the King, being much occupied with the souls of his subjects, spared it a share of his attention. It chanced that the post of Principal became vacant, and between the King and the Archbishop the choice fell on Fénelon. It was a form of missionary labour, and for this he had a natural inclination. Earlier in his life he had had dreams of a mission to the Greeks, dreams which his delicate health had completely broken;

but a desire to prove that heresy might be uprooted by gentle means had always remained with him. His new post could not appeal to his ascetic instincts, or touch his imagination as the eastern mission had done; it offered no delights of privation borne and danger braved in the name of Christ; but it seemed that for which Nature had especially fitted him, and life opened before him with countless opportunities of influence.

He was twenty-seven at this time. The habit of self-repression and sympathy for others had deepened his natural charm of manner; his intellectual powers claimed the interest of the more thoughtful; while his high birth and the outward graces with which he was endowed made his presence welcome to the frivolous majority of men. Society lay open to him in its most brilliant and seductive form, and according to the custom of the time his priest's orders were no bar to the fullest enjoyment of it; many a handsome abbé might be found among the pleasure-seekers of Versailles, sharpening his wit on any subject that came uppermost, without a scruple as to his sacred calling to hamper his weapon in the war of words. Society as it existed under the rule of Louis XIV. was generally acknowledged to be the most advantageous training-school for future cardinals and dignitaries of the Church; to obtain the favour of the King was to open the way to every goal of man's desire, and the King favoured none who did not add to the brilliant reputation of his Court. Therefore the most attractive path was that which led directly to future opportunity of influence, and thus might plausibly be justified. But M. Tronson had done his work thoroughly, and in defiance of custom and self-interest Fénelon held his priesthood sacred, and his contact with the world never brought it to dishonour.

When he left Saint-Sulpice he took up his abode with his uncle at St. Germain des Prés, and was thus brought into intimacy with the distinguished circle of friends whom M. de Fénelon had gathered round him. Foremost among these stood Bossuet, Bishop of Meaux, and the friendship between Bossuet and Fénelon, celebrated in its sequel and important in the lives of both, grew rapidly from their first introduction. Bossuet was the greatest of contemporary ecclesiastics; as a theologian he had no rival, and his eloquence equalled his learning. The notice of a man of such reputation was a high compliment to a young abbé; the bishop's fame as a scholar appealed to Fénelon's intellectual instincts, and he found additional attraction in the austere and spotless personal conduct which made Bossuet one of the rare examples of virtue in the high places of the Church. Fénelon accorded him a reverence approaching to devotion in those early days, and Bossuet responded with proofs, constantly renewed, of the pleasure he derived from the young priest's society. It was his custom to retire to his country house at Germigny when he required rest from a life of constant labour, and at these times he claimed a right to solitude; but at an early stage of their friendship he made Fénelon welcome to his retreat, and in the ease of familiar intercourse there their intimacy had the fullest opportunity of ripening. Fénelon was well able to appreciate the privilege of conversation with his host. Bossuet had a fund of learning which was

THE EARLY YEARS OF FÉNELON 19

inexhaustible, and to listen to him was to receive the fruit of a powerful brain long concentrated in thought on the most important of all subjects, thought which was often original, and therefore of immeasurably greater value than the close-packed information of the schoolman. He was, in fact, in advance of his profession and his generation in liberality of view. After the intense and watchful solicitude of M. Tronson, Fénelon's mind required bracing, and intercourse with such a man as Bossuet made it necessary for him to think for himself, to strain to keep in touch with an intellect far more developed than his own, to sound the depth of his own powers as he realised the greatness of his friend. Bossuet, on his part, must have valued Fénelon; but he owed nothing to him,—the influence and advantage were all on the side of the younger of the pair, and no subsequent contention or ill-treatment could obliterate the debt that was thus incurred.

In sharp contrast to Bossuet, both in the popular esteem and in Fénelon's regard, stood de Harlai, Archbishop of Paris. A courtier and a man of the world, skilled in all graceful accomplishments, and as careless of morality as the King himself, he was, from the point of view of expediency, not ill-suited to his post, for he was a diplomatist, a good administrator, and possessed of the keen insight into character which is the most valuable attribute for a ruler. Having brought Fénelon from obscurity within range of the public notice, he was disposed to raise him further, for he detected the capabilities of his protégé and the credit he might reflect upon his patron, and seems also to have been personally attracted by him. But Fénelon's tolerance, so wide towards heretics, was not extended to de Harlai; the archbishop's loyalty to the Church was not sufficient screen for his notorious life in the eyes of the young priest, and no consideration of expediency could induce him to pay his court to his superior. Consequently de Harlai's early liking changed ere long to pronounced enmity. "You desire to be forgotten, and you will be, M. l'Abbé!" was his greeting when Fénelon did present himself at one of his receptions, and his animosity increased as the friendship between Bossuet and Fénelon became recognised and established. Bossuet was his rival in the favour of the King, though the Bishop of Meaux made his way at Court by very different means, and maintained his sturdy independence even in that atmosphere of flattery.

Probably the influence of de Harlai was a disadvantage to Fénelon, for his age was no bar to preferment for which his rank and recognised abilities gave him a claim, and which the King, on more than one occasion, is supposed to have wished to offer him, had it not been for the influence of the archbishop. But Fénelon's happiness did not depend upon preferment. The ten years during which he held his post at the Nouvelles Catholiques were probably the sunniest of his life; he was discovering the infinite possibilities of his own powers; there might be infinite opportunities awaiting him in the future, and, meanwhile, his way lay clear before him. M. Tronson was near at hand to point him to ever fresh aspirations; Bossuet to direct him towards deeper study; he had work for which he was fully competent, and an ever-widening circle of friends outside his recognised

THE EARLY YEARS OF FÉNELON

work who looked to him as an influence for good. Under such conditions he could afford to be independent of the machinations of the archbishop.

The spirit of controversy was in the air. In 1685 the King revoked the Edict of Nantes, and set himself to stamp out heresy. Proselytising was, for the moment, the work most applauded by the popular voice, and Fénelon was thus brought into a prominent position. The validity of orders in the Huguenot ministry was naturally a matter of deep importance to the Huguenot faction, even to such as had been converted to the Roman faith. Fénelon had strong convictions on the subject, and the treatise[1] in which he embodied them established his reputation as a writer and attracted the notice of the King.

The point of this essay may be rendered briefly thus: "The majority of Christian people being unable severally and individually to decide for themselves amid the intricacies of dogma, the Divine Wisdom had provided them with the means of preservation from error in an external authority—that possessed by a priesthood succeeding directly and in unbroken line from the Apostles of Jesus Christ." Taking his stand on this assertion, he repudiated the authority claimed by the pastors of the reformed faith by virtue of their election by their flock. He is unflinching in his claim on apostolic succession; to him the Divine Grace communicated in the sacrament of ordination was a fact above the reach of argument, a part of the faith which was the reason of his being. But, strong and deeply rooted as were his convictions on

[1] *Traité du Ministère des Pasteurs*, printed 1688.

the subject, his treatise is free from that harshness of expression which it was the custom to accord to heresy in any form. For himself, he esteemed his consecration to the Church the highest privilege conceivable: it was the foundation of his life, his shield against all temptation to personal indulgence, as dear to him as his faith, because inseparable from it; and it was with an honest desire to convince others of their errors and admit them to a share of his own happiness that he employed his keenest powers of argument and logic against "a vain philosophy that would bring natural things to bear on that which is in its essence supernatural."

The effect of his endeavour upon convinced Protestants is not recorded; but it made an impression on the King, as testifying to a sincere desire for their conversion, and soon after its appearance he was entrusted with the control of the mission to the heretics of Poitou and Saintonge. The King was eager for a plentiful harvest of conversion; the Edict of Nantes having been revoked, and the welfare of his realm thereby imperilled, he desired certain and immediate results to compensate for future possibilities of loss. Moreover, by depriving so many of his subjects of their chosen pastors, he bound himself to provide for their direction, and, according to his lights, he was fulfilling his responsibility towards them when he sent them Fénelon.

The animosity between Catholic and Huguenot had never really lessened, and the baser of the Catholic faction had realised that the surest means of destroying their adversaries was to lure them on to break the peace. The Reformers of Vivarais were the first victims to such machinations. In 1683 they took up arms against the Catholics, and shortly afterwards there was a similar tumult in Dauphiné. Taken in conjunction, it was easy to magnify the tidings into a report of concerted insurrection. It was a part of the policy of government adopted by Louis XIV. to keep troops continually on the march through the provinces, ready to quell sedition wherever it might arise, and towards the Reformers he was only awaiting a pretext for severity—their need of suppression seemed to him even more urgent than for enlightenment. It is recorded of Mme. de Maintenon that at this crisis she fanned the flame of his intolerance. It is the gravest charge that is brought against her, and it is certain that if it was so her influence was seconded by all the power of party spite and Court intrigue. But it was a flame that needed no stirring from without; had the King been left unsupported in his resolution, the natural bias of his mind towards tyranny was sufficient to fix it, and, as soon as the recklessness of the Reformers gave him an excuse for persecution, their fate was sealed.

It is evident that the conversion of the Huguenots was ardently desired by Fénelon; but in the quiet years of his labour at the Nouvelles Catholiques he had too little influence in the world of active life to incur any responsibility for the suffering inflicted on them; and if in his retirement he had any detailed knowledge of the conflict, he must have deplored the means employed to attain the end he coveted, and admired the courage and resolution they displayed. But the highest courage is of no permanent service against overwhelming numbers; the resistance of the Reformers only aggravated the King's animosity and pitiless severity towards them. It is difficult for his warmest advocates to defend his proceedings, and Fénelon, not being among the number of his blind admirers, would have accepted his post less readily had he been cognisant of the crimes perpetrated in the King's name before he visited Poitou, and even when he arrived upon the scene it is possible that much was concealed from him. No honourable man could condone the treachery resorted to in dealing with the Huguenots, and it is difficult to understand what object, beyond the infliction of additional torture, can have been served thereby. Amnesties which excluded all whom they appeared to benefit, and general pardons which only revealed on the closest scrutiny that their conditions made them useless to the guilty, were constructed with all the ingenuity usually attributed to the Jesuits; prisoners accused of heresy were nominally granted trials, but practically they were condemned and sentenced before their defence was heard. The dragoons under the Duc de Noailles were quartered in the offending provinces, and their cruelty towards their victims is too hideous to bear recording.

Undoubtedly the King may be held responsible for the conduct of his representatives. He knew what was to be expected from his soldiery, and that they would have free licence; and if he was ignorant of the details of their behaviour at the time, he must have had knowledge of it afterwards, and he never censured it. There would have been sufficient reason had his repose been haunted by the cries of the victims of his fanaticism, as was the fate of Charles IX., but no such weakness ever disturbed the dignified composure of the great monarch. Nothing in his after-life testifies even to regret for his conduct at this time; he was acting in the name of the Church, and he was incurring an almost certain loss to the commercial prosperity of his kingdom, without any corresponding advantage, either personal or political. The position is a curious one: for the Church whose name he used to shield his tyranny was the Church to which Fénelon was loyal, and Fénelon was an ardent lover of justice and of peace; moreover, the end he sought to attain by a succession of barbarous crimes was not less dear to Fénelon. Both alike seem to have believed sincerely that death would deliver the Reformers to endless torment, and consequently that their conversion was the greatest benefit they could receive; but their resistance aroused a tyrannous instinct in Louis's nature, in which Fénelon could have no part, and therefore the King was ready to adopt expedients which to the priest would have seemed unavailing.

The dragoons did all that terror could do, and a system of bribery, by which a fixed sum was paid to every convert, appealed to the cupidity of a few; but the majority remained staunch to a faith that was stronger in its influence than either fear or greed, and having proved by bitter experience that justice and mercy were denied them in their native land, numbers of them fled to England and the Netherlands, and thus France was deprived of many of her worthiest subjects.

Fénelon left no record of his impressions when he reached Poitou; but he must have felt the inconsistency

of employing torture or bribery in the name of the
Church of Christ, for he refused to admit the dragoons
as fellow-workers, and he insisted on their withdrawal
from every place under his jurisdiction. Some stories of
their cruelty must have come to his knowledge; but being
once installed as the King's representative, he could do
better service to the sufferers by checking further persecution than by raising an outcry which would have had
no effect against the royal mandate. Moreover, Louis
was a despot. His servants accepted his commands:
secretly they might disapprove, but publicly they did
not question them; and Fénelon was still young, and had
been reared in the habit of obedience. It is only by in-
ference that we can arrive at any idea of his opinion.
He changed the whole system that he found when he
was installed at Poitou, and from thence it may be
deduced that he disapproved of it, though he made no
public comment. Gentleness and patient argument were
his weapons against a people whose opinions he condemned as heartily as did the King himself, but whose
conversion he esteemed as valueless when induced by
fear and not by reason, in opposition to the general
opinion that the most abominable persecution was justified if the dying heretic could be coerced into acknowledging his errors.

It was his first appointment to a position of
authority. He had been at the Nouvelles Catholiques
for seven years, and in the constant society of men
whom he regarded as greatly his superiors in piety and
learning, a condition not conducive to self-assertion;
and in the position in which he found himself it would

have been easiest to follow the course sanctioned by the Church and the King, and in the blind obedience that was often the result of priestly training, forget the dictates of humanity. But on this occasion Fénelon gave the first public proof of that independent strength of character which was destined to ruin his worldly prospects, and his missionary labours were carried out on the system which his reason and his conscience recommended. With those who gauged the success of a mission by statistics he can have found no favour, and he was keen enough to see the emptiness of much of the work that had been done. After six months of experience he gave some account of his work in a private letter written from Saintonge. "It would be easy enough to prevail on our sailors in their present condition to confess and communicate if—for the glory of our mission—we chose to do so" is one of his observations; but the Church's privileges seemed to him too precious to be thus pressed on unwilling recipients. "Of what avail is confession to those who do not acknowledge the true Church, nor her power to forgive sin?" That was a question that troubled him when he heard tidings of forced submission; for his own part, he "feared to bring a curse upon himself by hasty work that will not last."

It is strange, in view of his former dealings with the heretics, that Louis should have chosen Fénelon for the work: he was not yet developed, and the King may have formed a mistaken estimate; but there were many who would readily have filled the post who might have been relied on to maintain the system favoured by their royal master. There was no room in Fénelon's heart for sympathy with the spirit of the Inquisition, and though his tolerance was in this instance a matter of practice rather than principle—for he was bigoted in his hatred of the Huguenot errors—it was none the less a weapon made ready for the use of his future enemies. Doubtless he shrank from the infliction of needless suffering, but he shrank still more from the sacrilege of using force to win men to the Church, or bribery to induce them to accept its privileges. His view was calmer and at the same time deeper than that of his contemporaries; in those days of tyranny and persecution he kept the real end before him, and formed his judgment of a method by the permanence of its result.

Five years later M. de Noailles wrote to him for his opinion on the treatment of heretic mercenaries. He had then been in touch with the Court for a considerable time, had felt the King's pervading influence, and realised the strength of his desire to root out heresy wherever it should spring up, at whatever cost; yet he replies from the standpoint of a sincere and thoughtful man, unprejudiced by controversy. "It does not seem to me desirable," he said, "to torment foreign heretic soldiers with efforts to convert them; it does not succeed; it forces them into hypocrisy instead, and they desert in shoals. It is enough to forbid them the public exercise of their religion as the King desires."[1] In a case of illness he considered further effort admissible; but he was invariable in his conviction that

---

[1] *Correspondance de Fénelon*, ii. 5, July 1684.

THE EARLY YEARS OF FÉNELON

admission to the Catholic Church should be regarded as a privilege, and that all converts must so regard it before they could be made welcome by her ministers.

At the time of the most strenuous persecution the priests were in the habit of forcing themselves into the presence of the dying, expelling those who had the strongest claim to tend them, and making their last moments terrible by the vilest threats. Fénelon believed with them that a Huguenot who was deaf to argument forfeited his chance of salvation, but such a condition filled him with pity, and while reason remained he did not lose hope; if his fellow-priests were dishonouring the very name of their religion, it was given to him sometimes to strike the true note of Christianity. If the dying relented as their breath was failing, he had words ready, words, of humble confession of error and trust in the mercy of God: "Thou knowest, my Saviour, that I desire to live and die in the truth. Forgive me if I was mistaken."[1] Such was the conclusion of the prayer which he had written for those whose conversion came at the eleventh hour, and in the tenderness of thought lies the secret of his influence among them. It is not wonderful that he was censured by those who approved the other method, or that many a convinced and resolute heretic confessed to loving him. He put his heart into the work and spared no pains, but he was exiled from those to whom he looked for help and inspiration, and he had no love for the life of the country; he regretted the quiet of his former post, with its larger opportunities for study and reflection,

[1] *Correspondance de Fénelon*, iii. Appendix, p. 4.

and longed for the time when he should be free to return to Paris. In a letter to Bossuet he threatens gaily to bring suspicion of heresy upon himself to give an excuse for his recall; and the hint was not wasted, for the King, probably at the suggestion of the bishop, summoned him back to his post at the Nouvelles Catholiques.

Bossuet had made the young priest's fortunes his especial care. He had obtained his appointment to the southern mission, and intended that it should bear fruit in bringing him into personal intercourse with the King, whose eagerness concerning heresy was too great to be satisfied with a report at second-hand. Fénelon had everything to gain by an interview; the King was notably susceptible to outward impression, and the appearance and bearing of the young abbé were in his favour; moreover, he could tell his tale smoothly and well, with no misgivings as to its effect upon his listener, and afterwards be well content to retire to the routine of a life from which he had been summoned by the call of duty rather than ambition.

When he left the southern provinces he recommended that those who were to carry on his work should be chosen from among the Jesuits, a matter worthy of notice, because even at this early period it shows the bias of his opinion to have been in their favour and against the Jansenists, a sect which would indeed have welcomed him, but against which he had a violent prejudice throughout his life. This was the end of his controversial work among the Huguenots: it was work for which, according to the popular belief, there was the utmost need, and it had brought him into notice; the envious might cavil at his methods, but the general impression of the results obtained was good. If his moderation and humanity, in an age when such qualities were not esteemed, were remembered against him when other clouds were gathering, and contributed to his ultimate ruin, they add no less grace to the record of his life, and must have deepened his influence with those whose eyes were undimmed by prejudice and bigotry.

He returned thankfully to his work at the Nouvelles Catholiques and the friends whose intercourse was his keenest earthly interest and enjoyment. He was beginning to realise that his pen was a tool that might work great results; the path of learning and research stretched before him. He had been taught that the highest blessings were found more readily by those who lived retired from the world, and he accepted such a condition; but those who knew him best, and regarded the progress of the nation, knew that the world had need of him, the more because he was independent of its opinion.

Bossuet's interest was ranged against de Harlai; but Bossuet was not so apt a courtier, and the weight of his reputation might never have outweighed the power of the archbishop's flattery. It was due to lay influence that the King's favour was once more directed towards Fénelon.

Among his closest friends were the families of de Chevreuse and de Beauvilliers. The duchesses were sisters, daughters of the famous Colbert, and were linked by the strongest bonds of sympathy and affection; at Court they had attained a reputation for extreme piety and purity of life; to be admitted to their intimate society was a hall-mark of honourable living, and Mme. de Maintenon was their frequent guest. It was to assist Mme. de Beauvilliers in the instruction of her eight daughters that Fénelon wrote his treatise, *De l'Education des Filles*, which, when it was made public, greatly increased his literary reputation. It is a proof, not only of the versatility of his powers, but of his sympathy and faculty of intuition, that a court-lady (herself risen from an obscure family, and therefore the more likely to be worldly in her ambitions), should have turned to him for help in such a matter. He had been dedicated from childhood to his sacred calling, shut off from any experience of some of the strongest of life's influences, and therefore would not seem likely to prove an apt adviser; but those who loved Fénelon the most believed that he possessed the secret of the truest wisdom, that what he taught was drawn from too high a source to be affected by the limitations of personal experience. Throughout his life it was the power of sympathy, of entering into the difficulties of others, of realising temptations that can never have been present with him, that made his influence so comprehensive, a power rarer and more marvellous than the greatest of intellectual gifts.

His intimacy with M. de Beauvilliers began when he was a pupil at Saint-Sulpice, and after his appointment to the Nouvelles Catholiques he became his confessor; their mutual trust and friendship was therefore of long standing, and M. de Beauvilliers was as eager for Fénelon's advancement as Bossuet himself. When the King was forming the household for his grandsons, the Duke of Burgundy and his brothers, he selected M. de Beauvilliers

THE EARLY YEARS OF FÉNELON

as governor, and no sooner was the appointment confirmed than the new-made governor recommended Fénelon to the notice of the King as tutor to the princes.

The post was one much coveted; he who held it was in perpetual prominence at Court, and might prepare his way to almost any goal. At the moment when it was assigned to him Fénelon was very popular. His position at the Nouvelles Catholiques had left him leisure for other duties, and his reputation for purity of life and rigorous self-denial had struck the imagination, perhaps had touched the conscience, of many among the courtiers, both men and women, so that they turned to him when any sudden influence revealed to them the emptiness of perpetual frivolity, and dissipation—even if innocent—grew loathsome. If he had leisure, his help was always at the service of those who craved it; but he knew that the penitence revealed to him was often but a transitory sensation, an interlude amid excitements of another type, and, accordingly, was severe in his requirements, and would not accept the easy methods of the confessors who suited themselves to the spirit of the Court. His influence was definite and recognised; there was a charm about his quiet independence, and those who eschewed all clerical authority deferred to him; but when he accepted his new appointment he abandoned all other offices, that he might concentrate all his power of insight and reflection on the character and welfare of the princes.

In former years the King had selected Bossuet as tutor to the Dauphin, and Bossuet had taken the gravest view of the responsibility of the position; in the hours of friendly intercourse at Germigny he must have often referred to that period, although neither could have foreseen that a similar task awaited Fénelon. It was not a post to be refused, for it represented a possibility of limitless influence for good, and it was one of the strongest principles of M. Tronson's teaching that all the affairs of life were subject to and directed by the will of God, not nominally, but in absolute reality. With Fénelon principle and practice were consistent; he had many gifts which fitted him to train the future King, and when he undertook the charge, he did so in the belief that it was given him by a higher Authority than King Louis. It seemed to be the crisis of his fortunes: the world was smiling on him and setting its best gifts within his reach, so that the way of duty was made smooth; yet the smoothest way was one which he felt he must tread only with apprehension and misgiving—the way of the Cross is not that of success and gratified ambition, and it is likely that his heart had room for much regret when he exchanged the quiet of the Nouvelles Catholiques for the glories of Versailles. Misgiving was also the paramount sensation which the news of his advancement awakened in the breast of M. Tronson. There were friends in plenty eager to shower congratulations on him till he was almost overwhelmed by the warmth of their enthusiasm; but it required the confidence of a love stronger than ordinary friendship to strike the note of warning among the general acclamations. To the end of his life, in spite of the clouds that came between them at a later time, Fénelon attributed all that was best in himself to M. Tronson. The strength and extent of the influence is almost impossible to gauge; but at this point M. Tronson's warning admits us for a moment to their intimacy, and reveals in the older man a love pure enough to disregard the worldly advantage of its object. There can be no question that M. Tronson is the most important figure of those surrounding Fénelon in early life, and in the following letter he gives in his own words some glimpse of himself and his relations to his former pupil:—

"SAINT-SULPICE, *August* 1689.

" Perhaps you have been surprised, Monsieur, to miss me from the crowd of those who congratulate you on the honour his Majesty has just done you; but I humbly request that you will not be offended at this brief delay. I thought that, in a matter which concerns me so deeply, I could not but begin by praising God for His care of you, and asking Him to continue His mercies towards you. I have tried to do both as little unworthily as I might. And I can now assure you of the real joy it gave me to hear you had been chosen.

" In this selection the King gives fresh and reassuring evidence of his piety and discrimination. His Majesty has given you the charge of an education which is so important to the welfare of the State and the good of the Church, that if one is a Frenchman and a Christian one must rejoice to see it in good hands.

" But I candidly acknowledge that there is much apprehension mingled with my pleasure in view of the dangers to which you are exposed; because it cannot be denied that, in the natural course of events, promotion makes the way of salvation harder; it opens the door to the prizes of the world, but beware lest it close it on the enduring gains of Heaven. Doubtless you can do great good in your new post, but you may also be guilty of much evil: there is no medium under such conditions; success or failure will have incalculable consequences. You are in a land where the Gospel of Jesus Christ is little known, where those who know it make use of it for personal advancement. You now live among people whose conversation is practically pagan, whose example tends to dangerous things. You will find yourself surrounded by everything calculated to indulge the senses and awaken dormant passions: it will require great grace and great faith to withstand such impressions. The dust of evil which prevails at Court is enough to cloud the clearest and most obvious convictions. A very short time suffices to make familiar maxims seem exaggerated, however confident of them you might be when you thought of them at the foot of the Cross—to make the most evident obligations doubtful or impracticable; a thousand occasions will arise when even prudence or charity seem to bid you go with the stream. But it is a strange condition for a Christian—especially for a priest—to be bound to make terms with the devil. In truth, Monsieur, yours is a dangerous position; it must be candidly acknowledged that it will be difficult to remain steadfast in it, that you will need the highest principles to sustain you.

"If ever you needed study and meditation on the Bible, it is now; until now you have looked to it to strengthen you with the Truth, and inspire you with good thoughts, now you will need it to banish evil ones and shield you from lies.

"Above all else think constantly of death, when all the glory of the world must vanish like a dream, when everything you cherish slips away. Doubtless your friends will reassure you on the plea that you did not seek this post, and that is a support and one of God's mercies to you. But you must not hold to it too much; one is more responsible than appears: it is not often that elevation is sincerely shunned and feared; it is rare to find any one who has reached that degree of regeneration. There are some who make no effort for advancement, but nevertheless remove such obstacles as might hinder it. They do not curry favour with the influential, but they are not adverse to making the best impression; it is the little human self-revelations that often win advancement, and thus no man may feel that he had no part in his own promotion. Exhibitions of wit, though they may be almost unconscious, are to be shunned; it is better to crush them beneath contrition and humility of heart.

"You will perhaps esteem my letter somewhat over free and over long; it may seem a misplaced sermon rather than an apt congratulation. I should be more brief and less outspoken if I were not so eager for your welfare. If there be anything in my letter less respectful than is fitting, refer it to the fulness of a heart deeply stirred for your true interests. After so many finished compliments as you will have received, you have enough to counterbalance my plain-speaking."[1]

The warning was scarcely needed, for the attractions of that brilliant world did not dazzle Fénelon; but assuredly

[1] *Correspondance de Fénelon*, ii. 9.

it was not resented, and may have set him on his guard against some of the spiritual perils which haunted the imagination of the writer. To M. Tronson Versailles appeared as a battlefield from which the best-equipped of warriors could hardly hope to escape unharmed. But the dangers which awaited Fénelon at Court were of a different nature from those his old director pictured; his new office proved the ruin instead of the foundation of his fortunes, and there was deeper reason than he knew for M. Tronson's warning—written at a moment when all the world was greeting him with half-envious applause —"In truth, Monsieur, yours is a dangerous position!"

CHAPTER II

LOUIS, DUKE OF BURGUNDY

FÉNELON'S pupil, who now became the absorbing interest of his life, was a child of a most remarkable type. His father—the Dauphin—was slow and phlegmatic, weak of will and purpose, in every detail a contrast to the King; but the younger Louis promised a reproduction of some of the royal qualities. He was precocious from his cradle, and at seven years old—the age he had reached when Fénelon undertook his new office—he was pronounced by his governors to be utterly unmanageable. His royal birth and the prospect of his magnificent inheritance loomed so large in his outlook upon life that every claim of deference and obedience was dwarfed by the consciousness of his own importance; he made no effort to govern his passionate temper, and when crossed would rage like a wild beast.

"He was so impetuous as to desire to break the clocks when they struck the hour summoning him to do something he did not like, and fell into the most extraordinary fury against the rain when it interfered with his desires. Opposition threw him into a passion, as I have often been a witness in his early childhood." This is the testimony of Saint-Simon—not the most veracious of chroniclers, but one who possessed the faculty of grasping the salient features of a character and conveying an impression which is vivid, even if it be exaggerated.

The prince's intellectual faculties were as strongly developed as his faults, but his keen wit and quickness of understanding increased the apprehensions of those who watched his infancy and attempted to forecast a manhood so momentous to the fate of France. An influence such as Fénelon's was sorely needed, and he devoted himself entirely to the task of controlling his turbulent charge.

The first results of his efforts were evident in a few weeks. The personal charm that gave him so close a hold on the hearts and minds of all with whom he came in contact was not lost on Louis, and he yielded to influence when he would have rebelled at discipline. Hitherto he had been absorbed in himself as the future King of France, the principal object of thought in the minds of those about him—a personage whose whims and fancies must be treated with consideration; but now he met with one who was no king, nor held any prospect of kingship, who had no wealth, neither military or political reputation, but who, nevertheless, was so incontestably above himself, that the glories of his royalty seemed to fade before his puzzled vision, and he was forced to recognise that life held higher things than the grandeur of his future heritage.

Fénelon understood the extreme difficulty of the task he had undertaken, and he threw himself into it unreservedly. His letters testify that he adhered punctiliously to his duty to the prince at the risk of offending his closest friends, and at first he would permit himself no distractions, for his method was one of constant individual attention. It was, indeed, necessary that he should acquire the most intimate knowledge of the character on which he had to work, which, though the child was only seven, absorbed all his powers of sympathy and intuition, for the gravity of the prince's faults demanded correction, which his position rendered difficult. Fénelon was rewarded by winning the love and confidence, without which all his efforts would have been useless, and thus gave the strongest proof of the wisdom of his methods. When Louis yielded to the transports of passion that had darkened his infancy, his attendants were bidden to serve him in absolute silence, to ignore him entirely, or listen to him with the pitying deference accorded to the raving of delirium. Such a course was the destruction of his self-complacency; he ceased to find relief in swearing when his hearers ceased to be disconcerted by his abuse, and, being left to reflect on the situation in solitude, he saw himself for the first time as others saw him. Fénelon had studied childhood, and knew how deeply rooted is a child's fear of ridicule; in the prince it was exaggerated by his abnormal vanity, and a system which showed him how he degraded himself and lost all shadow of dignity when he lost self-control was the surest to produce a radical reform. The fables Fénelon wrote for his pupil are a further development of the same plan; they are almost all personal, the identity of the hero being very thinly veiled, and their chief point the contrast between what he might have been and what he was. In spite of their graces of expression and fancy, they can hardly have been pleasant reading to the little prince; but their author had won his heart, and thenceforth might mould him as he would.

There are still two pledges of his childish repentance in existence, testifying to the difficulty with which his faults were conquered.

"I promise, on my word as a prince, to M. l'Abbé de Fénelon, to do what he tells me immediately, and to obey him directly he forbids me to do anything; and if I break it I accept any kind of punishment and disgrace. Delivered at Versailles, November 29, 1689. Signed, LOUIS."

This promise, in spite of the word of a prince, was probably broken, for many months later he enters on another engagement, pathetic in its brevity.

"Louis, who promises afresh to keep my promise better. This 20th of September. I beseech M. de Fénelon to take it again."

Even at this later time he was but eight years old, and already the shadow of exaggerated gravity was upon him. Probably his serious responsibility towards a child who would be the future king influenced Fénelon, and he cannot have foreseen the disposition towards melancholy that became the failing of his later life. The child loved him passionately (he was intense in all things, a characteristic which was the cause of suffering all his life, and especially while the evil inclinations of his early years were still unconquered), and when the spell of Fénelon's personality fell on him, changing him almost magically, the new self came into violent conflict with the curiously precocious depravity of the old, and years which should be peaceful were passed by him in a series of desperate struggles. Such a result was inevitable. Fénelon ruled his own actions on a system of self-sacrificing piety which was the practical expression of his teaching; it was his deliberate opinion that a law of self-denial and self-restraint is the best law for a man's life, that in obedience to it—and by no other method—a man may learn to imitate his Master, and so fulfil the purpose for which his life was given him. He believed that such a doctrine was the best for all alike, and he impressed it on his pupil. In giving him his own view, he was giving him what he esteemed the best; but he himself had not been surrounded from his cradle by the temptations of the flesh and the devil in their most insidious form, and could scarcely realise how heavy a demand was made by the practical religion of Saint-Sulpice on the grandson of Louis XIV. It was natural that there should be occasional reactions, but the little prince found Fénelon more severe than a child of lower degree would have done; he had determined never to stoop to conciliation, but to rely entirely on the ascendancy he had won at his first coming to Versailles, and he would not deviate from this rule.

It was Louis's instinct to prize royal blood and regal dignity above all things; Fénelon had been the first to suggest to him that his royalty would not help him in the realities of life, and sometimes his old traditions came uppermost again. It is recorded that on one occasion he refused to obey an order, exclaiming, "No, no, sir; I remember who I am and who you are!"

It was impossible to pass over such a speech and maintain authority. Fénelon waited till the storm was passed and the prince had regained his reason, but before the routine of the following day had begun he went to his room and described his view of their relative positions with great clearness. In case, however, said he, Monseigneur de Bourgogne had received the impression that he valued his post in the royal household very highly, it was his intention to accompany him to the King and ask his Majesty to choose some other person more competent for such a charge. This was no idle threat, for Fénelon had always been determined to resign the tutorship directly he felt himself to be failing in it, and the prince was obliged to weigh his pride against his love. His love was proved the greater; life had been different since Fénelon came into it, and no sacrifice of his vanity was too galling, no pledge "on the word of a prince" too comprehensive, if he might cancel his offence and keep his friend. For a day he was left in suspense as to the result: it was necessary that he should receive a lesson that he would remember; but his remorse was sincere, Mme. de Maintenon interceded for him, and Fénelon consented to remain at Court.[1] Those were days when religion was the fashion. There was much profession and outward appearance of it, and the austere life of Mme. de Maintenon was imitated by all who desired favour; but a religion which was a matter of policy did not satisfy Fénelon, and the King had no true knowledge of him when he sanctioned his appointment to the Court. The priests of the period were constantly attempting to prove the possibility of serving two masters; but Fénelon had no such ambition, and although he recognised that it was well for the heir of France to be learned, courtly, and efficient in all manly accomplishments, he believed it

[1] *Saint-Simon Memoires*, vol. viii.

to be infinitely better that he should be religious. Therefore he attempted to train the passionate child who was given into his charge to habits of self-denial and self-control as rigorous as those of the future priests at Saint-Sulpice; and when the master himself was banished from him, the prince clung to his master's teaching, for Fénelon had studied him with limitless devotion, trying to realise every fact of his position, to forestall temptation and nourish better instincts, so that there was no harshness in the rigour of his discipline.

He gave five years of his life entirely to the royal children and the routine of their schoolroom duties. It seems a strange lot for a man of Fénelon's gifts and attainments; but he accepted it as a worthy one, and those five years are important in his history. M. de Louville, in a memoir (1696), describes the training appointed for the princes in graphic detail, and during those five years the life of Fénelon was merged in theirs.

"They lived plainly," he said, "being only allowed dry bread in the morning, but as much as they liked of the simple food served them at dinner and at supper. They kept Lent more or less according to their age, Monseigneur de Bourgogne having begun to observe it scrupulously. As for their other rules, no citizen of Paris would risk such a system. They wear nothing on their heads even when riding or when it rains. They go out daily, whatever may be the weather, and take violent exercise, sometimes, when at Fontainebleau, remaining out the whole day.

"The hardening system is due to M. de Beauvilliers, who believes that an infirm prince is useless, especially in France, where he is called upon to lead his army. So far it has succeeded admirably.

"They rise at 7.45 and go to Mass, then to the levee of the Dauphin for a moment, then to the King, remaining till 9.30. From 10 to 12 they study. They then dine together, and amuse themselves in their own apartments till 2.45. In summer they study till 5; in winter they spend the same time out of doors. At 8 they sup, and afterwards play at indoor games till about 9.

"They go out together, and three or four young lords with them; but they are alone the rest of the day. They are forbidden to whisper to each other, but must always speak out to every one.

"On Sundays and fête-days their lessons are religious, but they keep the same hours. At Fontainebleau they have some degree of holidays. M. de Fénelon has a horror of pedantry, and dwells chiefly on the study of politics, history, and military tactics. The object is to teach them everything that is beautiful and curious and useful in all arts and sciences, but nothing to be specialised, a definite pursuit being regarded as unworthy and ridiculous in a prince.

"Monseigneur de Bourgogne had to work harder than the others. Histories were drawn up for him, and he was required to join in discussions on the policy of foreign rulers and of the earlier French kings. He had an extraordinary memory for dates and chronology.

"They were punished rigorously, being sent to bed or kept indoors, but never whipped. They never required punishment over their lessons."[1]

---

[1] *Correspondance de Fénelon*, ii. 32.

M. de Louville was equerry to M. d'Anjou, the second son of the Dauphin, who afterwards became Philip V. of Spain; and Fénelon had given much thought to the character of the younger prince, although the Duc de Bourgogne was his primary charge. It was not their royal blood which gave these children such importance in his eyes, but the immensity of the power which would one day be entrusted to them; and this thought being present with him constantly made his life a perpetual strain to do the best for them that was possible. From the statement of M. de Louville it would seem that familiar fellowship between the brothers was not encouraged; but this was probably the result of Mme. de Maintenon's influence. Fénelon was disposed to cherish family life whenever possible, and, in the case of the Duc de Bourgogne it would have been especially salutary, for it was difficult in his early days of arrogance to induce him to admit his brothers to any kind of equality. He termed them "the children," though the difference in age was slight, and, while exalting them above the level of ordinary humanity, placed them on a far lower plane than himself. It is said that Philip took delight in irritating him when, under the influence of Fénelon, he was endeavouring to control his temper; and there is never a hint of any love between them, or of any effort to foster such a sentiment. From first to last, indeed, the life of Louis was curiously isolated and loveless; he spent it groping after an ideal of kingship—an ideal which was rather the dream of a priest than the worthy hero of a loyal people—and so missed his grasp on happiness. He never had the opportunity of proving that his ideal was practical; and Philip not being imbued with Fénelon's opinions, his succession to the crown of Spain is of little importance with reference to his tutor. Fénelon had not devoted as much attention to the younger brother; but when he was severed from the Court, and had no further recognised link to the princes, he made one effort to span the gulf that divided the isolation of Cambrai from the regal glories of Madrid. He wrote to M. de Louville in October 1701, and his letter proves how much anxious reflection he had given to the prospects of the young king. There is no extravagant eulogy of his character; he had found in it a foundation of good feeling, but much depended on the tact of those about him. It was inevitable that he should be surrounded by flatterers, and he was unusually susceptible to flattery—so much so that Fénelon compares his probable condition to that of M. Jourdain dispensing fees to those who paid him compliments, in blissful ignorance of the connection between the avarice and the admiration of his companions. But, though he could smile over his weaknesses, he was sincerely interested in Philip; it was no cant when he said that he prayed for him daily, and he is eager to give M. de Louville the benefit of his reflections and experience.

"From his childhood," he wrote, "he has had a high sense of honour and great courage. He requires courage other than that of a soldier as a defence against intriguing ministers, indiscreet favourites, and women who desire to be royal mistresses. He requires it in face of flattery, of amusement and self-indulgence, in work and in failure, in misrepresentation, and to confront importunity so as to refuse without impatience or discourtesy. The courage of warfare, albeit more brilliant, is far inferior to that required for the whole of life and for every hour."[1] The letter is interesting, as showing how deeply he had entered into the circumstances and temptations of royalty, and when he proceeds to give M. de Louville advice as to his conduct in a position of which he had some personal experience, he reveals his personal knowledge of the dangers that attend upon a courtier.

M. de Louville was in an unusually difficult position at the Court of Madrid, for the Spaniards regarded him with suspicion and jealousy. Fénelon preached silence as a safeguard against intrigue, and the most scrupulous honesty when silence must be broken. No one of his enemies had ever, in fact, been able to rake up so much as a suspicion of his probity during the seven years he passed at Court; but his standard made severe demands on impecunious office-holders, for he himself was plunged every year more deeply in financial embarrassment, and would seek no compensation in the form of benefits to confer upon his friends.

"You will easily understand that I come to Court with no claim for myself or my family," he wrote to M. de Noailles in 1690; "such esteem as is extended to me is only founded on the belief that I am looking for no interest."[2]

He never wavered from this resolution, and only urged upon others what he was practising himself; but doubtless the fact of his profession was a support to him, and he

[1] *Correspondance de Fénelon*, ii. 63, October 1701.
[2] *Ibid.*, ii. 14.

had few true followers on so steep and unfruitful a path of virtue.

At twelve years old, in 1696, M. de Bourgogne was considered to be approaching manhood, and was betrothed to a daughter of the Duke of Savoy, an arrangement that ended a long and disastrous war. To Fénelon it was an important year, as being that in which he prepared his pupil for his first Communion—the most serious epoch in the development of life. In the pseudo-religious atmosphere of the Court under Mme. de Maintenon, much outward recognition was bestowed upon it, prayers were offered for the spiritual welfare of the prince in every church in Paris, and there was much talk and discussion on the condition of his soul.

The boy himself went into retreat some days before the event, and, by his conduct then and afterwards, proved how deep a hold the teaching of his tutor had taken upon him. Had he held any other position in life, Fénelon might have made a priest of him, for, by means of his own personal charm, he had led the prince to such a realisation of the power of religion that no after influence ever obliterated it. Thus he had accomplished the great purpose of his coming to Court, and it must have been a consolation to him amid the clouds of anxiety that were already shadowing his life. A year earlier, in 1695, the See of Cambrai had been conferred upon him. He demurred at taking it, not being able to reconcile his idea of his duty to the princes with the necessary labours of his new office; but the King insisted, and his friends were confident in their expectation of seeing him enrolled among the cardinals in the near future.

He seems to have given more thought to the arrangement of his double duties than to any anticipation of coming honours. He wrote the smallest details to the Abbé Fleury from Cambrai, giving exhaustive and elaborate directions for the instruction of the Duc de Bourgogne, and naming the books—mainly historical—to be studied in his absence. The prince's letters to him are charming in their simplicity. The following might, with the exception of the final passage, have been written by a schoolboy of to-day.

"FONTAINEBLEAU, *October* 23, 1696.

"My cold is much better, even quite done with; I have been going out the last two days. We have had horrid weather till then, almost constant rain. We return to Versailles the day after to-morrow, and I shall go back to my usual ways, interrupted a little by this illness. When I left Versailles the canary had ceased to moult and begun to sing again. I have finished the 'History of Francis I.' and am in the middle of the Fourth Book of Tacitus. I hope to finish in three weeks. I desire to see you again very soon, and in good health. Till then, I beseech you be well assured of my love for you. Do not forget to write to me now and then: your letters always give me pleasure."[1]

It is pleasant to think that Fénelon—already beginning to be involved in the labyrinth of the Quietism controversy—was interested in these items of information, and had thoughts to spare for the moulting canary bird;

[1] *Correspondance de Fénelon*, i. 13.

but the completeness of his sympathy made him the greater loss to his pupil when the time for parting came.

Fénelon's promotion was, in fact, his ruin, not only because it made him enemies among those who were less fortunate, but because the opinions of the Archbishop of Cambrai were criticised when those of the simple abbé might pass unnoticed. He had never sought after the favour with the King which would have secured his position at any crisis, and therefore he fell an easy prey to the machinations of intriguing rivals, the first result of the Quietism slanders being his banishment from Court and complete severance from the prince.

It was natural that the King should not entrust his grandson to the care of a priest suspected of heresy. But his precautions came too late; he could not break the chain of deep affection that bound them together, and the records of Fénelon's sojourn at Cambrai prove how large a part he played in the life of the Duc de Bourgogne. Nevertheless, the most prosperous and hopeful period of his life was over; the years at Versailles had been sunny ones, in spite of his subsequent protestations that he had no desire to return to Court, and those that ensued were full of mortification and disappointment. That he cherished the memory of Versailles is proved by the fact that after fifteen years he could write as detailed and graphic a description of his pupil as if he had only just been deprived of office. On the death of the prince he was called upon by Père Martineau to search the storehouse of his recollections, and though the shock and pain of that unlooked-for loss had shaken him, he did not shrink from the melancholy task, but despatched the following response:—

"CAMBRAI, *November* 14, 1712.[1]

"I shall be only too glad if I can send you anything worthy of your great subject; but it is so long now since I was separated from the prince, that I can bear no witness to the doings of his riper age. . . . Of his childhood I can, at least, assure you that I always found him open and sincere, so much so that one only needed to ask him to discover his misdeeds. One day he was in a very bad temper, and in his anger desired to conceal that he had disobeyed. I urged him to speak the truth before God. He fell into a great passion, exclaiming: 'Why do you ask me before God? As you have asked me thus I cannot deny that I have done such and such a thing.' He was beside himself with anger, nevertheless religion had sufficient power to force a humiliating confession from him. We never corrected him unless it was absolutely necessary, and only then with much discretion. As soon as his excitement was passed he would come to whoever had rebuked him, acknowledge his fault, make it up with them, and bear no ill-will to them afterwards. I have often known him say—when he might speak freely— 'I am leaving the Duke of Burgundy outside the door, with you I am only little Louis.' This was when he was nine years old.

"Whenever he wished to talk on subjects that would instruct him, I gave up lessons at once. This happened often. We came back to lessons very easily, for he was fond of them, and I wished him to be fond of sensible conversation also, to make him sociable and ready to get a knowledge of people in society. The progress that

[1] *Correspondance de Fénelon*, iv. 305.

he made during these conversations in literary, political, and metaphysical subjects was evident. . . . By such treatment his temper grew sweeter; he became gentle, good-natured, and merry: he delighted every one. He was no longer arrogant, and found better amusements than the children's games, wherein he so often lost his temper. I have never known him care about praise; he took no notice at first, and if this was observed would say simply that he knew his faults too well to accept praise. He has often told me that he should remember the pleasure he found in uninterrupted study all his life. He cared so much for the things he desired to learn that I have known him ask to be read to during his meals and dressing. Moreover, I have never known a child so young listen to the gems of poetry and oratory with such appreciation. He grasped the most abstract ideas with ease. If he saw me doing anything for him, he would set to work to do it in the same way, not waiting to be told to do so. Except when he gave way to his temper, I have always found him very reasonable, his judgment being grounded on the pure maxims of the Gospel. He had a friendly regard for a certain number of worldly people whom he considered deserving of it, but he reserved his confidence for those who were honestly religious. One could not tell him of faults in himself that he did not recognise and acknowledge, and he would listen gratefully. I have never known any one to whom one could tell the plainest of home truths with so little risk of offending; I have had extraordinary experience of this.

"With years, and experience of things and people, and

a position of authority, he acquired a strength in which he was somewhat lacking formerly. Constant occupation diverted him from trifling pleasures, and gave him a dignity of which his nature was always capable. If it seemed to him that the interests of religion, of justice, of honour, truth, or commercial integrity were concerned, he took his stand with a firmness that could not be assailed.

"These are all the outlines that I can remember, should more come back to me I will write them to you."

Among the records of the time, many shades of opinion regarding the Quietism controversy are presented to us; but there is no means of knowing what form it took in the eyes of the young Duke of Burgundy. In after years he was zealous in arranging ecclesiastical disputes; but this must have been a vague and shadowy enigma to him, and a thing to be resented for the loss and sorrow that it brought him. His love for Fénelon was far deeper than mere boyish admiration, as he proved by the faithfulness of a lifetime, and all that Quietism can have meant to him was the banishment of Fénelon to Cambrai. Outwardly the separation was absolute, and after seven years of the closest intimacy with so marvellous a personality, the prince was left to prove, unsupported, the value of the training and example that had led him from a repulsive unmanageable childhood to youth of unusual promise.

The King's methods were sweeping: Fénelon offended him, and straightway all the friends of the offender were included in the ban of his displeasure. M. de Beauvilliers himself was within an ace of losing his post as governor;

it was only the worth of his wisdom and integrity—qualities which had been proved and tested repeatedly—that saved him. All who corresponded with Fénelon were in danger of sharing his fate, and those who braved it were forced to convey their letters surreptitiously, and veil the names in cipher. Fénelon was thus deprived of all possibility of giving further direction in the training on which he had concentrated all his best powers for seven years; but, while he accepted his fate with proud resignation, his interest and anxiety remained undiminished.

"I am sorry never to see you, my dear Duke," he wrote to M. de Beauvilliers towards the end of 1699, "you and the duchess and a very few other friends. As for everything else I am glad to be well away from it all; I sing the song of deliverance, and nothing would cost me more than to take it up again.

"I must love M. le Duc de Bourgogne in spite of his worst faults. I beseech you to let nothing lessen your friendship for him; let it be disinterested friendship, rooted in faith; it is your part to nourish him—painfully—till Christ be formed in him. Encourage without flattering him, instruct without wearying him, concentrating yourself upon the chances and opportunities given by Providence, which must be used faithfully. Tell him such truths as you must needs tell him, but shortly, gently, with respect and tenderness. It is providential that he does not respond to those who seek your undoing. In the name of God you must not lose him. He must feel that your heart is open towards him as a harbour in the storm should he fall into any great sin."[1]

[1] *Correspondance de Fénelon*, i. 21.

It is curious to see how his heart warms to his subject as he writes, how he yearns over the boy who had so long been the chief object of his thoughts, so that it is a little difficult to believe in that song of deliverance which he endeavoured to raise in the solitude of Cambrai. The prince was not unworthy: four years of boyhood give time for much forgetfulness, to one of his degree the world was more than ordinarily full of new interests and experiences, and its claim on him was continually antagonistic to the teaching of that voice which was never to be heard again in Paris or Versailles; nevertheless, after four years he snatched at the first chance of communication, and could write to Cambrai thus:—

"VERSAILLES, *December* 22, 1701.

"At length, my dear Archbishop, I have a chance of breaking a four years' silence. I have suffered much in that time, but nothing that hurt me more than the impossibility of telling you all that I felt for you. Your misfortunes have made my love the warmer instead of chilling it. I think with delight of a time when I shall see you again, but I fear that time is still a long way off. It must be left to the will of God, of whose mercy I am ever finding fresh proof. I have forsaken Him many times since I saw you, but He has always recalled me to Him, and, thanks be to God, I have not been deaf to His voice. For some little time I have seemed to hold more firmly to the right way. Ask Him to give me grace to confirm my resolutions and not let me be again His adversary, but to teach me Himself to follow His holy will in all things.

"I still continue to study alone—for the last two years I have not done so regularly—and I love it more than ever; I care most for metaphysics and morals, and am never weary of working at them. I have done some writing which I wish I might send you that you might correct it as you used to correct my exercises. What I am writing is disconnected, but that does not signify.

"I cannot tell you here how I loathe the treatment you have received, but one must accept the will of God and believe it is all for our good. Do not show this letter to any one except M. l'Abbé de Langeron, if he is at Cambrai; I am confident of his secrecy—and remember me to him, assuring him that separation does not lessen my love for him. Do not make me any answer unless by very safe means, and enclosing your letter to M. de Beauvilliers; I have confidence in him only, knowing how disastrous it would be to him if it were known."[1]

If this had been written during Fénelon's temporary absence from Versailles it would not be especially remarkable; but after four years, during which there had been no lack of voices to whisper every rumour injurious to his reputation, he must have been astonished and overjoyed to find the prince opening his heart to him as freely as of yore. To him, perhaps, the sadness of the letter was no cause for regret: he was glad to know that the allurements of the world had not taken a strong hold upon Louis; but when we remember that the prince was but eighteen, it seems unnatural that he should have

[1] *Correspondance de Fénelon*, i. 33.

discovered the emptiness of his great inheritance, of his favour with the King, and the unlimited possibilities that lay before him, so early. Fénelon had desired to impress upon him the magnitude of his responsibilities, and he did his work too thoroughly for the prince's happiness. The natural instincts of youth were in perpetual conflict with aspirations after holiness, and the prince had not the buoyancy of spirit required to support so perpetual a strain. Contemporary memoirs depict him exaggerated and injudicious in his piety, but those who judged him were apt to forget how prematurely he was deprived of the friend who might have guided him. He must have had many terrible moments to live through when he was left alone, with the memory of the exhortations and example of an ascetic such as Fénelon as his sole defence against the temptations of the regal glories of Versailles.

"I have suffered much in that time," he wrote after four years, and in the years that followed he did not cease to suffer. Fénelon watched his career with eager anxiety, noting and deploring his failings, but never diminishing his love, for he was able to understand the infinite difficulty attendant on the position of the prince, and to make allowance for his lapse from the ideal that he professed to cherish. The prince's professions in his letters to Fénelon are indeed very difficult to reconcile with his way of life when he was first emerging from his state of tutelage. Yet, in all likelihood, he was no hypocrite; the impression of Fénelon's teaching had gone deep, and when the thought of his master was foremost in his mind, he was again possessed with those aspirations after piety and self-renunciation which had been the salvation of his childish character. The reverse of the picture, as described by contemporary diarists, was almost an inevitable development; with good reason may it be said that princes should put a special fervour in the prayer of every Christian, "Lead us not into temptation," for their temptations are more pressing, more ubiquitous, than those of other men. Self-indulgence was expected, almost demanded, of the Duke of Burgundy; every day in the years of his early manhood was given up to a round of futile trifling that conferred no benefit upon himself or others. It was enough for him to be the Duke of Burgundy, the heir-presumptive of the Great Monarch—humanity could ask no further effort from him; such was the point of view impressed upon him by the younger courtiers, and a youthful love of ease made its acceptance easy. For a time he followed in the footsteps of his father, and shared in his pursuits. He passed from Fontainebleau to Versailles, from Versailles to Marly, as the King directed. He gave entertainments and attended them; he devised costumes for the masked balls which were the chief delight of the young duchess; he hunted hares and deer and wolves with the packs that were always kept at the disposal of the princes. These things in themselves were innocent enough, but they were not worthy of the character on which de Beauvilliers, de Chevreuse, and Fénelon were resting all their hopes for the future of the nation.

The spirit of gambling was among the most disastrous influences in the Court of Louis XIV. It had not yet undermined society to the same degree as under the

Regent a few years later; but it was especially prevalent among the princes of the blood-royal, and the Duke of Burgundy did not escape the infection. Dangeau—the most detailed of Court chroniclers—bears witness to the hold it took upon him, not as a matter of regret, but rather as evidence that he was taking his natural place at Court.

"*Tuesday, March* 4, 1700, à Marly.—Monseigneur and Monseigneur le Duc de Bourgogne played the whole day, and went together to hear the music in the evening, as usual."[1]

Such an entry as that—and they are of very frequent occurrence—tells its own tale. Monseigneur le Duc de Bourgogne was in danger of forgetting that there was a higher power in the world than that of Louis XIV., or a higher ambition than that of being King of France. His grandfather had given way to frivolous tastes and self-indulgent habits all his life, and had learnt to regard them as the fitting attributes of royalty. He was pleased when the young prince evinced the same desires. "Monseigneur le duc de Bourgogne a few days ago asked the King for money. The King gave him more than he asked for, and in giving it said that he did it with the utmost pleasure, because he asked him directly instead of approaching him through any one else, that he should always act with the same confidence, and that he might always play without anxiety, that he should never want for money, and that losses were of no importance to such as he."[2] It must be acknowledged that the testimony of

[1] *Journal de Dangeau*, vol. vii.
[2] *Ibid.*, vii., Versailles, May 15, 1700.

these daily chroniclers of the Court is sufficient to explain the shortcomings and inconsistencies of the young prince, without convicting him of intentional hypocrisy, and his failure was only temporary. A year or two later the claim of religion had once more become paramount, and the austerity of his private life was so marked as to be offensive to the King. It would appear that the right mean between asceticism and indulgence was beyond his reach, and the conflict was severe; but, though there was much to darken his experience of the world, there is one bright and pleasant side that should not be omitted in any attempt to picture his position. Before Fénelon left him he had married the Princess of Savoy, and every softening influence in his life was due to her. The King of whom he stood in awe was arrogant, domineering, often contemptible; but the King who loved and petted his child-wife revealed the capabilities of a nature which flattery had ruined. The glitter and magnificence of the royal palaces and the royal hospitality are wearying until the figure of the little duchess appears upon the scene. At her touch all doors were opened, at her demand all etiquette was put aside. She filled the King's carriage with her favourites; she kept him playing with her long after his usual hour for retiring; she was the spirit of every festivity, the softening influence in periods of gloom; she won a love that had never been accorded to any of the King's descendants, and when the duke (her husband) was threatened with a disgrace that endangered the dignity of his position, it was she who won for him the justice he despaired of, and contrived to share with him the favour that was hers in so large a measure. And although it may be difficult to recognise the tyrant who coerced the Pope and exiled Fénelon in the kindly gentleman whom she tormented and caressed, he was, none the less, the Great Monarch of Voltaire, the hero of a thousand myths and chronicles.

It is due to the little duchess that he stands revealed in this unfamiliar aspect. It is due to her that the Duke of Burgundy was admitted to the Councils of the State, and given the opportunity of proving that the high qualities with which he was accredited were his in truth; and she was in addition so far linked with every enjoyment, not only of the King's, but of all those surrounding him, that, when she died, it was mournfully admitted that the Court had lost its gaiety for ever.

CHAPTER III

MADAME DE MAINTENON

DURING the eight years that Fénelon was tutor to the Duke of Burgundy he lived among the celebrated figures of the Court of the Great King, in the gay and brilliant world which countless memoirs have depicted. Thus, as has been intimated already, he came in contact with one who may take rank among the strange phenomena of history, and whose life—although, in spite of endless records of its details, it remains in some degree mysterious—is a proof that the power of personality can master every law of custom.

Mme. de Maintenon was born in 1636. As François d'Aubigny—the child of a man of scandalous reputation and spendthrift habits—she had a hard battle with the world. Her mother was almost penniless, and left her dependent upon charitable relatives. She came of a Calvinist family, and the tenderest recollections of a childhood which contained much rough experience were linked with a Calvinist household. Yet at an age when conversion was still an easy matter, she was placed in a Parisian convent, and never afterwards wavered in allegiance to the Church of Rome. She was still only seventeen when—to escape the pressure of dependence in the present and anxiety as to the future—she consented to become the wife of Scarron, a writer of comic poetry, and the victim of a disease which so distorted him that he was hardly human in appearance. To live with him was a lesson in self-repression: he had become a cripple in the prime of life, with every faculty for enjoyment unimpaired; but he saw a humorous side in his own deformities, and ended the groans which pain forced from him with a laugh.

The select and intellectual circle which later welcomed Fénelon was beginning then to be a feature in Parisian life. Its influence raised the tone of society; but it led to a strange transformation in social laws, for the Hotêl de Rambouillet accepted wit and learning as a passport to its gatherings at the same time that Scarron, in the purlieus of the Quartier du Marais, was discovering that he might mingle the gallants of the Court with his own boon companions. The levelling tendency left a marked distinction between the two grades of literary society nevertheless; in the salon of Mme. de Rambouillet fine sentiments expressed in high-flown phrases were the surest tender for applause, and every luxury was provided for the indulgence of taste and sight and hearing. Scarron had not the means for open-handed hospitality, but his suppers (to which it was said that every guest brought his own provisions) were not lacking in attraction, and the fun sometimes became too riotous to suit those who had any leaning towards decorum.

The presence of his wife, young as she was, was a check upon his guests. She made and held a unique position in the irregular society which centred in her new home, and, when Scarron grew too feeble to enjoy it, she devoted herself wholly to him in his solitude. When he died, five years after their marriage, she faced the world again almost as destitute as she had been before it; but, although marriage had not saved her from poverty, Mme. Scarron was in a better plight than François d'Aubigny: she was welcome at the Hôtel de Richelieu, and had caught the fancy of Mme. de Sevigné, and, had she desired it, might have found a home with one or other of her wealthy friends. She preferred, however, to struggle for independence. Life had many good things to offer; she was young and pretty, and as attractive to women as to men; she was, moreover, thoughtful and observant, and intelligent as well as vivacious in conversation.

Society was then at a frivolous stage, but extravagance was not its sole distinction; a current of religious thought mingled with the frivolity, and, periodically, detached one or two, touching imagination only in some cases, but occasionally something deeper, so that the attractions of Versailles were dimmed, and the favour of the King was no longer the highest goal for aspiration. For those who were irrevocably bound to the Court by ties they had not strength to sever, the easy doctrine of the Jesuits was welcome; but in a first reaction austerity is more inspiring than indulgence, and the impossibility of reconciling ease and pleasure with the sharp rule of Port-Royal attracted many repentant souls to the subtleties of Jansenism.

Pascal's letters appeared about the time of Scarron's death, and Bossuet was beginning to preach in Paris. Such influences were not long in reaching Mme. Scarron,

MADAME DE MAINTENON 67

for during her married life she had adhered to the external regulations which the Church prescribes, and in her solitude directed all her actions by the advice of her confessor. She had chosen the Abbé Gobelin for this office. He was a Jesuit, but one of the severest type; himself an example of one of those sudden conversions which were the glory of the Church, he was rigid with his penitents, and Mme. Scarron complied implicitly with his exactions.

The office that saved her from destitution is hard to reconcile with any ideal of religion or morality, but it opened the door to her extraordinary fortune. Her first meeting with Mme. de Montespan was at the Hôtel d'Albret, when the latter was celebrated only as a beauty and a wit, and there was no intimacy between them until her future rival had won the ruinous favour of the King. The personality of Mme. Scarron was sufficiently remarkable to make an impression even in a chance meeting, and the favourite remembered her when she was in need of a trustworthy confidante. Mme. Scarron was required to conceal the birth of the children of the King and Mme. de Montespan, and to bring them up in secret. Extreme poverty had almost driven her from the Paris that she loved. The glory that surrounded Louis XIV. was supposed to blind his subjects to his sins, and he laid his command upon her. Nevertheless, she obeyed reluctantly, and the recollection of that first step towards her future glories must always have been repugnant to her.

But the Jesuit confessors had methods of their own for justifying conduct. The Abbé Gobelin retained the direction of Mme. Scarron's conscience in spite of her questionable office, and later Bossuet joined him in the task of persuading her that she was the chosen instrument for the conversion of the King. To understand her subsequent position, it is necessary to follow her along the path that led to it. She was faithful in all she undertook: she kept the secret of Mme. de Montespan until it had ceased to be one, and loved the King's children as if they had been her own. The world had buffeted her before her intercourse with the King began, and she was older in years than he. It is not likely that the charm which captivated Louise de la Vallière affected her; but the King's supreme claim on the deference and consideration which she had always coveted impressed her. Bossuet may have inspired her with the highest motives for opposing Mme. de Montespan (whose influence on the King was unquestionably evil), but there was room in her heart also for ambition, for gratified vanity, and, finally, for triumph.

Bossuet was a righteous man, and impatient of the loose morality that satisfied his fellows, but he joined his powers of reasoning to Mme. Scarron's more subtle methods of persuasion to attain the end which each desired. "No other friend has ever received such care and attention from the King," wrote Mme. de Sevigné. "I often say that she opens a new world to him, that of the intercourse of friendship, easy and unconstrained: he seems enchanted with it."

Mme. de Montespan struggled hard to retain her empire, but the combination against her was too strong; the religious element, so powerful an influence in the complex character of the King, was in favour of Mme. Scarron. She concerned herself deeply in his spiritual welfare. "All schemes are useless," she wrote to a confidential friend in 1676; "only Père la Chaise can make them succeed. Twenty times has he joined me in deploring the King's shortcomings, but why does he not absolutely forbid him the Sacraments. He is satisfied with half-conversion. Père de la Chaise is a worthy man, but the atmosphere of the Court blots the purest and softens the severest virtue." Its religious aspect only complicates the story of Mme. Scarron's successful rivalry: after the King's children had passed out of her care she remained at Court in attendance on the Dauphine, a post to which her rank gave her no claim, and for several years before the death of the Queen the King spent hours daily in her company. Their marriage, when he was free to marry, is the only explanation of her after-life, and Louis XIV. was too proud a man to have married her had the slanders on her name been true. The Abbé Gobelin was noted for his strictness, and Bossuet's reputation is unassailable: these two were familiar with every stage of her gradual conquest, and the respect with which they treated her increased as her position became more established; moreover, the most searching scrutiny of envious eyes failed to bring to light any proof of former misdoing, and her intimacy in youth with Ninon de l'Enclos, and later with Mme. de Montespan, is the most serious blemish that affects her private character. It may be assumed, therefore, that she was the strict moralist she appeared to be, and did not owe the ascendancy she gained over the King to arts acquired from her vanquished rival. She had fought a hard battle with life, and in winning it had won the mastery over herself. She had learnt to listen, to be silent, to influence without showing that she did so, to be incapable of passionate affection, so that she could calmly repudiate a friendship which interfered with her ambition. Thus she escaped the complications that hampered others in an intriguing age, and held upon her resolute way armed with the qualities that command success.

Such was the woman who ruled at Versailles when Fénelon came into office there in 1689. She had, probably, concerted with Bossuet for his appointment, for it was not their first meeting; he had excited her interest six years earlier, before his mission to the heretics or his literary powers had won him celebrity. "Your Abbé de Fénelon is very well received," she wrote to Mme. de Saint-Géran; "but the world does not do him justice. He is feared; he wishes to be loved, and is lovable."[1]

Bossuet's influence was in Fénelon's interest, and Godet Desmarais, who succeeded Gobelin as confessor to Mme. de Maintenon, had been his friend and fellow at Saint-Sulpice; but it was not necessary that she should be prepossessed in favour of one whose purity of character could not fail to win her admiration. Even when she joined the general outcry against him, it is plain from her letters that, secretly, she regretted his absence from Versailles. Saint-Simon declares that he took pains to win her, and that the successful part of his career was the result of perpetual intrigue. But even if such state-

[1] December 20, 1683.

ments bore the appearance of truth, there is sufficient evidence to contradict them in the case of Fénelon, towards whom that celebrated scandalmonger shows himself more than ordinarily venomous. The strongest interests in the private life of Mme. de Maintenon were those connected with the Church, and Fénelon's religion seemed to promise her a more tangible hope of peace than that which satisfied the other priests who came and went about the Court; moreover, she was a lonely woman, and Fénelon had the gift of sympathy. As time went on she found herself too closely tied and bound by ambition to follow in his footsteps; but in those first brilliant years at Versailles, when the cleverest and best of men and women were full of his praises, and no goal to which he might aspire was beyond his reach, it seemed that he had learnt the secret of winning man's favour by devotion to God's service, and she, who was perpetually torn betwixt the two, looked to his teaching to solve the difficulty of her life.

She looked to him in vain, for the definite choice betwixt God and Mammon had not yet come to Fénelon. M. Tronson imagined that it was given when the temptations of the Court were offered to him, but it lay in the future, and it was to be unmistakable. When he reached the turning-point he did not falter, but those who had been eager to follow while the way was smooth were left behind.

His intimacy with Mme. de Maintenon began with his arrival at Versailles. "I saw the Abbé de Fénelon again to-day," she wrote, when he was established there; "he is very clever, he is still more religious; that is exactly what I like."[1] His friends could not have desired a more favourable impression; but he was more than clever and religious. Those terms might have been applied to many Jesuit priests, who, sincere to their Order, were sincere in nothing else, and were but useful tools in the hands of those set over them. Fénelon had reserved the power of independent thought; he strove to rid his mind of personal desires that he might understand the thoughts of others, and when he endeavoured to help them in their blind groping after a higher life, he dealt with them as honestly as with himself.

The atmosphere of the Court was not really congenial to Mme. de Maintenon; she was past the period of life when splendour may be satisfying, and her sense of its emptiness was intensified by the continual war between piety and self-interest inevitable in her situation. The reality of this conflict is made evident by her letters; even while success was new to her, and the world had hardly recognised her strange position, she was fully alive to its dangers and its drawbacks.

"Though the favour I receive brings the rest of the world to my feet, it need not affect a man who controls my conscience and to whom I look to lead me in the right way unflinchingly;" it was thus that she wrote to her confessor. "Do not fear to offend or weary me: I wish to find salvation; I ask you to help me; never refer to any obligation to me; consider me, apart from my surroundings, tied to the world, but desiring to give myself to God."[2]

There is something tragic in the appeal; it seemed

[1] April 16, 1691. [2] July 27, 1686.

as if she could not seek a refuge from her new dignities even in religion. It may be believed that Fénelon would have been unaffected by them, but had he been her director, it is hardly probable that Mme. Scarron would ever have become Mme. de Maintenon. The last words of her letter summarise her condition; the knot once tied was almost impossible to loosen, for she clung to her privileges while she proclaimed their emptiness. " A frightful blank remains in all conditions," was her verdict; " anxiety, listlessness, craving for something else, because nothing is entirely satisfying."[1] Truly it is not wonderful that Fénelon, with his theory of a condition which was entirely satisfying—even upon earth—should have been welcomed with eagerness and only abandoned with regret.

The King was devoted, but he was exacting, and it is doubtful whether years of intimacy can have increased esteem which was never rooted in affection. He is impressive as history depicts him, and doubtless was so among contemporaries to whom his will was law; but with the woman who was his wife, and yet was not a queen, he could dispense with ceremony, and there was nothing to blind her to his defects. It was her part to listen and dissemble her own feelings, to tolerate the expression of opinions which she disapproved, to submit the disposal of her time, her tastes, and devotions, and desires to the ruling of his whims. Whatever were her faults, therefore, she did not lead a self-indulgent life, and all the self-mastery taught by her early experiences was requisitioned. Perhaps the idea that gave her

[1] To Mme. de Maisonfort, 1698.

courage for the protracted struggle with Mme. de Montespan remained to solace her in the tedium of her afterglory. It was worth some suffering to secure the spiritual welfare of the greatest of kings, and Mme. de Maintenon was ever on the watch for opportunities; but her hopes of a turn in the right direction must have been frequently dashed, for it pleased him better that she should brighten his hours of relaxation with her own comments upon men and manners than that his mind should be raised above the pressure of worldly cares by the works of Fénelon or any other saintly person.

Père de la Chaise was the most indulgent of Jesuit confessors, and invaluable to the King, but Madame de Maintenon had no veneration for him. She had once called him "a worthy man," but withdrew even that half-hearted commendation as she learnt to know him better, and to those in whom she had confidence she did not conceal her sentiments. "There is no rest here," she wrote wearily to Cardinal de Noailles, "the King comes to my room three times a day. Everything I have to do is stopped. . . . I see with sorrow that no desire for righteousness shows itself either in personal effort or in toleration of the effort of others. There seems to me to be less piety: yesterday vespers were not desired. Such instability is more than I can bear, and destroys all the enjoyments with which I am surrounded. 'What will the King become,' I cannot help saying to myself, 'if I die before Père de la Chaise?'"[1]

His respect for all that concerned the Church was a marked trait in the character of Louis XIV.; but it blinded

[1] September 9, 1698.

him to the political effects of intolerance without affecting his personal conduct, for he could banish a courtier on an accusation of heresy at a period when he himself was leading a life of open immorality. In the early days of her influence Mme. de Maintenon may have dreamed of moulding and developing the King's religion to a likeness of her own, but experience taught her that on this point more than on any other he was unassailable; without the smallest attempt at practice he was in principle a bigot, and she—who was accused of ruling him in affairs of State with which she had no concern—was forced, as time went on, to deny the theories that were most congenial to her, and betray the friends in whom she had most confidence. The King would not have sanctioned Fénelon's appointment if he had not regarded him with favour, but the violence of enthusiasm with which he inspired Mme. de Maintenon was, in fact, one of the causes of his misfortunes. Her strictness of life was already a rebuke to the Court, and his influence was towards increased austerity. He impressed on the King's grandson that royalty was no excuse for self-indulgence; but such teaching, if it penetrated to the apartments of the King, would not have been acceptable. Nor was it in accordance with the traditions of the Court that his choice of society should be quite independent of royal favour; popularity was supposed to depend on the direction of the King's smiles; it was a subtle tribute accorded to his judgment; but the foundation of Fénelon's friendships went deeper, and Louis XIV., who had no inclination to examine the motives of his conduct, missed in him the outward tributes of veneration for his character to which he was accustomed, and would not recognise the combination of piety, scholarship, and personal charm which made the young abbé so welcome to Mme. de Maintenon.

In truth, Fénelon, for all his gentleness, was stern and unbending in his judgments. He could be loyal to the point of silence, but he could not flatter even when flattery was a means to influence; those who chose him as confessor required to be sincere in their professions, for he was not lenient to the claims of custom and society. At one period—on the death of Gobelin—it was supposed that Mme. de Maintenon would turn to him; such a choice would have resulted in unfathomable complications, and it was well that she selected Godet Desmarais, another pupil of M. Tronson's, as the director of her conscience. There is, however, a letter written by Fénelon to Mme. de Maintenon from Cambrai during his first sojourn in his diocese, which is evidently in answer to one from her desiring to know his judgment on her character. Such a request throws a curious light on their mutual position; it is plain that throughout their intercourse she, whose favour was so important a possession, is humble, and ready to defer to his opinion, while he is independent.

The letter almost reaches the proportions of a pamphlet, and the following extracts seem to convey the estimate he had formed of her during his six years at Court; subsequent experience may have modified it considerably:—

"You are genuine and candid, whence it comes that you are very good to those you like without needing to reflect, but over cold to those for whom you have no liking.

"You have naturally a great deal of pride, of that kind which one regards as good and justifiable, but which is all the worse because one is not ashamed to think it good: the most exaggerated vanity is easier to overcome. A great deal of this pride still remains to you though you are unconscious of it. Your sensibility in such things as would wound it to the quick proves how far it is from being extinguished. You still cling to the good opinion of good people, to the approval of great ones, to self-complacency because you bear your high fortune with moderation, to all, in fact, that shows you have a soul above your place. The self of which I have so often spoken remains an idol that you have not thrown down.

"You are naturally kindly and confiding, perhaps even a little too much so; but when you begin to draw back, I fancy you harden your heart too much: genial and confiding people generally do so when they are obliged to draw back. There is a medium between excessive confidence and that distrust which, having lost one thing it put faith in, knows nothing else to which to hold.

"The world says that you love goodness sincerely; for a long time many believed that a false vanity influenced you, but I think every one is convinced and does justice to your purity of motive. They say, however, and apparently with truth, that you are hard and severe, that you do not allow any one to have any faults, that being hard on yourself, you are so also with others, that when you begin to discover weakness in those whom you have hoped to find perfect you are disgusted too soon and press your disgust too far.

"It is said that you do not take sufficient part in the affairs of the nation. Those that say so are prompted by a desire to mix themselves in the government, by spite against those that distribute promotion or by the hope of reaching it through you. It is not your part, Madame, to try and rearrange what is not in your hands. Your eagerness for the King's welfare must not make you overstep the bounds which Providence seems to have laid down for you. There are a multitude of things to be regretted, but we must await the time which God only knows and holds in His power.

"And because the King is far less apt to go by principles than by the influence of those who surround him, and whom he permits to represent him, the great point is to lose no chance of bringing faithful people round him, who will work with you upon him to fulfil his duties in their true sense, of which he has no inkling."[1]

He was even then on the brink of the troubles which ruined his career, but he writes with the confidence of secure friendship and a fearless candour which may have hastened his downfall. Mme. de Maintenon was in the habit of discussing with him, not only religious questions, but her own personal concerns, including that which lay nearest to her heart, the foundation and organisation of Saint-Cyr. Saint-Cyr was her one unfailing relaxation and resource; no honours which the King could bestow upon her were so dear to her as her position as its foundress, and there were plausible reasons for consulting Fénelon as

[1] *Correspondance de Fénelon*, v. 40.

the author of the celebrated treatise, *Sur l'Education des Filles.*

The Ladies of Saint-Louis established at Saint-Cyr were a community pledged to a devout and holy life, with the special object of educating and training five hundred girls, daughters of the poorer nobility. Mme. de Maintenon had originated the idea of this foundation; it grew under her direction, and her judgment and strength of character were displayed to the best advantage. But even this delight was not without its shadows; she had many difficulties to contend with, and much to learn from experience, for the ladies of the sisterhood were not easy to control, and she wrote of the girls when the school had been long established: "From morning to night I am settling their quarrels; I would rather have an empire to govern!"

As her original scheme was based on Fénelon's treatise, it was natural that she should frequently consult him; moreover, his spiritual view of life was an infinite solace to women bound by the conventual rule, yet near enough to the Court to throw a backward glance towards the delights which in some cases were abandoned more by compulsion than by choice. He knew that there was danger in such consolation. "I would, above all, keep pious women and the sisters of a community deprived of books on high spirituality," he wrote to Mme. de Maintenon; but she was convinced that his influence was good for all, including the foolish and hysterical, and encouraged the sisters to seek his counsel, while she recommended his writings for their study.

"You are naturally kindly and confiding; but when

you begin to draw back, I fancy you harden your heart too much;" such, as we have seen, was his description of her, and it was curiously prophetic of his own experience. In her first enthusiasm for his character she was carried beyond the bounds of prudence, for he possessed a power more far-reaching than she realised, and in one characteristic instance she had reason to regret that she had made use of it, even to gain a much-desired object.

Mme. de la Maisonfort, known as "La Chanoinesse," was a well-known figure at Court; she was of noble birth and unusual beauty, and her name was connected with certain romantic stories which excited the interest of society without dimming her reputation. Her personal charm had made a deep impression on all who knew her, and she was regarded as a saint. Mme. de Maintenon, desirous of turning all things to the profit of Saint-Cyr, determined that Mme. de Maisonfort should feel it her vocation to be one of the Ladies of Saint-Louis, and was in no way daunted when she found that La Chanoinesse did not respond to the idea. In her dealings with other women she was relentless, and opposition made her the more resolved. Having satisfied herself that her friend was specially designed to be the mainstay of Saint-Cyr she pronounced her resistance to the call to be distinctly inspired by Satan.

Mme. de Maisonfort's closest friends were also intimate with Fénelon—Mme. de Beauvilliers, Mme. de Chevreuse, Mme. de Charost, and others of the same set, and she shared in their admiration for him. She was, moreover, eminently impressionable, and religion was the constant subject of her thoughts. The easiest means of influencing her was, therefore, not difficult to discover. Fénelon at that time believed that membership in a community was a privileged condition for man and woman, and was induced to help Mme. de Maintenon in her attack on La Chanoinesse. The interest of others whose reputation was of weight was enlisted also, such as de Noailles and Godet Desmarais, until Mme. de Maisonfort was at length overcome by the spiritual pressure put upon her, and consented to abide by the decision of five priests (of whom Fénelon was one).

They assembled on the 12th of December 1690 to consult whether there was sufficient reason to believe that God summoned Mme. de Maisonfort to be one of the Ladies of Saint-Louis. They believed they would be divinely inspired in their verdict. She spent the period of suspense kneeling before the high altar in excessive agitation, but she must have known the result to be a foregone conclusion. The decision accorded with the wishes of Mme. de Maintenon, and Mme. de Maisonfort entered on her novitiate forthwith.

In spite of her confidence in Fénelon, she shrank from the fate to which he condemned her, and in later years, when experience of life had ripened his judgment, it may be believed that he would have acted otherwise. Nevertheless, what he did he did in all sincerity, and Mme. de Maintenon was more responsible for the disastrous results than he was. The life of a convent was ill suited to La Chanoinesse. The emotional side of her character was already too much developed, and finding herself confined within such narrow limits, she sought relief in what may be termed ecstatic religion, and in the

F

end her presence proved fatal to the peaceful conditions of Saint-Cyr. The King in former years had acknowledged and approved her saintliness; but the shadow of his displeasure fell upon her, and by his orders she was, after years of difficulty and friction, expelled from the community.

It is a disastrous history, and Fénelon cannot be entirely absolved from blame; but she had looked especially to his support in the condition to which she had submitted at his bidding, and it was ordained that he should pass out of her life for ever.

At first, however, Mme. de Maintenon, overjoyed at the accomplishment of her desire, was ready to encourage her victim with her sympathy. "I have not shown you the full extent of my delight," she wrote on the very day of the great decision; "but I feel sure that you must know it. I thank God with all my heart for that which He has done for you and for us. You are going to find peace. You are now in the depths of that abyss where one begins to find foothold—you know from whence I get this expression.[1] I shall see him to-morrow, and show him what Monseigneur de Chartres appointed for your retreat."

The half-veiled allusion to Fénelon indicates that Mme. de Maisonfort looked to him to help her in those depths of despair which she was sounding, and that Mme. de Maintenon recognised the position. But before long she began to have misgivings as to the prudence of her novice. Mme. de Maisonfort was cousin to Mme. Guyon, and her ardent admirer; but Mme. de Maintenon,

[1] It was one of Fénelon's.

even while she countenanced Mme. Guyon, does not seem to have had unbounded confidence in her, and afterwards bitterly regretted the encouragement she gave her.

"Submit yourself simply to the Abbé de Fénelon and Monseigneur de Chartres," she exhorted La Chanoinesse. "I always give in to the opinion of these two saints. Accustom yourself to live by their rule; but do not spread the abbé's maxims among such as have no taste for them. You talk perpetually of a condition of perfection, and you remain full of imperfection. As for Mme. Guyon, you extol her excessively: we must be satisfied with keeping her to ourselves. It would not do for her any more than for me to direct our ladies. It would expose her to fresh persecution." [1]

Mme. de Maisonfort was prepared to submit unreservedly to the direction of Fénelon, and having done so on Mme. de Maintenon's advice, may well have thought herself free from any possibility of blame; but the difficulties which were appearing at Saint-Cyr could not all be attributed to Mme. Guyon, and the foundress, while retaining her belief in the vocation she had imagined, wrote to her chosen novice somewhat impatiently: "You are intended to be a foundation stone of Saint-Cyr, my dear daughter. You must one day support this great erection by your own regular life and good example. But do not be so eager; talk less; and above all things, do not be carried away by your feelings. You say that one should not trouble oneself about anything; that one should forget oneself, never reverting on oneself at all. Such expressions are a cause of difficulty to many of our ladies.

[1] 1691.

You know as well as I do that there is a time for all things. My lack of experience made me resist M. de Fénelon when he did not wish his writings to be shown. He was right, however. All minds are not well balanced. They declare the freedom of the children of God to some who are not His children, and who claim such freedom that they may disown all subjection."

This last phrase sums up one of the chief complaints against Quietism; one which would naturally appeal to the Society of Jesuits, and had sealed the fate of Molinos. If subjection were in truth disowned, there would be little power remaining to the priesthood; and no form of heresy was therefore so sharply condemned as this.

A month after receiving this protest from Mme. de Maintenon, Mme. de Maisonfort made full profession to Fénelon, and became a member of the Community of Saint-Cyr. For three years she was sustained by his sympathy and counsel; but then suspicion fell upon his doctrine, and he and Mme. Guyon were pronounced to be dangerous teachers for the Ladies of Saint-Louis. With the first muttering of the storm, Mme. de Maintenon reviewed the situation, and decided that her only safety lay in retreat; but she did not find it easy to convince others of the necessity. La Chanoinesse proved rebellious, and required such vigorous remonstrance as the following:—

"MARLY, *August* 6, 1695.

"Submit yourself, therefore, quickly to your bishop as a Christian, and as a nun to your superior. As for the writings of Monseigneur de Cambrai, why must you keep them? Do you believe yourself to be supported in your singularity? You know that we showed them against his will, and what was the result of our imprudence. He has said and written to us many times that they were not fit for every one; that they could even be very dangerous; that they were intended for each individual to whom he was replying."

Mme. de Maisonfort was now a nun, and probably was forced to yield to conventual discipline, and surrender the letters she had received from Fénelon; but in the correspondence of Mme. de Maintenon there is a series of exhortations addressed to her, generally beginning with rebuke, for she was evidently fretted beyond endurance by the restrictions set upon thought as well as conduct, and full of regret for the world she had renounced against her will. With Fénelon banished to Cambrai, and Mme. Guyon in prison, she found herself isolated from all consolation and chained by her vows; it was not wonderful, therefore, that she was restless, and disturbed the peace of the community. Bossuet himself exerted his keen powers of reasoning and logic to convince her of Fénelon's heresy; and when she was expelled from Saint-Cyr, she was removed to a convent in his diocese, that he might await an opportunity of bringing her to a better mind. In the end there was some degree of friendship and esteem between them; but, though she might have been a happier woman had Fénelon never crossed her path, she could never be persuaded to deny the purity of his doctrine.

The story of her ill-advised renunciation gives a glimpse of that straining visionary section of society which had its definite place even in Saint-Simon's portrait-gallery.

Fénelon's ideal condition for human life was one of constant effort to come in touch with hidden mysteries, to lay hold on certainty, to hear the voice of God in distinct answer to impassioned prayer. This mystic view of his is well expressed in the words of Cardinal Newman: "In spite of this universal world we see there is another world quite as far-spreading, quite as close to us, and more wonderful; another world all around us though we see it not, and more wonderful than the world we see. For first of all, He is there who is above all beings."[1]

To touch this world, in spite of individual hindrances and imperfections, was the aim of Mme. Guyon, of Mme. de Maisonfort, and many others: such would have been the endeavour of Mme. de Maintenon had she been independent of the favour of the King. Knowing how deeply rooted were his prejudices against all novelty, it is strange that she ever allowed herself to become involved in any suspicion of heresy, for, though she drew back as soon as danger threatened, she did so at considerable cost to her self-respect, and the case of Mme. de Maisonfort is only one among many which were the fruit of her untrustworthy enthusiasms and her love of dominating others. As late as 1704 Fénelon was still the cause of contention at Saint-Cyr although his voice had been silent for so long, and Mme. de Maintenon felt it necessary to write to the Ladies of Saint-Louis a letter far more injurious to herself than to the teacher she attacked:—

"You know what my intention was in bringing you into contact with Monseigneur de Cambrai and his writings. He was a man of high reputation, and seemed to

[1] "Life and Correspondence of Cardinal Newman," vol. ii.

me to be a saint. I have never had anything of value that I did not desire to share with you, and consequently I filled the house with his works. You know the evil that ensued.

"I heard a great deal about Jansenism in my youth. I did not forget its tenets, and, by God's grace, I have always hated it. But I knew nothing of Quietism, and therefore became imbued with the theories of Monseigneur de Cambrai in ignorance of their danger. I lost faith in him as soon as I found him challenged by his colleagues and his best friends; and when it was set before me, I soon saw the error from which it had pleased God to preserve me. Whilst awaiting the judgment of Rome I often found myself in a difficulty between my ardour to attack this doctrine and the friendship which summoned me to defend Monseigneur de Cambrai. Rome condemned the doctrine of Monseigneur de Cambrai; he accepted and submitted to its condemnation, and I found myself in another difficulty: could I believe in the sincerity of this submission when I could not see the prelate becoming, like St. Paul, a preacher of the faith he had assailed. I only believe in conviction of error when I see it attacked as fiercely as it has formerly been supported."[1]

This last is a hard saying, though it may be characteristic of the woman, and those of the community who had known Fénelon, and remembered the many proofs of Mme. de Maintenon's esteem and admiration he had received when the world was smiling on him, may have felt their faith in their foundress somewhat shaken by

[1] July 1704.

so candid a statement of her difficulties in reconciling friendship and expediency. They were near enough to the Court to know that there had been a moment when her influence with the King might have saved Fénelon from ruin; but it would have been at the risk of the King's displeasure falling on herself, and she esteemed the risk too great. That Fénelon had looked to her in his distress she betrays in a letter to Cardinal de Noailles, to whom she was especially outspoken:—

"MARLY, *February* 21, 1697.

"Monseigneur de Cambrai spoke to me privately a moment. He realises the bad effect of his book, and his defence of it convinces me more and more that God means to humble this great mind, which has perhaps been too self-reliant. He told me Père de la Chaise had reported to him a conversation with the King, after which he felt he must speak to him. I was ready to fall in with anything, but from what I gather of the King's inclinations, Monseigneur de Cambrai will not gain much by explanations. I also spoke a moment to M. de Beauvilliers, who was evidently troubled by the King's silence. . . . This antagonism is not my doing; it is the King's attitude towards all novelties. I know that I am held responsible; but the truth is your due, and I tell it to you. Finally I am prepared to do my duty on so important an occasion."

It is characteristic that she should require the support of an idea of duty when it was her interest that was obviously concerned; it is plain that she was on the defensive with her conscience, for there was a foundation of honesty in her nature inimical to the policy of betrayal which she adopted in the case of Fénelon and of others also. It seems, indeed, to have been her fate to feel herself called upon to sacrifice her friends; she ruined Racine with the King, and he died of a broken heart, and when suspicion of heresy fell upon de Noailles their years of intimacy did not protect him—she deserted him even as she had deserted Fénelon.

Yet she was not without some instinct of fidelity; she was true—according to her lights—to her great object of working the salvation of the King, although it would be hard to imagine a less hopeful object of endeavour. It is difficult to determine what degree of power she held in the State. She constantly declared that she had none, but, considering the type of woman that history proves her to have been, it seems probable that she seized every means of influence within her reach, and certainly the odium of many an act of tyranny fell upon her, especially with regard to the Reformers, among whom her name was execrated. Fénelon knew her intimately; even in his exile he was kept well informed of the proceedings of the Court, and, undoubtedly, he regarded her as the mainspring of affairs when the King's reign was drawing towards its close. This view may have increased his bitterness towards her, which, after fifteen years, was deeper than when he left the Court. Age made him gentler towards others, and personal resentment had had time to fade; but he was jealous for the honour of his country, and found her wrongs difficult to forgive. When the Duke of Burgundy was dead, and the position of France appeared to him to be desperate, he realised how much depended upon Mme. de Maintenon. "I am only too much afraid that she will be absorbed by jealousy, pique, prejudice, and feminine intrigue. I am only too much afraid that she will support only feeble, superficial schemes to keep the King calm and blind the public, that do not touch the pressing needs of the State."[1] This was his verdict on her—a very different one from that which he wrote so candidly sixteen years before. Yet the two estimates are not wholly contradictory: in the first he showed that he knew her character to be many-sided; in the second he can see nothing but the darker side. While he was with her he had drawn out all that was truest and strongest in her, and there had seemed to be a fellowship of aspiration between them; she was not false in this though she was faithless; his teaching was the expression of her inmost thought, but expediency remained her rule of conduct, and when the King died, and she was free at length to follow her own will, Fénelon was already beyond the reach of prejudice or favour.

[1] *Correspondance de Fénelon*, i. 176.

CHAPTER IV

MADAME GUYON

THE contemporaries of Mme. Guyon found it difficult to form a just judgment of her life and theory. The lapse of two centuries has not lessened the difficulty. Her theories grew with her, developing as her life developed, and though their personal intercourse was limited, her name has been inseparably linked to that of Fénelon, and she was the primary cause of his disgrace and exile. She was the cause also of the most deplorable warfare of tongue and pen that ever scandalised society, of severance of friendship, of endless bitterness and persecution at a time when persecution had no limits, and men died because their thoughts were not pleasing to the King, therefore her name was utterly abhorrent to the many in whom her novel doctrine awakened no responsive echo.

She made confession of her life's experience, and, in spite of its wildness and exaggeration, it has its foundation in reality. In her Autobiography there are very many sentiments and phrases which revolt the reader's sense of reverence—phrases which sink into the memory and spring up rapidly to prejudice all future judgment, and yet have not sufficient real significance to convict their author of anything more heinous than an uncontrolled imagination. She has many fellows in her desperate groping after truth; she had countless disciples in her lifetime; successive generations have paid tribute of devotion to her memory, and she is at the present time held in especial honour by the Society of Friends, although she remained a member of the Church of Rome till her last hour; but few among her followers have reached the confident assurance that supported her. There is something sublime in her egotism, in her certainty that she had found the solution of the mystery of human living, in the isolation that she claims for herself by virtue of her nearness to the spiritual world; yet, in spite of all her claims, she excites pity rather than reverence, and her record is most pathetic when it is most triumphant.

There was nothing in the surroundings of her early life to account for her phenomenal experience. She was of gentle birth, but she was given in marriage, without any reference to her personal feeling in the matter, to a citizen of middle age and great wealth. Her new home was uncongenial, her husband's mother treated her harshly, her husband was indifferent; but these distresses were but the common outcome of the matrimonial system of her country, and many a young wife has had the like to bear. "I was alone and helpless in my grief," she sighs; but such a belief is common to morbid minds. Hers was evidently of an introspective tendency, which was fostered by lack of sympathy with her surroundings. She had had little education, but she turned to books for consolation in this early period of depression, and the spell of Thomas à Kempis fell upon her. Thenceforth she eschewed secular reading; she reflected constantly upon her sins, keeping a written record of them, and thus the first step on the steep path of her religious life was made. Many may reach firm foothold after such a step, but few aspire to scale such giddy heights as Mme. Guyon afterwards attempted. She was still very young, and her character received impression from various persons with whom she came in contact. She records how deeply she was influenced by a Franciscan monk, a devotee who had spent five years in absolute solitude that he might seek communion with the Almighty. In his first interview with her he bade her "Seek God in her heart!" The phrase, though Thomas à Kempis might have made her familiar with it, had a striking effect upon her; she thought that it revealed to her her former error in seeking God "as though by mercenary purchase of external service," and her future doctrine sprang from the seed thus sown. "I felt at this instant deeply wounded with the love of God," she writes, and the words were set down in all sincerity. This interview was the first landmark. The Franciscan remains nameless, but he may be held responsible for some of the extravagance that made her name so notable in the religious world. Five years of solitude, of self-discipline, of wistful aspiration after gifts that God withholds, were not likely to result in the well-balanced judgment most fitted to control the waywardness of a young enthusiast.

It is strange that, with all her self-examination, she never realised her own egotism. She is sincere in her groping after God. She thinks her mind is filled with the consciousness of the greatest of all mysteries. She thinks that Truth itself has been revealed to her; that she stands upon a pinnacle above the clinging thicket of everyday experience through which her fellow men and women must struggle blindly; yet in her exaltation she never forgets private grievances. Writing long afterwards, she still holds the petty details of her sufferings in remembrance, and glories in self-pity while she imagines that she has immolated self. The extreme practice of asceticism was the natural result of the condition of her mind. Her record of her self-imposed penances is incredible unless the extraordinary force of religious mania be recognised, and, even allowing for its potency, it is hard to understand how a woman, whose mind centred on contemplation of the love of God, could tear her flesh with pointed spikes and bruise herself with whips and nettles, with the deepest assurance that she thus did Him honour. Here, in the very beginning of her spiritual history, is the warp that twists it to the end. The word which is so often on her lips, the name of Love, which she declares she can never hear without a conscious sensation of delight, has no true significance: call it Majesty, Mystery, Omnipotence, and she is no longer inconsistent; but we learn, as the alphabet of life's experience, that human love suffers with those who suffer, and therefore love at its purest must shrink from a sacrifice of useless pain.

Another misconception of the ideal of love caused her much suffering: the natural instincts of youth revolted against the strain she had put upon herself. She went to Paris, and while there the allurement of the gay world proved too much for her. Her backslidings appear to have been innocent enough; but on her return to the quiet of the country she was overwhelmed by a sense of her own iniquity. "My Beloved was offended," she exclaims; "for above three months He withdrew the favour of His presence from me. I could see nothing but an angry God before me."

Undoubtedly she was sincere in this impression and in the distress it caused her, failing entirely to see how she wronged the sense of Fatherhood: the God she strove to serve was indeed an incarnation of jealousy if a passing sense of pleasure in lawful joys could so offend Him. It is strange that despair did not alienate her from the stern idol she had created, but a curious incident, probably much magnified by imagination, occurred about this time to renew her fervour. On her way to a service at Notre Dame, whither she went on foot attended by a servant, a man of shabby appearance accosted her. His first words showed her that he did not desire alms. She observed an air of authority about him; and without preamble he exhorted her to live a religious life, for God required that her heart should be holy. She was as much impressed as she had been formerly by the Franciscan hermit; but her life had deepened since that first conversion (she was at this time two-and-twenty), and such a claim upon her had more significance. "From this day, this hour," was her resolve, "if it be possible, I will be wholly the Lord's. The world shall have no portion in me."

The temptation to vanity was reduced soon afterwards by very severe smallpox, and she accepted the loss of her beauty as a touch from the hand of God, refusing any remedies intended to restore her complexion, a course which she finds keen after-pleasure in recalling.

From this time her mental excitement became more pronounced and more continuous. To understand what manner of woman she was, it is necessary to accept the phraseology which she permitted herself even when presumption seems to lead her across the borders of profanity. Never for a moment does she lose sight of her own highly-developed sensibility, every vicissitude is magnified, every sorrow becomes a cross directly sent with reference to her "state," and in her untiring contemplation of herself she ceases to reason, and aims only at the picturesque. But absolute obedience to the Will of God is the loftiest of aspirations, and it was at this she aimed. Her desire for its attainment was a stronger factor in her character than self-complacency. It was a part of all her schemes and ambitions, or else her description of herself is completely false. If we admit the sincerity of her confessions, it is extraordinary that she should have believed herself endowed with the highest of all gifts; that, with a mind susceptible to an overpowering sense of awe, she could be confident that she had attained to a condition of full and perpetual communion, which she describes as follows: "If I had a will, it appeared to me that it was like yours, O God; like two lutes in perfect accord—that which is not touched giving forth the same sound as that which is touched: it is only one same sound and one single harmony." If such words as these are considered in their full significance, comment upon them is impossible; but their writer, in her swift flow of expression, had no leisure for revision.

A fevered brain struggling with the perpetual thought of things too great for it has no room for tranquillity. Its excitement craves to be supported on fresh sensation. Mme. Guyon was a wife and mother, and possessed considerable wealth, therefore life gave her full scope for the practice of religion. Nevertheless she could not be content without a continual variety of " states." To her it seemed that every event, not only in her own life but in the lives of others, occurred primarily that it might affect the condition of her soul. For that all natural courses were diverted. For that the sun shone and the rain fell. No secret consecration of herself could satisfy her. She required an external pledge that in possible after times of stagnation might touch her fancy and kindle the dramatic side of her disposition to renewed fervour. To the Romanist devotee the marriage-contract that she drew up and signed is not a novelty; but it probably is unique in detail, and it is characteristic of her point of view. The closing sentence, which conveys the spirit of the rest, runs thus: "Pledged as I am to be His, I accept, as part of my marriage-portion, the temptations and sorrows, the crosses and the contempt, which fell to Him."

Thenceforth each difficulty of daily life became a martyrdom in which she revelled; misfortune ceased to be regarded as common to mankind, it was concentrated upon her who had accepted it as marriage-portion. "Since that time," she writes, "crosses have not been spared me, and although I have had many previously, I may say they were only the shadow of those I have had to suffer in the sequel." To be the confessor or director of such a being was no desirable post. At times she evidently delighted in confession; but she detected a spiritual danger in such indulgence, and checked herself firmly. Nevertheless she was the prey of swiftly changing moods which reduced her advisers to despair, and one at least resigned the office.

The death of her husband (in 1670) withdrew the authority which had limited the outward expression of Mme. Guyon's eccentricities. Her own description of her conduct towards him and towards the mother-in-law whom she regarded as so severe a cross, accounts for the unhappiness of her married life. To her view his claim was on her forbearance only. A long illness made him irritable, and she bore his reproaches in silence. She delighted in performing the most menial offices for him, but she defied his wishes when they clashed with her fantastic whims. If he asserted his authority she wept unceasingly. She fasted to the damage of her health, and marvelled at his lack of sympathy for her consequent illness. Her innocent candour reveals the true conditions of her married life: the stern, worldly woman who ruled the household, her son, a wealthy merchant of high reputation, and the girl-wife whom he had chosen for her beauty, with no suspicion of the extraordinary developments of which her character was capable. It was a dreary little drama—all the drearier because religion was the cause of discord, and Mme. Guyon, in childish self-complacency, regarded herself as a martyr to her faith.

Her husband left her great riches, and after a time she separated from his mother, taking her youngest child only with her. She might have married again, and the prospect was not without attractions; but a more visionary future pleased her better. Confessedly the conduct of her life depended upon impulses; the most serious decisions resulted from a sudden thought regarded as an inspiration. Such a condition is susceptible of the most extraordinary developments. She loses herself in a maze of superstition, till it is impossible to separate the actual from the imaginary. She believed she had wrought cures more miraculous than any of those chronicled at Lourdes. She believed that the waves were arrested as they broke that the boat she sat in might receive no damage; that when she rode on horseback for the first time the devil was forcibly pushing her off. She does not disguise the full extent of her credulity, nor realise for a moment the extraordinary presumption that gave it birth; rather she regarded with compassion all who did not accept her as a chosen messenger of the Almighty, and prayed that they might be enlightened. She never seems to have prayed that she herself might see her error if she were only self-elected as a teacher of mankind.

After a period of quiet widowhood she undertook missionary work in the diocese of d'Aranthon, the Catholic Bishop of Geneva, and in the five years thus spent away from the surroundings of her early life, she seems to have formulated her theory of "Quietism," a theory the dangers of which are sufficiently obvious, but which possesses an extraordinary attraction for a certain order of deeply religious mind. In its most favourable form it is contained in the *Moyen Court de faire oraison*, a work written under the excitement induced by her missionary travels, but guiltless of the worst defects of her later writings.

She begins by stating that religion is entirely dependent upon prayer, and then defines her conception of what prayer should mean, "not the formal offering up of specific petitions," but "that state of the heart in which it is united to God in faith and love." Words cease to have value and prayer becomes a mental state, or, as she expresses it, "a silence of the soul." From this silence of the soul proceeds the indifference of pure love, the condition of unquestioning resignation which is the essence of Quietism. "But this cannot be without the principle of *abandonment*, by which we resign, abandon, or consecrate ourselves entirely to God. . . . Such a soul is resigned in all things, whether for soul or body, whether for time or for eternity. . . . When we have given ourselves to God in *abandonment* and have exercised faith in God that He does *now*, and that He will ever, receive us and make us one with Himself, then God becomes central in the soul, and all which is the opposite of God gradually *dissolves itself*, if one may so speak, and passes away. . . . When the soul has reached this degree of experience it is disposed to practise the Prayer of Silence, so called, not merely because it excludes the voice, but because it has so simplified its petitions that it has hardly anything to say, except to breathe forth in a desire unspoken, *Thy will be done!* This prayer, so simple and yet so comprehensive, may be said to embody the whole state of the soul. . . . When St. Paul speaks of our being led by the Spirit of God, it is not meant that we should cease from action, but that our action should be in harmony with and in subordination to the Divine action."

As if some realisation of the danger of her doctrine dawned on her, Mme. Guyon closes her essay with a passage on "False Pretensions to a State of Sanctification." "Men may *pretend* to be wholly the Lord's," she says, " by harmony of affection and will, and by being in entire moral union with Him, but *if they are not so* there will certainly be something in look, in word, or in action which will show it." At the time of writing she was giving practical demonstration of this final truth. It is not necessary to convict her of hypocrisy. She was self-deceived, though her hallucination was as disastrous to her credit as though she had practised deliberate imposture.

The two chief dangers attendant on the Quietist theory are these: (1) The indifference to morality consequent on the indifference to salvation that Mme. Guyon indicated as the highest proof of pure love; and (2) The self-confidence which, relying on the direct inspiration of God, disdains the laws of tradition and conventionality whereby the lives of others are controlled. On this last point Mme. Guyon exhibited the defects of her own belief. In her celebrated connection with her confessor, Père La Combe, she appears, not as a divinely directed saint, but as a victim to a subtle form of hysteria fostered by complete independence of control. In a scandalous age so notable a woman could not hope to escape calumny; but Mme. Guyon is so open in her relation of her own proceedings that it is impossible to distrust her sincerity. The simplicity of her egotism stamps it genuine, and she never attempts to disguise the degree in which her life centred around the priest, or spares a detail of their intimacy. She regarded her own character as above suspicion, and it may be accepted that it was so; they were united by mutual enthusiasm, but he does not appear to have broken the bonds of reason as effectually as she did, and her reference to him savours occasionally of compassionate contempt as to one less advanced, spiritually, than herself. Nevertheless, it was his fate to suffer an equal martyrdom for her theories. No doubt the links between them were strengthened by personal attraction, and the priest acknowledged what the woman would never have admitted. Once, on her way to Paris, she appeared suddenly at Verceil, where Père La Combe was living, and found him "strangely displeased, so that he even could not hide it from me." Her surprise at his displeasure is remarkable, for she had been informed of the scandals spread by her enemies concerning herself and her director, and that a censorious world refused to recognise their spiritual union.

La Combe appears to have regarded her as "the chosen vessel" she claimed to be; but he knew that dwellers in the world must not ignore its judgments, and that their spiritual privileges would not account for their meeting at Verceil. Moreover, he had won himself a place at Verceil, which was infinitely precious to him. He had gained an influence among the soldiers of the garrison, men of depraved life, to whom his eloquent tongue and practical example of self-denial was an inspiration towards virtue, and he had left Mme. Guyon and her spiritual transports behind him. Possibly he had discovered, by stern self-examination, that their intercourse was not without temptation; and when she pushed herself once more into his life, he realised that she heralded misfortune.

The scandal that her recklessness thus created is a

deplorable complication of her case. It was used as a weapon against her in subsequent controversy, and even her friends found it difficult to defend her. If the accusations brought against her had been limited to the question of her orthodoxy, her position would have been precarious enough; but the imputation on her moral conduct was still harder to refute, her own views of her connection with La Combe being the only innocent explanation of her proceedings. It was, however, greatly in her favour that this incident, of which she made no secret, did not exclude her from the society of the strictest of the ladies of the Court. The fame of her strange theories had preceded her. There were stories whispered of the visions she had seen, of messages communicated to her direct from another world. All eyes were turned on her with awe and wonder, and those who aspired to a reputation for piety vied with each other in doing her honour. The group that centred round Mme. de Maintenon were debarred from many of the excitements afforded by the Court. Mme. Guyon was welcome as a novelty. Her somewhat reckless originality inspired fresh interest in the questions of doctrine and ceremonial, which were growing wearisome to those whose piety was chiefly a matter of expediency, and any attack upon the reputation of the devotee would at that time have raised an outcry among the strictest of the courtiers. Therefore her position morally appeared impregnable, and the recollection of this, the most prosperous period of her career, could never be wholly effaced from the minds of her contemporaries.

There were some, doubtless, who were not carried away

by the tide of enthusiasm, who desired more knowledge of these spiritual novelties before accepting them, and were not prepared to follow the lead of Mme. de Maintenon without reflection. Considering the subsequent connection of their names, it is curious that Fénelon should have been numbered among these. Possibly he was inspired to some feeling of resentment that an enthusiastic woman, with but little education and no claim on the esteem of her hearers, should thus proclaim to all comers, and at all seasons, the thoughts which were dearest and most sacred to his soul. His own agreement with the new theories which were now on every lip revealed to him their danger. The lack of reticence which distinguished Mme. Guyon offended him, and he disliked the conjunction of her religious views with her conduct regarding Père La Combe. He regarded her, therefore, with suspicion; nevertheless, he was attracted by her against his will, a fact for which the fundamental sympathy between them must be responsible. "The person that you mention to me has a bad reputation," he wrote of her; "she makes use of an appearance of piety, and is not to be trusted. It is true that I have seen her at Mme. de Charost, and once or twice besides in good company, and that I was impressed by her, but I have given her no introductions."[1]

The letter is dated June 1694, and Mme. Guyon, supported by Mme. de Maintenon, had made her own way to general favour, and was independent of Fénelon's opinion, but her memoirs reveal that she was possessed with a singular desire to number him among her

[1] *Correspondance de Fénelon*, ii. 23.

following. The society which had received her doctrine with enthusiasm included many of his friends, and, although he avoided personal meetings, his reputation must have been familiar to her. The journey from Verceil was practically the end of Père La Combe's career. From thence onwards his life became a tragedy, and Mme. Guyon, in the loss of his support, may have hoped to find a friend of similar calibre in Fénelon. Undoubtedly her enemies deliberately ruined her Barnabite confessor. It was true that he travelled with her from Verceil to Paris; yet such a course was sufficiently in accordance with the custom of the time, and he could prove that he had business in the capital. But the world did not ask his reasons or accept his proofs; and, knowing as he did that slander had already been busy with his name and hers, he showed culpable recklessness. Père La Motte, Mme. Guyon's brother, was awaiting an opportunity of vengeance on La Combe. His own designs on her large fortune led him to pursue them both with relentless animosity, and within a year of the journey from Verceil he had obtained the arrest of La Combe on a charge of heresy. An obscure priest whose teaching had in any way diverged from the straight lines the Church laid down had very little possibility of self-defence. La Motte's purpose was easily accomplished, and his victim spent the twenty-seven years of life that still remained to him in close imprisonment. His mind was not sufficiently imbued with the philosophy of Quietism to be proof against his sufferings, and his reason gave way a few years after his arrest. His is a melancholy and sordid history, and their connection

is the most damaging incident in the career of Mme.
Guyon; but both were to a great degree responsible
for their own misfortunes, the details of which would
be unworthy of record but for their after effect on
Fénelon. By a strange freak of fortune, their ill-con-
sidered actions were the cause of the sharpest anguish
which he was ever called on to endure, although there is
abundant proof that he had but little personal intercourse
with her, and had never met La Combe.

According to Mme. Guyon's own account, characterised by her usual candour, the presence of Fénelon had
an exciting effect upon her; it is possible that she modified her habitual phraseology that it might not be offensive
to his ears, and after a time she succeeded in overcoming
the prejudice with which he had at first regarded her.
The basis of their opinions was similar: the realisation
of God's presence; the recognition of His perpetual and
complete direction, not only of the external circumstances, but of the actual minds of believers, was the
stimulus of his daily life. If this were Quietism, then
he was as guilty as the visionary herself. Misfortune
was threatening Mme. Guyon when Fénelon expressed
approval of her doctrine; the fate of La Combe was a
shadow in the background, and her enemies were growing bold enough to whisper suggestions of Molinos and
Mysticism when her name was mentioned. Every instinct
of reasonable prudence should have urged avoidance of
her, but—where he hoped to sift truth from falsehood—
Fénelon did not listen for the voice of prudence. He
studied the published books of Mme. Guyon, and found
in them an echo of his own belief. He might wish

to modify her statements, but he was ready to support them, and thus he took the first step towards his own ruin. The full purity of his reputation was needed to support it against the subsequent onslaught of personal calumny, and in this respect only did he escape uninjured; but even the power of the King was not sufficient to create proof of evil-doing in connection with such a character as his.

Mme. Guyon was the cause of infinite suffering to others; but she also suffered much herself, and there are many details of her experiences which must have resulted from deep personal animosity towards her. It is impossible to disentangle the web of motives which were responsible for the Quietism controversy, but it may be assumed that the defence of the Church was but a secondary influence on the minds of the disputants. Nevertheless, the doctrine of Molinos had been accepted as a grave danger to the Church, and it cannot be disputed that that of Mme. Guyon had many essential points of similarity. The two volumes of her writings which attained celebrity (besides *Le Moyen Court*), *L'Explication du Cantique des Cantiques* and *Les Torrents Spirituels*, contain passages that implicate her in the worst errors imputed to the Spanish mystic, while the licence of expression she permits herself is often offensive, and sometimes approaches perilously near to blasphemy.

Her independence of the outward forms of religion, including confession, excited the suspicion of Godet Desmarais, Bishop of Chartres and confessor to Mme. de Maintenon. In this last capacity he was brought into constant intercourse with the Ladies of Saint-Louis at

Saint-Cyr, and he detected that the influence of Mme. Guyon was inimical to the authority of the Church. Consideration of her writings increased his alarm, and he charged her with the heresy known as false Mysticism. She appealed to Fénelon for advice, and at his bidding, laid the matter before Bossuet as the foremost theologian of the day. Fénelon was deceived in his opinion of his friend, and had not calculated on his virulence of opposition, to the whole idea of Mysticism. He himself was in no danger from the chief temptations that the doctrine offered to sincerely religious minds—indifference to salvation and passive contemplation that set no value upon efforts for the good of others—and he had given deep study to the mystic writings of the Saints. Bossuet, on the other hand, never understood the true meaning of Mysticism, and does not seem to have realised the extent to which it was supported by the writings of the Saints; he was a sincerely religious man, but his God was transcendent, Almighty but not Immanent, and the speculations and assertions of Mme. Guyon roused him to such fierce indignation that his opposition had not long been declared before it assumed the aspect of personal enmity.

In fact both Fénelon and Bossuet approached the question of Mme. Guyon's heresy under the influence of differing misconceptions. Fénelon greatly undervalued the dangers arising from the development of her theories; while Bossuet would not acknowledge the sanction to some of her assertions which may be found in the books of St. Francis de Sales and other of the Saints especially cherished by the Roman Catholic Church. The point is important, because their celebrated quarrel originated in this difference, but at the beginning of their examination of Mme. Guyon's doctrine they were still, outwardly, in accord. In conjunction with de Noailles, then Bishop of Chalons, and M. Tronson, they met at Issy, by the King's order, to give formal consideration to the charge of heresy brought against Mme. Guyon. The conferences continued at intervals for some months, and resulted in thirty resolutions especially bearing upon Quietism, known as the Articles of Issy. The wording of these articles is very ambiguous, and Fénelon had no difficulty in subscribing to them, although they implied censure upon Mme. Guyon.

The rumour of accusations brought against Mme. Guyon effected an extraordinary change in the opinions of her friends; those who had never wearied of applauding her avoided the mention of her name, they forgot that they had gloried in echoing her sentiments, and believed they had always observed her with suspicion; and if she needed proof of the evanescence of human friendships she found it at this moment. Her adversaries were wholly without scruple; they laid every species of trap to beguile her into damaging admissions, and they were secure in the support of Church and Crown. She, on the other hand, stood practically alone. She was imprisoned in a convent where she was the victim of constant petty ill-treatment, and debarred from seeking advice from any who were friendly to her. Yet though it was easy to prove her reckless and misguided in speech and conduct, it could not be denied that the strength of her defence lay—not in a natural claim on liberty and justice—but in her confidence in the Love of God. This was a stronger power than her vanity, her egotism, or her self-consciousness, and in defiance of menace, civil or clerical, she persisted in her belief that she had found a truth of which no earthly power could deprive her.

From the moment that Bossuet drew attention to the heresy of her opinions, there was no cessation to the suffering she was required to endure. The most atrocious forms of slander were linked to her name and generally circulated. She was hunted from every place where she sought refuge and retirement, and the minds of her remaining friends and followers were poisoned against her by selections from the wildest of her literary efforts, so chosen and distorted that the sense became revolting. Yet until age and imprisonment had broken her physical strength she retained the strange serenity of Mysticism. Secure in the confidence of her disputed doctrine that all her thoughts were of God's suggestion, and therefore necessarily sinless, she justified her faith by maintaining a composure which the most fiery assaults of indignant Churchmen could not ruffle. She was ready to admit that others might fail to reach a similar condition of detachment, and so fall into error, but she had no misgivings as to her own privileges. She considered that she had yielded her will entirely to God by a permanent act of renunciation, and that He had accepted her renunciation. If her Autobiography is a true representation of the doctrine of Quietism it is not convincing, for the Self of Mme. Guyon is never absent, it never ceases to glory in her sufferings and in her patience under them, to witness to her mystic privileges, to contemplate the sensation she created in the minds of others; and if she, who was certainly pure in her aspirations, could be thus deluded, the possible effect of her doctrine upon persons with temptations stronger than their sanctity is quite incalculable.

It was left to Bossuet to raise the cry of warning, but the fallacies of Quietism should have been patent to ordinary minds. The King had, from the first appearance at Court of Mme. Guyon, deprecated the encouragement she received from Mme. de Maintenon. It is no injustice to Bossuet to assume that this fact influenced his action; but he had other incentives, and his treatment of her was consistent with his professed opinions.

He was a devout Churchman and a scholar. His keen reasoning faculty rebelled against the claims of Mysticism, and he detected the exaggeration in Mme. Guyon's account of her experiences. He was, in fact, as sceptical of the supernatural as she was credulous, and they had no common ground on which to start discussion. In argument he vanquished her. His ready flow of words was seldom checked to give her a moment for reply, and an interview with him generally reduced her to complete exhaustion. Nevertheless, his logic was thrown away upon her; he even failed to convince her that the intervention of saint or priest was necessary to obtain her salvation, and she would not recognise his claim to speak at all on the doctrine which was everything to her, for, in the phrase of Molinos: "To those who have not proved them, these things are as colour to the blind or music to the deaf." This is the summary of a point of view which is absolutely unassailable, and constitutes a formidable stumbling-block in all theological controversy, for those who hold it honestly, possess a shield which the sharpest arrow of reason or of ridicule cannot pierce, and from behind its shelter can regard the efforts of their unenlightened adversary with compassion. Thus armed, Mme. Guyon was invulnerable to the shafts of Bossuet's wit, and her belief in the heavenly messages so constantly accorded to her, in the miracles of healing which had preserved her feeble life, in the tangible demons she had exorcised, remained unshaken.

The history of the resolute attack made upon Fénelon by Bossuet is an interesting study in the frailty of human nature, but it is not necessary to seek deep motives for his antagonism towards Mme. Guyon. Her attitude of calm conviction that her knowledge came from a source higher than any to which he, after the labours of a lifetime, had access, was maddening to a man whose intellect and learning were held in veneration by every student of theology, to whose opinion the most eminent men and women of the day deferred as to an oracle; and it is no marvel that his resentment should have been implacable against the half-educated visionary who thus, in full view of his contemporaries, set him at defiance.

Fortune had seemed to smile on Mme. Guyon when Mme. de Maintenon admitted her to intimacy, but her transient favour was her ruin. When she had once crossed the threshold of Saint-Cyr, the King directed his attention to her, for he shared Mme. de Maintenon's enthusiasm for the institution while it was still a novelty, and would permit no whisper of possible heresy in the ears of those who received their training under his patronage.

The doctrine of Quietism was, in fact, exceptionally pernicious to undeveloped minds, and was proportionately attractive, for it gave boundless scope to sentiment and imagination, faculties which are blighted by the monotony of school and convent life. Mme. Guyon perceived at once that she would find fertile ground at Saint-Cyr; the Ladies of Saint-Louis, no less than the scholars, were ready with their sympathy, and she sowed the seed of her new theories with a generous hand, foreseeing that the opportunity would not be lasting.

As has been demonstrated, Mme. de Maintenon made a fatal mistake when she opened the door to those sacred precincts; she herself might have found such teaching sufficiently innocuous, and its novelty stimulating to her jaded taste, but her imprudence was far less excusable than in the corresponding case of Fénelon's admission. The mistake was decisive of the fate of the enthusiast; it drew suspicion on her patroness, and precluded her from even an attempt at defending the proscribed doctrine. Fénelon's support was useless, for the King had already declared himself, and Mme. de Maintenon loved power far too well to let it waver in the balance. Mme. Guyon realised that she was deserted, but she was not long in discovering that there remained one friend on whom she might rely. "Do not talk of me, I implore you," she wrote to M. de Chevreuse when suspicion was gathering round her, "unless it be to M. l'Abbé de Fénelon, in whom I can confide; to him my heart is open."

Yet, as her case grew hopeless, she appealed many times to Mme. de Maintenon, seeking to move her to pity of her desolate condition; she was deceived, perhaps, by the endeavour made by that calculating lady to give her disaffection a gradual appearance. But though Mme. de Maintenon's inclinations were in favour of Quietism, she never really wavered; the royal fiat was to her as absolute as to the humblest subject of the King. To an intimate correspondent, Mme. de St. Géran, she reveals her secret leanings towards the visionary, even when she was ready to condemn her publicly. "I have had a copy of *L'Explication du Cantique des Cantiques* for two months," she wrote in May 1694; "there are some involved passages, some instructive, and some which I do not in any way approve. L'Abbé de Fénelon tells me that one may find the highest form of devotion in the *Moyen Court*. . . . I read a piece to the King, who pronounced it to be raving. He is not far enough advanced in religion as yet to appreciate its perfection. I have entreated Mme. notre Superieure to forbid our ladies to have these books in their hands in future. Such reading is too strong for them; they require milk suited to their age. Mme. Guyon edifies them, nevertheless I have asked her to discontinue her visits; but I cannot forbid them to read letters from one of such piety and virtue. M. de Paris seems much incensed against her; but he owns that the danger of her errors lies not in themselves but in their result, and that there is more to fear than to condemn."

Mme. de Maintenon evidently found it difficult to retreat with the dignity befitting her reputation; it was not easy to sacrifice Mme. Guyon and retain any claim to consistency, and already, looming in the distance, she saw the possible necessity of sacrificing Fénelon. That apprehension was not likely to soften her heart towards the cause of her anxieties; yet it was difficult to read appeals, of which the following is a specimen, and remain heedless.

"Madame," wrote Mme. Guyon, "so long as I was only accused of praying and teaching others to pray, I was content to remain hidden. I believed that every one would be satisfied if I neither spoke nor wrote to any one, that I should appease my enemies and calm the agitation of certain worthy people who were disturbed by calumny; but I find myself accused of that which concerns my honour—that crime is spoken of. I believe it to be due to the Church, to my family, and to myself, that the truth should be made known. Therefore, Madame, I ask of you such justice as is not refused to the most depraved in the most unenlightened countries: to let me have my trial, and to give me judges—half lay, half clerical—people of recognised standing and unprejudiced, for honesty is not enough when slander has prejudiced so many. If you obtain this favour for me—and, by the wounds of Christ, I beseech it of you, Madame—I will go to whatever prison it may please you or the King to commit me."

Indignation had inspired Mme. Guyon's pen; her righteous wrath had banished affection, and Fénelon himself could not have written with more obvious sincerity. "Yet another letter from Mme. Guyon; the woman is importunate!" was Mme. de Maintenon's comment to her favoured correspondent. "Truly she is very unlucky." She proceeds to give a possible scheme for the trial her suppliant desired; but her thoughts wandered to Fénelon, who was not in any way involved in the arrangements. "M. l'Abbé de Fénelon is too spiritual not to believe that one can love God for Himself only, and too wise to believe that one can love Him in the midst of the most shameful vices. He assures me that he only interferes in the matter to prevent careless condemnation of the opinions of true saints. He is not Mme. Guyon's defender although he is her friend; he is the defender of Christian godliness and piety. I trust in his word because I have met few men as honest as he is; and you may tell him so."

There is no evidence that Mme. de Maintenon made any effort to save Mme. Guyon once the tide had turned against her. All her energy was concentrated on ridding Saint-Cyr of the traces of her heretical instruction, and re-establishing her own tranquil authority; the cause of all her difficulties was abandoned to such justice or mercy as she might receive at the hands of Bossuet. Mme. Guyon's first experience of imprisonment was of six months' duration in the diocese of Meaux, where she could not escape from interviews sought by the bishop, and had no defence against his arguments and threats; but no power was strong enough to shake her faith and belief in a passive condition of prayer. She was ready to admit errors in her writings, misuse of words that conveyed a false impression (she often lamented the paucity of terms expressive of her sentiments), but the conviction that her thoughts had been directly inspired by God made it blasphemy to admit a fault in them. This was her faith, and in this she was immovable.

Bossuet, moved at length to admiration of her resolute endurance, set her free from the convent, and as she was willing to remain thenceforth in complete retirement, it seemed likely that her troubles were at an end. But her name had become the mainspring of numberless petty intrigues; it was impossible that she should sink into oblivion. The ladies of the Court, stirred by her teaching, had turned from those amenable confessors whose leniency had reconciled conscience and inclination to others more severe, and the resentment of the deserted priests fell upon Mme. Guyon. Bossuet's weaknesses made him an easy power to move for their revenge. It was whispered that the Quietist had defeated him in argument, converted him to her own theories, that in future he might be found working with Fénelon for her defence. The rumour carried a suggestion of mockery which was insupportable to the bishop's pride, already galled by the resistance of those who should have deferred to his opinion; he was secure of the King's sympathy, and the Quietist was consigned to the prison of Vincennes in the winter of 1695. Mme. de Maintenon had not then cut herself off from intercourse with Fénelon, and so long as they met face to face, his influence over her remained. It was at this point, therefore, that Mme. de Maintenon made her only decisive effort on behalf of the prisoner; she obtained her release from Vincennes, but only on condition of her remaining in the closest durance in a convent at Vaugirard.

During the year that followed Fénelon left the Court for the last time. He never saw Mme. de Maintenon again, and she interfered no more to soften the fate of

Mme. Guyon. By a final act of royal tyranny the Quietist was committed to the Bastille, and her enemies were satisfied at length. To her highly-strung temperament the associations of hopelessness and suffering inseparable from the very name of the great State prison were overwhelming; in some ways her treatment was much less rigorous than during her confinement at Vaugirard, but she was never permitted the solace of a friendly face, and had every reason for believing death the only end to her sufferings that was possible. She acknowledges that the five years spent in that gloomy place were terrible. She magnified the fretting grievances of early life into tragedies, but the details of that period of solitude and persecution are not recorded. There is no human language for describing such an experience as she was required to endure; it must perforce go down into silence, and the silence is significant.

Considering how unsparing had been the King's severity towards her, and the danger of displaying even compassion for her misfortunes, it is remarkable that she should ever have become an object for the royal clemency; it came too late to preserve her health, but it probably prolonged her life. She was permitted to remove to her son's house at Diziers for six months' change, under strict supervision, and when the moment came for her release she was found to be so shattered in nerve and physical strength that she had to be carried thither in a litter. This was in 1702, when Fénelon's fate had been long decided and Quietism no longer engrossed the public mind; she was suffered, therefore, to remain in comparative freedom. The fourteen years of her life that remained were passed at Blois in close seclusion; she was too much broken by persecution to be a further danger to the Church, her active life had ended when the gates of the Bastille closed upon her, and she could not have survived another year of imprisonment. The few who knew her after her release bore witness that she was never heard to complain of those who had used her so cruelly. "They believed that they did well," was her comment, the accuracy of which is open to question. The object of her enemies had been to silence her, and in this they were successful; but it is difficult to admit that the means employed conformed to any standard of well-doing.

She could sum up the lesson of her life in a few words, worth all the unrestrained extravagance of her writings. "It was God's will to humble me," she said; "I am not yet humbled enough. Blessed be His name." Her declining years exhibited the strength and endurance of her faith to noble purpose; she had proclaimed it when her world was listening to her in the hush of speechless admiration, and it had not faltered before the test of general contumely. The test was not a light one, for five years' confinement in the Bastille was an ordeal calculated to bring a man or woman down to reality, and the tissues woven by imagination and self-complacency fell to pieces when the applause and sympathy of others was withdrawn. Mme. Guyon declared that her God was all-sufficient for her, that her soul was so merged in Him, so irrevocably lost, "as a drop of water in the ocean," in the greatness of His glory, that she had no further part with earthly things, and it was ordained that she should put this self-annihilation to the proof. When she acknowledged that she endured terrible moments, she was admitting that it failed her, for if her theory had been absolutely valid, if self could be so lost in God that every thought was but an impression of His Spirit, then life could have no terrors, no sorrow, and no joy. In admitting that, as a lonely persecuted human being, she suffered, she convicts herself of inconsistency; but in her endurance of her suffering, in her fortitude and resolution under it, she testified that her faith was not the hallucination of a visionary but rather the venture of a pious soul, grasping too much and therefore failing, but still taking hold of a great truth that had power to keep her steadfast, in defiance of every trial inflicted by prejudice and intolerance.

It is difficult to estimate the value of her contribution to the history of human thought. In its ultimate result it ranks lower than less sensational doctrine; but, although her imagination often carried her away and her revolt against the restraint of the world's opinion misled her fatally, the actual force and courage of her conviction claims the reverence of all seekers after truth. In a society so loose in morals and degraded in ideals as was that of France under Louis XIV., she turned from the beaten track to a steeper and less alluring path; she realised the greatness of religion so keenly that the contrast between its infinite importance and the pettiness of the aims of daily life overwhelmed her, and her reasoning faculty was not strong enough to counterbalance the strength of the impression. The claim of human fellowship, the family ties which Christ Himself sealed and sanctified, were ignored in the ardour of her pursuit of a phantasm, and for many years of her life she was convinced that the supreme grace she pictured had been accorded to her.

Age and experience at length overthrew this arrogant certainty of Divine selection; she learned, perhaps by solitude, to find herself, and rest content with a calmer faith in the indwelling and fellowship of God; but in spite of all her errors and exaggerations, in spite of the suffering and discord whereof she was the cause, it should be remembered to her honour that her aim, however ill-directed, was above all else to solve the enigma of our human life, to understand the mystery of prayer.

CHAPTER V

THE QUIETISM CONTROVERSY

HISTORICALLY, the Quietism controversy is the central point in the life of Fénelon, and it may also be termed the central point in the development of his character. During the earlier period of his career every circumstance seems to have combined to smooth the path he had chosen; if he resolutely turned away from the delights of the world, he had every inducement of personal friendship and general veneration to keep to the way of self-denial. "He desires to be loved," Mme. de Maintenon had written of him many years before; in the intimate circle of de Beauvilliers and de Chevreuse he obtained his desire to the full. It is idle to speculate on what he might have become if the world had continued to smile on him; undoubtedly the highest honours were within his reach, and he would ere long have obtained the dignity of cardinal. Nevertheless, his years of exile at Cambrai are a more impressive conclusion to a life begun under the auspices of Saint-Sulpice than any of the glories of the Papal Court could be. The gradual unfolding of his character is evident from the time when he drank in M. Tronson's exhortations to self-surrender and disinterested love, through the years in which his mind lay open to the scrutiny of Bossuet, until the crisis came when he found himself arraigned as a traitor to

THE QUIETISM CONTROVERSY

the Church he loved by the friend whom he had trusted; and throughout, whatever bypaths of ambition or desire may have temporarily beguiled him, he held to the supreme purpose which had inspired his earliest reflections.

The controversy that convulsed the Roman Church at the end of the seventeenth century has long ceased to engage attention; its details are, however, not without interest to the historian. It reveals Mme. de Maintenon trimming her sails to the breezes of expediency with the most convincing distinctness, and the differing characteristics of Bossuet, de Noailles, and many another distinguished pilot of the Church are depicted with a vividness impossible of attainment otherwise. The primary cause of it was nominally the King's eagerness to root out every sign of heresy within his realm; this had turned his attention to Mme. Guyon, and inspired a general criticism of the Quietists; but also he resented the growing friendship between Fénelon and Mme. de Maintenon. Bossuet also, in a different way, was jealous of the friendship, and ready to work on the royal prejudice as soon as he detected it. Fénelon's appointment to the duke and subsequent archbishopric were the result of his favour with the public rather than with the King; his spiritual religion never appealed to Louis, who was easily disposed to rank him as a dangerous charlatan in the same category with Molinos.

Bossuet waited till every circumstance was propitious for his attack; his bitterness towards his former friend must have been of gradual growth, originating in some sort of rivalry. In the days of their familiar intercourse at Germigny he had recognised Fénelon's ability, his gift of graceful speech and his literary power, and he knew that at any moment the post he held might place him foremost among rulers, for if the King died the eyes of the nation would be turned towards the young Duke of Burgundy, while the Dauphin, Bossuet's own pupil, could never be more than a crowned nonentity. Bossuet, after so many years of pre-eminence, could not face the possibilities unfolded by such speculations; his way of life had not fostered his affections, and, between envy and ambition, his love for Fénelon withered rapidly, and he traded on the unsuspicious nature of his victim.

It has been shown already that Fénelon did not yield to the attraction of Mme. Guyon's doctrine till her period of favour was near its close, and even during their brief personal intercourse he was always reluctant to recommend her or her books to others. He expressly states that he never gave a copy of the latter to any one, and it is probable that only his intimate friends were conscious of the degree of sympathy existing between them. From Bossuet, however, he had no concealments. While he was reflecting on the worth of Mme. Guyon's theories he would have discussed them freely with him, and, if he had remained the simple abbé of the Nouvelles Catholiques, M. de Meaux might have left him to dream and speculate unchallenged. But he was the friend of Mme. de Maintenon, and the King made him Archbishop of Cambrai; that constituted his original guilt, and Bossuet, in his zeal for the Church, did not scruple to bring up their confidential discussions as evidence of heresy, declaring that the

THE QUIETISM CONTROVERSY 125

accused book was less heretical than the opinions its writer had expressed in his hearing, and constantly repeating his assertion in the society where Fénelon was most revered.

"Observe (and you may protest on my behalf)," Fénelon wrote to his agent in Rome when he heard of this treachery, "that we had but two conversations on this topic, wherein we only talked vaguely, without entering on any special question."[1]

Even these two conversations were before his appointment to the See of Cambrai, and he was consecrated by Bossuet himself, although suspicions of Quietism were already in the air. This fact should have told in his favour, for those who knew him knew that he would not have disguised his real opinions. Bossuet deftly turned his own inconsistency in the matter to his own advantage, however, by subsequently making elaborate and somewhat theatrical apologies to the King for having taken any part in a ceremony so prejudicial to the Church, and Fénelon refused to attach any importance to the incident. "He never asked me if I was of his opinion," he says; "such a question would have been utterly improper. Agreement with the Church is what is necessary, not with one particular bishop."[2]

Bossuet could hardly expect a man of such strong intellectual powers to remain perpetually submissive to him. Fénelon's independence was late of development. He clung to a condition of tutelage endeared by custom long after his personal influence and authority were

[1] *Correspondance de Fénelon*, viii. 258, to de Chanterac, September 1697.
[2] *Ibid.*, viii. 327, January 1698.

recognised by others; but when the moment came that their opinions clashed, his fundamental sincerity of thought made submission impossible, and Bossuet, when he applied his decisive test, must have foreseen the probable result. It was fortunate for him that his desires accorded with those of the King. The King had declared against Mme. Guyon and her theory of prayer as represented in her celebrated pamphlet, *Le Moyen Court;* the moment was, therefore, opportune for another work treating the same subject from another point of view, and Bossuet seized it to compose his *États d'Oraison.* This purported to be a commentary on the Articles of Issy, and in it Mme. Guyon's doctrine received no mercy. His pen was a sure weapon, and she was defenceless. If he had aimed only at her downfall he was secure of success, but he desired to shake the foundation of Fénelon's influence also, and that was a more complicated matter. His method of accomplishing his purpose was ingenious: he sent his book to Fénelon to read and sanction before it was published, knowing that by consenting his colleague must admit error in his own expressed opinions, and thus weaken his position in the Church for ever, while the consequences of refusal were incalculable, and might possibly be fatal to his career.

In the spring of 1695 Fénelon, at the Conference of Issy, had agreed in the Articles regarding Quietism, and he imagined that it would be equally easy to agree to the book which he knew to be in preparation. He was at Cambrai when the manuscript reached him, and therefore could not take counsel with any of his confi-

THE QUIETISM CONTROVERSY

dential friends. As he turned the leaves and skimmed their meaning, it appeared to him to be impossible to endorse the opinions they contained, and he found that his implicit confidence in Bossuet had involved him in a position from which he could not escape without some degree of inconsistency, for, in his opinion, the book accused Mme. Guyon of the most mischievous tenets of the corrupt followers of Molinos. "If, by a public subscription to it, I supported this explanation of her system," he wrote in one of the many pamphlets of the controversy, "I should help to convince the world in general that the imputation on her is true, and that she is, in consequence, the most accursed being upon earth.

"I have often seen her; it is well known that I have, and I respect her. I have allowed people of high reputation, who trust me, to hold her in high esteem. . . . I could not esteem her without going to the very foundation of her theories; I have got more to the bottom of them than her examiners could possibly have done, because she was more open and free with me, and confided in me completely."[1]

The view here expressed is a somewhat exaggerated one, nevertheless it is obvious that his code of honour bound him to support the accused woman as far as possible, despite the loss in friends and reputation she might cost him, and in this he was hampered by the faith in Bossuet which he had so openly professed. Such expressions as the following were not easy to forget, yet it was little more than a year since he had written them.

[1] Œuvres de Fénelon, iv., p. 91.

"VERSAILLES, *December* 16, 1694.

"I must simply obey always, for it is neither the man nor the learned doctor that I see in you—it is God. Even when you are mistaken, my absolute obedience is not mistaken, and mistakes made in humility and under the control of those who have authority in the Church do not trouble me. Once again, Monseigneur, if it were possible for you to be doubtful of my entire compliance, test it, and do not spare me. Albeit your mind is more enlightened than that of others, I pray that God may darken it, leaving you the light of His only. All my life, Monseigneur, I shall be equally full of respect for you."[1]

It is impossible to form a fair estimate of Bossuet's conduct if we ignore such evidence as this, and Fénelon himself found it as difficult to reconcile his new attitude of defiance with his former absolute humility as to retract his expressions of agreement with Mme. Guyon. Her desolate condition went far towards deciding him in his choice, and if he had yielded to Bossuet at such a crisis he would have found it hard ever to claim his independence. He was loyal to the Church even when it condemned him; he was in complete agreement with the whole system of authority, but as Archbishop of Cambrai he owed no allegiance to the Bishop of Meaux, and he was asserting this principle when he refused to add his name to those of de Noailles and Desmarais, who were ready to sanction the *États d'Oraison*.

Bossuet may have expected him to take the safer course of agreement, even though it left him open to

[1] *Correspondance de Fénelon*, vii.

future attack; but from the moment that his refusal was made public the most powerful brain in the kingdom was at work to compass his downfall, and the celebrated friendship which had edified society for so many years was at an end. Fénelon's grief at the rupture of the bond between them was deep and sincere. "God alone knows what pain it is to me to give pain to one for whom, in all the world, I have the most attachment and respect,"[1] he wrote, even when he was defending himself from the most virulent attacks, and he would not have called God to witness to a profession that was not absolutely sincere.

The *États d'Oraison* is founded on the teaching of the Saints and Fathers of the Church, carefully cited so as to contradict the assertions of Mme. Guyon. Bossuet summarises Quietism as "Indifference between salvation and damnation, between the favour and disapproval of God, the suppression of desire, of action, of effort, of all direct employment of free-will,"[2] and he will allow no other meaning to the expressions "abandonment" and "consecration," so constantly on the lips of Mme. Guyon.

As the book professed to be an enlargement of the Articles of Issy, the Church's judgment upon Mysticism, which had been signed by Fénelon, it was necessary for him to defend his refusal to support it if he would escape a charge of gross inconsistency, and it was with this object that he wrote his own commentary on the Articles, which he entitled *L'Explication des Maximes des Saints sur la Vie Intérieure*. This treatise, being merely an arrangement of the opinions attributed to the

[1] *Œuvres de Fénelon*, iv., p. 101.   [2] *États d'Oraison*, liv. v.

Saints, with the false deductions drawn from them by Molinos and others, is now very difficult reading, and is the weakest of Fénelon's works from the literary point of view, but it was the epitome of his own view of the question, and therefore of infinite interest at the period of writing. It was, in fact, a defence of the Saints, whom he felt to be involved in the attacks on modern Mysticism. The most superficial knowledge of the writings of such visionaries as St. Teresa or St. Catherine of Genoa will indicate their affinity with the teaching of Mme. Guyon, but it was with the doctrine of St. Francis de Sales that Fénelon was especially concerned. Throughout his life he continued to. recommend the maxims of St. Francis as themes for meditation and incentives to self-conquest, and it was of vital importance to him that no reflection, even indirect, should be cast upon their purity. It can hardly be disputed that the writings of St. Francis are susceptible to the imputation of what was known as false Mysticism. Before the arraignment of Molinos many propositions had been not only tolerated, but approved by the Church, which Bossuet would have convicted of heresy, and therefore the failure of any effort to exonerate the Saints from some of the charges proved against Mme. Guyon was a foregone conclusion, for—to choose one instance from the many—St. Bernard of Clairvaux is quite as explicit on the question of passive or contemplative prayer as the Quietist writer of *Le Moyen Court*.

Fénelon had, in fact, attempted the impossible, and had ventured every hope and ambition of his life on the attempt. The comment attributed to Innocent XII.—" Monseigneur de Cambrai errs from excess of love, Mon-

THE QUIETISM CONTROVERSY 131

seigneur de Meaux from lack of it "—describes the situation. It was easy for Fénelon to find support for his own doctrine in the writings of the Saints, and he did so in his *Maximes;* but when he endeavours to prove that his doctrine and theirs is absolutely distinct from Quietism, he becomes hopelessly obscure. He was, however, so confident in his book that he submitted it to de Noailles, Archbishop of Paris, and to his old master, M. Tronson. He consulted a representative of the Sorbonne also, and when he had complied with the few alterations suggested, the book was pronounced to be *tout d'or*. De Noailles recommended, however, that the *Maximes* should not appear till Bossuet's *États d'Oraison* had been given to the public, and to this Fénelon agreed readily. The advice was good, but unfortunately his friends, prompted by most mistaken zeal, caused the book to be printed and distributed during his absence from Paris.

The result was most disastrous. *Les Maximes* was intended as an answer to the *États d'Oraison*. If they had appeared simultaneously its existence would have been understood, but, coming by itself, it was uncalled-for and superfluous. Moreover, to the general public its meaning seemed to be so involved that considerable self-confidence was required to profess an individual opinion of its doctrine. Its obscurity irritated those who had been eager to obtain it on account of their love for its author, and it lay at the mercy of theologians who might explain its subtleties as they pleased.

Theology was a favourite topic of conversation at that time among many who were not theologians, and a rumour of the discussion was not long in reaching the

King. Fénelon had held no communication with Bossuet on the subject of *Les Maximes*, a fact easily explained by their late disagreement regarding the *États d'Oraison*, but liable to misinterpretation, and it was easy to whisper that he was declaring himself a partisan of Mme. Guyon and Quietism, and to rouse the King to indignation that he had not been warned before. Having gained this point, Bossuet adopted the attitude most advantageous to himself and derogatory to Fénelon; he was full of contrition that affection should have made him hesitate to apprise the King of his suspicions earlier, and he undertook to do all that lay in his power to bring the Archbishop of Cambrai to humble acknowledgment of his errors, not forgetting to suggest the terrible possibilities of danger to the princes and the nation owing to the position of the culprit at Court and in the Church.

It is open to argument that Fénelon was mistaken in his original opposition to Bossuet. To the modern reader the *États d'Oraison* appears innocuous, except, perhaps, in its closing sentences, which are very explicit in their condemnation of every form of Mysticism; but Fénelon was sensitive to any reflection on his doctrine, and the persecution which Mme. Guyon was suffering aroused his indignation and his chivalry. Her burden was already so overwhelming that his censure could have added little to the load, and his intervention did not lighten it; nevertheless, even if he was wrong in his original defiance, his subsequent self-restraint and probity redeem his position, and *Les Maximes*, if one may judge by contemporary correspondence, was innocent of heresy in the eyes of unprejudiced critics. Its condemnation was, in fact, the

THE QUIETISM CONTROVERSY 133

result of the malignity of Bossuet, which every circumstance combined to foster, until his powerful brain was completely concentrated on it.

The excitement in Paris over the supposed heresy of the Archbishop of Cambrai was as great as that caused in Rome by the fall of Molinos, and those who trimmed their sails to suit the breeze that blew at Court were frequently in difficulties. De Noailles must be included in this category; he had openly commended the ill-omened treatise, and now, being altogether disinclined to stand in opposition to Bossuet and the King, was forced to veer round and contradict himself. The course taken by Mme. de Maintenon has been indicated already, and to Fénelon the defection of such friends as these was only less painful than the misfortunes that fell on those who remained faithful to him.

Bossuet was methodical and deliberate in action. In the March after the publication of *Les Maximes* he summoned de Noailles, Archbishop of Paris, and Godet Desmarais, Bishop of Chartres, to confer upon it. These two were not only eminent in the Church, but also closely connected with the Court, and conspicuous figures at Versailles. The one was confessor to Mme. de Maintenon, and the other her most intimate correspondent. It would have been an act of heroism for either of them to risk the alienation of royal favour, and the heroic faculty was lacking, therefore the Bishop of Meaux, whose opinion represented that of the King, ruled the conference, and the greater part of *Les Maximes* was condemned as heretical. It was possible that, in conformity with this verdict, every bishop in France would forbid the circulation of the book within his diocese, and so make Fénelon's position in the Church untenable. Many of his friends urged submission and the withdrawal of *Les Maximes*, but he, awaking all at once to the full menace of Bossuet's enmity, appealed to Rome.

He must have added greatly to his knowledge of human nature at that crisis, for in personal relation to himself he saw men with a vividness impossible while his experience was limited to the confessional. M. Tronson had been his guide so often that his first instinct was to turn to him.

"What does it matter that I do not believe Mme. Guyon to be either mad or wicked," he wrote, "if I maintain absolute silence, if I leave her to die in prison without taking part directly or indirectly in anything that concerns her? They could not desire to press me further if they did not believe that some dangerous mystery lay behind my aversion to censuring her. Yet the sole mystery is that I do not desire to speak against my conscience, that I do not desire to insult one whom I have reverenced as a Saint from all I have, personally, seen of her. Can they truly have doubts of my sincerity? Have I behaved as if I calculated or dissembled? Should I be in my present difficulties if I had been influenced by the world? Why should that be required of me which would hardly be required of an impostor? I conjure you to read all this attentively, and if you think well, to allow Monseigneur de Chartres to read it."[1]

There is infinite foreboding in this appeal, and he looked in vain to M. Tronson for support. The Superior

[1] *Correspondance de Fénelon*, vii. 99.

of Saint-Sulpice was advanced in years, and his habitual humility made it easy to convince himself that he had been mistaken in his commendation of *Les Maximes*. He shared the general opinion of Bossuet's erudition, and regarded him as the chief pillar of the Church in France, while he felt Fénelon, as his former pupil, to be open to his criticism. M. de Beauvilliers, who had been his pupil also, wrote to him almost simultaneously.

"I tell you with the honesty that you know to be mine that there is a cabal against Monseigneur de Cambrai. Mme. de Maintenon fancies that she will glorify God by being always ready to go to extremes against Monseigneur de Cambrai. As I have told Monseigneur de Chartres, there need be no anxiety regarding the princes, neither of whom knows that there is a woman called Mme. Guyon in the world, or a book called *Le Moyen Court*."[1]

No one knew better than M. de Beauvilliers that if Mme. de Maintenon went "to extremes" it would mean ruin to Fénelon, and, as their governor, he was the best judge of any point concerning the princes; but all his representations were unavailing. M. Tronson pleaded age and illness as an excuse for silence whenever possible, and when his opinion was peremptorily demanded, he gave it in favour of Bossuet.

Fénelon never reproached him, and his letters to him never ceased to be affectionate. He concentrated his indignation on Mme. de Maintenon, and addressed her with a candour which, in the midst of so much intriguing and diplomacy, is somewhat astonishing.

[1] *Correspondance de Fénelon*, vii. 100.

"Permit me to remind you, Madame, that after seeming to share our opinion on the innocence of this woman, you turned suddenly to the exact opposite. Ever since then you have been suspicious of my firmness, your heart has been closed against me; people who desire a chance of intercourse with you, and of becoming necessary to you, impress on you in roundabout ways that I am deluded, that I may be growing heretical. They resort to many methods to move you; you are struck by them, and pass from excessive confidence and security to excessive disturbance and alarm. This has been the cause of all our misfortunes. You dare not follow your own heart and your own instincts. . . . If you had spoken openly to me, I could, in three days, have brought all the disturbed souls of Saint-Cyr to peace and entire submission to their saintly bishop. . . . Do not fear that I shall contradict Monseigneur de Meaux; I shall never speak of him except as my master, or of his propositions [1] but as the rule of the Faith. I am willing that he should triumph, and that he should convict me of every kind of error: it is not a question of me, but of the doctrine." [2]

He was inspired, at any rate in the beginning, by a desire for the truth. He cared more for that than for any individual sentiments or ambition, although in the heat of the conflict then impending some personal resentment inevitably crept in. His sense of disappointment was perhaps stronger than his resentment; it was difficult for him to believe that the sun of friendship and popularity which had shone upon him so warmly could be

---

[1] The Articles of Issy.   [2] *Correspondance de Fénelon*, vii. 102.

THE QUIETISM CONTROVERSY 137

irrevocably clouded over. Once in the autumn of that disastrous year, 1696, he wrote to Bossuet in terms that recalled their old intimacy, in the vain hope of bridging the gulf which seemed to be rapidly widening between them. The failure of that attempt convinced him of the hopelessness of any reconciliation. Bossuet required complete surrender, and compliance appeared to Fénelon to involve a deliberate denial of the truth. From that moment he set himself to face the inevitable struggle with wisdom and self-control, qualities especially needed during the year immediately following, when he still held his post at Court, but was overshadowed by the cloud of his impending disgrace.

In his familiar correspondence his chief comfort to those in sorrow was the assurance that God directs all things. He aspired to that "prone submission to the heavenly will, seeing it, what it is and why it is," which is the essence of true Quietism, and his misfortunes gave him the opportunity of proving the consolation of religion, and showing with what resignation and self-surrender he could accept a lot which must be difficult, however fortune turned.

"Disinterested love should make us disinterested in all our opinions, impartial in all our views. I wish for nothing of my own. Everything belongs to the Church, our mother, holder of our trust. If what I say does not come from her, if I have not learnt it in her bosom, I hate and condemn all my thoughts and all my words." This, written to a brother priest while he was still engaged on his duties at Versailles, is an epitome of his views. It is necessary to follow it to understand his position, for while he endeavoured to think for himself, he intended also to be loyal to the Church, and looked to the Pope as the "holder of his trust"; and being hard pressed by his colleagues, it was the Pope to whom he appealed for justice. Considering his rank, he did his duty in so doing, and was within his rights when he asked the King for permission to go himself to Rome to support his letter and plead his cause before his Holiness; nevertheless the application was practically a declaration of war. The King refused consent, probably fearing the effect which Fénelon's personality might have upon the Pope, and accompanied his refusal with a peremptory order to the archbishop to retire to Cambrai, and remain within his diocese till he received the royal permission to leave it. The letter was dated August 1, 1697, and it was, in fact, his sentence of perpetual banishment. Fénelon obeyed immediately, and left the Court for ever.

Even such a blow as this does not seem to have made him realise the full strength of the forces ranged against him. He must have known the later history of the Church and the influence of Louis XIV. on its proceedings, but he refused to acknowledge that the power of the King could be greater than the justice of the Pope, although that power was the reason of his condemnation. The far-sighted among his friends, such as de Chevreuse and de Beauvilliers, foresaw the outcome, and those who believed they detected discrepancies between his professed doctrine and his book, such as Tronson and Desmarais, regarded him as condemned already; but in his exile at Cambrai he had a little band of loyal priests around him, encouraging him by their confidence

THE QUIETISM CONTROVERSY 139

in his ultimate victory, and spurring him on to renewed efforts with brain and pen, efforts which resulted in disappointment, and can only be deplored.

From August 1697 the scene of the struggle changed to Rome. Fénelon was not allowed to be there in person, but from the date of the King's letter to him until the papal decision was pronounced all his interest in life was centred on the Vatican. He had selected the Abbé de Chanterac as his representative and confidential agent, and the abbé's letters to him depict the extraordinary tangle of intrigue and chicanery which gathered round the trial of his book, till the original reason of the dispute was completely lost and almost forgotten by all but Fénelon himself.

It was, in fact, very difficult for the Pope to condemn the *Explication des Maximes des Saints* even in compliance with the desire of Louis XIV., because such condemnation involved the denial of much that was admitted by the Saints, a dangerous position even for the Pope. The book was given to the ten "Consulters" of the Holy Office for examination. Their conferences began in the autumn of 1697, and they met three times in the week (which gives an impression of the intricacy of the subject). After a year, that is to say in the autumn of 1698, five of them persisted in pronouncing the book to be absolutely orthodox, in defiance of every influence that could be brought to bear upon them. That year was, therefore, wasted, and the proceedings had to be begun again. The period of suspense promised to be of long duration, but the duel of pamphlets waged between Bossuet and Fénelon never ceased, Bossuet becoming more and more reckless in his animosity as each of his thrusts was parried by a hand as skilful as his own. It is melancholy that Fénelon's literary genius should have been so misused; but the vigour and rapidity with which, without being once betrayed into abuse or slander, he turned his adversary's weapons against himself is worthy of admiration. Most of the writings produced by the dispute are now devoid of interest, but at the time the excitement was intense, as they were successively distributed in Rome.

Bossuet's choice of an agent was to the advantage of his cause, but greatly to the detriment of his reputation; it fell on his nephew, the Abbé Bossuet, a man of great ability, well versed in knowledge of the secret springs that moved the powers of the Vatican, a diplomatist by nature, and thoroughly unscrupulous. He it was who kept the fire of controversy at furnace-heat throughout the lingering proceedings of the papal Court, feeding it again and again by personal attacks on Fénelon and innuendoes against his private character. He had good reason to take credit for the ultimate triumph of his chief, for de Chanterac was no match for him, but it required two years of patient labour to secure to him the papal Bull that condemned *Les Maximes* as containing heresy.

Fénelon lost in the struggle, yet the dignified submission with which he accepted his defeat won him universal reverence, while Bossuet, though he might glory in success, had sullied himself for ever by the means to which he had resorted to obtain it. The only work, of the many concerned with their dispute, that retains interest for the reader of to-day, is due to the pen of the latter; at a moment when society was growing slack in interest concerning a battle fought at so great a distance from Versailles, he wrote his *Relation sur la Quietism*.

His full cleverness as an author is here exhibited; from the first page to the last it is terse, graphic, and vigorous, a masterpiece of style; but, admirable though it may be in a literary aspect, it is, humanly, a disgraceful performance. Bossuet did not undervalue the influence of his name and reputation on the public mind; his book was intended for the general public, and might be read by many from whom Fénelon, in his exile, could never obtain a hearing. He professed to be writing a history of the celebrated dispute from the beginning, and it was natural that he should tell it from his own point of view and strive to leave a final impression favourable to himself, but his animosity carried him so far that he permitted himself to make suggestions of a criminal intrigue between Fénelon and Mme. Guyon. He explained his adversary's tenacity by the fact that he shared his doctrine with Mme. Guyon, and was defending her when he defended it. The moderate and deprecatory language in which this calumny is couched makes it all the more venomous, and he illustrates his theory by reference to a well-known story—Montan, a fanatic in the second century, roaming about the world with Priscilla, another man's wife, and proclaiming that their bond was one of spiritual sympathy, until their statement was conclusively discredited and their names became bywords of blasphemy and vice. Bossuet dares to draw a parallel between these two and Fénelon and Mme. Guyon, insinuating in his closing chapter—with mildness and hesitation—"that this Priscilla has found her Montan to defend her."

This is the most deplorable incident of the affair. The book was seized upon and devoured with delight; it lowered the tone of the controversy irreparably, and afforded much entertainment to the frivolous section of society. "The book of M. de Meaux makes an immense sensation here: we talk of nothing else. Its development is beyond no one's capacity; Mme. Guyon's folly gives general amusement. The book is short, brisk, and well-written: it is lent, snatched, devoured. . . . It has revived the King's indignation that we allowed him to make such an archbishop; he reproaches me violently: all the worry of this business has to fall on me."

Such was Mme. de Maintenon's comment on a production which contained the grossest of libels upon two of her intimate friends; apparently her sole reason for regretting its existence was the personal worry of which it was the cause.

The general amusement was not confined to Marly or Versailles; in Rome the dulness of an intricate controversy was lightened by the breath of scandal; the Abbé Bossuet fostered every attempt to amplify the story so dexterously suggested by his uncle, and priests and cardinals discussed it over their chocolate with covert smiles. The general effect of the pamphlet is described in de Chanterac's letters to Cambrai: he loved his chief with the most faithful and ardent devotion, and the *Relation* roused him to indignant wrath. Fénelon's instinct was to ignore it, and, had it been possible, that was, no doubt, the most dignified course; but the times were not ripe for any refinement of self-restraint, and de Chanterac considered a prompt reply to be absolutely necessary. Throughout he was a true representative of Fénelon; he would not condescend to touch the poisoned weapons wielded by his adversaries with such dexterity, but he had the shrewdness to see that they were within his reach.

"I don't know that it would not be more prudent of him to say no more of Mme. Guyon," he wrote when Bossuet was endeavouring to convince the Quietist by daily interviews and discussions, "for I have seen certain cardinals who were much interested in her stay at Meaux, and asked me if she was beautiful and young. I have never wished to listen to anything of that kind, and indeed I became so grave in speaking of his piety and his zeal for the instruction of this lady that they abandoned this sort of jest."[1]

The impression made by Bossuet's pamphlet at the moment was terrible, and Fénelon's friends were thrown into consternation, which was augmented by the production of a letter addressed by the unfortunate La Combe to Mme. Guyon, of which the following is an extract:—

PÈRE LA COMBE TO MME. GUYON.

"*April* 27, 1698.

"Honour and glory be to the one God.

"I sincerely acknowledge before God, Madame, that there has been delusion, error, and sin in certain matters

[1] *Correspondance de Fénelon*, viii. 337, February 1698.

wherein there was too great freedom between us, and that I regret and loathe all principles and conduct that depart from the commandments of God and of the Church, openly disowning all I have done against these holy and inviolate laws, and exhorting you to do the same, in the name of our Lord—to the end that we may undo, so far as it is possible to us, the harm our bad example may have done, and all that we have written which could do injury to the law of morality laid down by the Holy Catholic Church. . . . Once again I entreat you by the love of Christ that we may take refuge in the one remedy of penitence, that, by a truly repentant and absolutely regular life, we may efface the grievous impression our false steps have made upon the Church. Let us, you and I, confess our sins humbly before heaven and earth, blushing rather that we committed them than at their confession." [1]

La Combe was already insane when this letter was extorted from him, but de Noailles condescended to confront Mme. Guyon with it suddenly in the hope of surprising her into a like acknowledgment of guilt. "She changed colour on reading it, but afterwards observed that he must have been forced to write it by torture, or must be mad. She did not seem disconcerted. Being much pressed to confess, she acknowledged that on returning from a journey Père La Combe embraced her. More than this she would not say." [2] Nevertheless the

[1] *Correspondance de Fénelon*, ix. 391.
[2] Report by M. de Chetardie, Curé of Saint-Sulpice, on an interview held with Mme. Guyon, of which he was a witness (*Correspondance de Fénelon*, ix. 403, May 1698).

THE QUIETISM CONTROVERSY

letter served to blacken Mme. Guyon's reputation further, and Fénelon's enemies had succeeded so well in linking their names together that he suffered proportionately. De Chanterac felt the necessity of being candid even on so difficult a subject, and in July he wrote thus to Fénelon:—

"You know that for the last three months the most shameful things regarding the conduct of Père La Combe and Mme. Guyon are spread about: that they made him acknowledge the most detestable crimes; that they made him write to Mme. Guyon exhorting her before God to acknowledge them with equal humility. After this they produce a letter wherein you call this woman 'mon amie.' This is an odious word in Italy, and they add—to give additional weight to such testimony—that they daily discover more, still more surprising and convincing."[1]

It was a painful task to despatch such a report as this to Cambrai. Fénelon's enemies seemed to have had free entrance everywhere, and their hints were far more dangerous than their open accusations. A phrase which was innocent in the writer's native tongue became an acknowledgment of guilt when translated, and a misplaced comma a conviction of heresy. "They threaten and give glimpses of fearful things against him," wrote de Chanterac to the Abbé de Langeron, "and so confuse his book, his doctrine, and his conduct with Mme. Guyon, that it all becomes the same."[2] De Chanterac was, in fact, torn between his regret at giving pain and his desire to convince his master of the full urgency of the danger, but the sympathy that inspired his letters must have softened the disastrous news that he was forced to give.

[1] *Correspondance de Fénelon*, ix. 434.   [2] *Ibid.*, ix. 453.

"You will forgive me for all the evil that I tell you, Monseigneur. My heart is sometimes sharply pierced to have to send you such cruel and unjust things; but it is not possible for me to be silent when I see so clearly and absolutely that silence in itself may be your destruction. I am happier now the truth will be known. What can they decide against you? Can they condemn the pure love of God, charging you with all the evil motives which Monseigneur de Meaux imputes to you, and which you have so well refuted? I am assured again to-day that Rome will be immovable, and that I need not fear the least influence on the Holy See from all this explosion at the French Court."[1]

It was undeniable that silence would be fatal, and again and again Fénelon implored the Pope to stop the war of pamphlets, representing that it was impossible for him to leave attacks upon his reputation unanswered if he retained his position in the Church. He, at least, could see the anomaly of the situation, and shrank from the part that he was forced to play. With grim humour, he catalogued the letters already discharged upon the world: "Monseigneur de Paris gives me a fresh hold, and involves me in a fourth letter. Monseigneur de Meaux is publishing an immense book. As you say, the accused should have the last word, but we shall spend our lives tearing each other and scandalising the Church, if, after so many reprisals, they do not command silence."[2]

Bossuet fired off accusation and rejoinder with evident delight in every point scored by his brilliant logic, but

---

[1] *Correspondance de Fénelon*, ix. 464.
[2] *Ibid.*, viii. 360, to de Chanterac.

THE QUIETISM CONTROVERSY

Fénelon, while his sense of justice forced him to fight, could find no pleasure in the exercise, desiring only rest and silence. "I can proclaim their injustice to the world; shall I make this scandal, or is it better to let myself be blackened and made permanently useless to my flock?"[1] This is the frequent burden of his letters; but to the very last, in spite of every hindrance in printing and conveyance, in spite of ill-health, depression, and solitude, he was forced to strain every nerve to defend himself from the persistent slander of his foes. It was all unavailing, nevertheless, and it is curious to observe how the buoyant optimism of de Chanterac sinks gradually before the terrible conviction of defeat. It was impossible for him not to see that the battle was to be decided from Versailles; but it was contrary to Fénelon's loyalty to accept such a suggestion, and he combats it with a sort of despair in his opposition: "Condemnation after such frightful aspersions on my faith and conduct will cover me with infamy for ever. No solitude will be deep enough, no desert distant enough for me. As matters stand, to condemn me and to depose me will be one and the same."[2] Had he expected condemnation, he would not have expressed himself so strongly; he believed so sincerely in the justice of his cause that it seemed to him to be treason to the Pope to have doubts of the final decision. "If the Roman Church is influenced by the favour or disfavour of princes, she will fall (I dare to say it) into irrevocable error. Even the wisdom of the world and the interests of authority ought to prevent so false a

[1] *Correspondance de Fénelon*, viii. 292.   [2] *Ibid.*, x. 504, November 1698.

step."[1] So he wrote more than a year before judgment was pronounced, and this was the ground of his hopes until the very end. In this, at least, he was consistent, for he never flinched in his opposition to the influence of Versailles or in absolute submission to the Vatican, and it was hard for him to realise the intrigues that were entangling the controversy and explained the unexpected verdict. Contemporary letters are the surest guides to the truth of so confused a battle, and the glimpses that they give of Pope and cardinals and "Consulters" indicate that these were less divided in opinion than they appeared: that, in fact, the sympathies of the Roman world were with Fénelon, and the evil hour of decision was postponed from month to month, because some chance—the death of the King or Bossuet—might relax the pressure and allow the papal conscience to weigh against the papal policy.

De Chanterac gives a minute report of many interviews with Innocent XII., and, to the unprejudiced reader, the Holy Father does not emerge from his difficulties with honour. "I send you a copy of the King's letter to the Pope," de Chanterac wrote when he first arrived in Rome; "M. l'Abbé Bossuet is at great pains to make it public here. Nothing is talked of but the favour in which M. de Meaux stands at the French Court, as if this favour must carry the votes of all the examiners of the book. It seems to me that religion teaches a different notion of the decisions of the Church."[2] This impression was a hindrance to him, and he was always too ready to

---

[1] *Correspondance de Fénelon*, viii. 339, to de Chanterac, February 1698.
[2] *Ibid.*, viii. 262, to de Langeron, October 1697.

THE QUIETISM CONTROVERSY 149

accept the appearance of piety which the Pope assumed in his presence. In one description he relates how Innocent "greatly hoped this matter could be arranged in France," in reply to which he represented the many advances towards a peaceful understanding made by Fénelon, so that the matter must now await the judgment of his Holiness, to whom they hoped "the Holy Spirit would reveal the whole truth." At this the Pope appeared greatly affected; "joining his hands together, he drew them gently towards his breast, and remained thus for some moments with downcast eyes, like one absorbed in religious thought who is praying secretly."[1]

Considered in relation to the subsequent action of the Pope, this is a curious picture, but at the time de Chanterac thought it very reassuring, and continued—even when his hopes had dwindled to vanishing-point—to rally in a surprising manner after an interview with his Holiness. In November 1698 it was plain to all dispassionate observers that Bossuet's triumph was secured. It was said openly that the King had it more at heart than the succession to the throne of Spain. Innocent XII. had already yielded once to the will of the King of France, so that there was little room for uncertainty as to the course that he would choose. Nevertheless, he continued to practise the most elaborate dissimulation. De Chanterac's report convicts him:—

"ROME, *November* 23, 1698.

"I have presented your last letter to the Pope. This last audience gave me more satisfaction than all those which I have had till now, not only on account of his

[1] *Correspondance de Fénelon*, viii. 305, December 1697.

outward air of frankness, or rather—cordiality. He was eager to make me rise almost before I was on my knees. Formerly he has signed to me to lean upon his table, which stands between us. This last time he wished me to come round, that I might be nearer to him, and I leaned on the arm of his chair and spoke into his ear; but that which struck me most was a certain genial open manner, as between people who confide in each other and share the same secrets and the same interests."[1]

These details, so trivial in themselves, are very significant, and it is pathetic as well as humorous that the simple-minded abbé should have retained his confiding innocence through an experience of men and manners calculated to disillusion the most trustful. Even he, however, makes a plaintive comment after his final interview with his Holiness: "How great is the difference between what he says in private and the burden of his brief. We, all combined, have less grief than he alone appears to suffer for anything that could be painful to you in the judgment he has just pronounced, and he seemed changed out of all recognition. But his appearance gives little clue to his secret thoughts! He told me many times that he regarded you as a great archbishop—*piissimo, santissimo, dottissimo.*"[2]

It is a relief to find Fénelon expressing thoroughly human indignation in his reply. "Leave Rome with that noble and unassuming bearing which has been yours always,"[3] was his exhortation to de Chanterac,

---

[1] *Correspondance de Fénelon*, x. 510.
[2] *Ibid.*, x. 587, March 14, 1699.
[3] *Ibid.*, x. 612, April 11, 1699.

THE QUIETISM CONTROVERSY 151

"on my behalf ask neither interest nor commendation. By his own act the Pope has made it impossible for him to serve me, and he has done me so much harm that he can do me no good with the King. I am far from desiring to buy such futile service by my own degradation. As for the praise he gives me, I told you long ago that it was contradicted by his intentions. If he thought me *piissimo, santissimo, dottissimo*, he would not have wished to ruin me unnecessarily. That is what every man of common sense says about these compliments. May God preserve me from buying vague words, which are contradicted by him who utters them, so dearly. If my patience, my teaching, and my example cannot uphold me among my flock unassisted by such approbation, approbation will not suffice to uphold me."

He very seldom allowed resentment to master him even in confidential letters. The following is far more representative of the dignified submission of his attitude :—

"In all I do I wish to exhibit what I truly feel—that is to say, a heart without resentment, a sincere respect for the Holy See, and absolute submission to its decision, however stern it be. Otherwise I need do nothing more concerning Rome; after all that has passed there would be a certain meanness in advances towards her. All my life I shall remain loyal and submissive to her. But I desire that you should withdraw from Rome, and do only what absolute decorum demands before leaving. One must not murmur: one must submit sincerely and unreservedly; but one must not pretend to be pleased when one cannot be so really."

These are the words of a man who has been wounded to the quick, but who has the courage, nevertheless, to face the world in defiance of the pain. The forced inconsistency of his position was, perhaps, his greatest trial: because he was incredulous of the corruption of the Vatican, he had declared that the Church would dishonour herself if she bowed to the Crown of France, and he found himself forced to uphold her in her dishonour. He had declared that he would be so broken and disgraced by condemnation that after it he could retain no shadow of authority, and he found his Flemish diocese wholly unaffected by the decision of the Roman Court, and the affection and reverence accorded to him by his friends only augmented by his misfortunes.

He was forced to regard life from a new standpoint, perhaps to form a lower estimate of human nature as the result of personal experience, but he had learnt to look onwards to a vision of perfection which was the inspiration of his Mysticism, and his beacon through all the storms and disasters of his life.

The worst that could be dreaded had befallen him, but at least the fight was over, and he had only to accept his fate. That in doing so he was able to remain steadfast to the Roman faith and its doctrine of papal infallibility is a mystery difficult of solution; his reason told him that Innocent XII. was false and shifty, and that he had given judgment in a question of belief against his reason, to curry favour with the Court of France; but all the story of the life of Fénelon proclaims him true and pure of heart, and to those of his own faith these contradictions may seem less impossible to reconcile. His enemies sought in vain to find a flaw in his submission. " Your conduct is a living *Explication des Maximes des Saints*," wrote one of his

THE QUIETISM CONTROVERSY

followers; and the dignified humility with which he met misfortune restored the reputation which Bossuet's slanders had assailed, even if the sting of them still rankled in his own remembrance.

When the judgment was the sensation of the hour, numerous busybodies presumed to write their advice and sympathy to him. It was well that he could receive such attentions with half-humorous resignation. "Sometimes," he wrote to de Beauvilliers, "I am inclined to laugh at the fears betrayed by some zealous folk that I shall possibly be unable to make up my mind to yield. Sometimes I am harassed by others who write long exhortations to me to submit. They tell me of the glory I shall find in such humiliation, and the act of heroism I shall be achieving. All this wearies me somewhat, and I am disposed to say to myself, What have I done to all these people that they think I shall find it so difficult to prefer the authority of the Holy See to my own dim knowledge, or the peace of the Church to my own book? However, I am well aware that they are right in attributing much imperfection to me, and much shrinking from an act of humiliation, therefore I can easily forgive them."[1]

But thenceforth his renunciation of his chief enjoyments was not self-imposed, but involuntary. His prospects, formerly so brilliant, were darkened, as it proved, for ever; and though he might endeavour to persuade himself that he did not desire to return to Court, it is plain that his thoughts flew often to Versailles with longing and regret, and it was with a heavy heart that he faced the future.

[1] *Correspondance de Fénelon*, x. 595, March 29, 1699.

CHAPTER VI

BOSSUET AND "TÉLÉMAQUE"

THE news of the papal judgment had reached Fénelon on the Festival of the Annunciation, and from the pulpit of his own cathedral he preached on the duty of absolute submission. Nor was he content with that one public humiliation; he completed it by a pastoral letter forbidding any member of his flock to hold in their possession the book over which he had spent eighteen months of reflective labour. Thus, with lowered arms, he retired from the scene of a conflict in which he ought never to have taken part, and the Quietism controversy ended.

It was a strange and moving drama for those who watched, although after the lapse of centuries it may seem to turn only on complications of terms and phrases, and in it the fiercest human passions found expression, passions that had grown more violent from long years of bondage beneath the forms of priestly reticence and dignity. The world of talkers screamed and disputed and condemned, and Fénelon's enemies had reason to be thankful that, amid the general hubbub, the magic influence of his personality could not take effect on wavering hearts; for from his home on the Flemish frontier he could not, had he willed it, have obtained a hearing in his own defence; he could only accept defeat in silence. It had been, in fact, only a new outbreak of a struggle that, beneath the surface, is always going on, the wrestle between the dreamer and idealist and the man of logic—of all human efforts the most futile when the combatants are men of strong conviction, for it were as easy to bring parallel lines to meet as to fuse the creeds of Fénelon and Bossuet. Both might have served honestly in the same Church, nevertheless, and retained the semblance of their old friendship, but for the prejudice of the King and the miserable jealousy of Bossuet; and the result, in spite of the inconsistency into which Fénelon the dreamer was ruthlessly entrapped, has injured his final reputation far less than that of his opponent.

It was incumbent on all members of the Court to simulate satisfaction at the verdict, and many were so weary of the controversy that they welcomed any ending. There was a race to Versailles between the couriers of Cardinal de Bouillon and the Abbé Bossuet, wherein the former was successful, and the King made no attempt to conceal his joy, keeping the report upon the table beside him at his evening meal. The banality of that final race was no unfit conclusion to a history that contained so much pettiness and trickery; de Chanterac recorded it all in a letter to Cambrai, that his master might cherish no illusion regarding the King's attitude towards him. He realised how much that little detail of the supper-table meant, for Louis was not only King of France, he had now proved conclusively that his sway extended to the Vatican, and those whom he desired to crush must needs accept his fiat. It was a strange and arresting thought that the one man who held the lives of so many millions in his grasp, was himself long past his prime, and that his death—an event that would reverse the fortune and conditions of those who shone most brilliantly at Court—was left outside the calculations of ambition.

The Duke of Burgundy was a child no longer, and he had proved that it was impossible to undermine his faith in Fénelon. If the King had died it may be assumed that the great decision would have been tacitly annulled, and Cambrai have ceased to profit by the perpetual residence of the archbishop; but the King lived on, and Fénelon's exile only ended with his life. To understand the weight of the sentence passed upon him, it should be remembered that he had enjoyed unusual popularity and favour while he remained at Court. "He wishes to be loved," Mme. de Maintenon had written of him many years before, when life was only beginning, and the wish remained with him to the end; he had delighted in the love and sympathy of friends worthy of his friendship, and he was condemned to lifelong separation from them. Nor should it be forgotten that all men prophesied that the high honours of the Roman Church would be his ere many years had passed; his birth, his talents, and his untarnished reputation fitted him to take his place among the cardinals, and undoubtedly he desired that it should be so. Saint-Simon would have us believe that his whole character hinged upon ambition, that calculation was its mainspring. The history of his life hardly bears out such a theory, but undoubtedly the element of ambition was innate in him, and all the circumstances of his position at Versailles had fostered it, in spite of constant and watchful self-repression. His was not the nature of a recluse, and his brilliant genius and noble aims would have graced the most exalted post, fitting him to use the power that it gave him for the glory of God and the welfare of his fellows, even while he revelled in the possession of it.

Had he been less human, less open to temptation, he could not have remained such a living personality through the dividing centuries, nor been the guide and friend of a thousand troubled souls, who turned to him when the stress of life was overwhelming them, and found the help they needed in one who had himself struggled and suffered, and failed in hope and courage.

It was a hard lesson, and many tongues were ready to urge him to rebel against it; there was sufficient proof of injustice in the verdict to absolve him from disgrace in the eyes of reasonable men if it could be made known to them, and a clear statement of his case by an independent writer must have benefited him. But he would not accept such an advantage when it was offered to him. "It is not right or edifying that a writer should wish to keep the Church perpetually occupied with his personal concerns," was his reply to the suggestion "that he should prefer to prolong the contest everlastingly to taking up his cross with humility. When the real intention of a bishop is set forth in writing many times without effect, why should he go on protesting? He can only edify others and maintain his own dignity by absolute silence."[1]

[1] *Correspondance de Fénelon,* xi. 664, to Père Gerberon, Benedictin.

Absolute silence was indeed the best remedy for the injuries he had suffered; such a reputation as his would have recovered under the treatment, but it was destined to receive a new and unexpected wound. He was, indeed, not only a persecuted man, but a singularly unlucky one: he had intended to reserve the "Maxims" till he decided on the apt moment for its publication, and its premature appearance was most injurious to his cause in the subsequent controversy; now, when his submission had softened many hearts, and his quiet acceptance of injustice had claimed the popular sympathy, a new incident gave scope for the machinations of his enemies.

The Duke of Burgundy had profited by the literary power of his tutor. The fables written for his amusement and advantage have already been referred to; they bear the light impress of a master-hand, and are perfect in their way; but they were not intended for the public, and Fénelon was content that they should fulfil their object in catching the imagination of his wayward pupils. With a similar purpose, he wrote *Les Aventures de Télémaque*, jotting it down at odd moments, and giving it to the prince in fragments as it proceeded, little dreaming that it was destined to be the most celebrated of his works. He permitted a few of his friends to read it, for it was written while he was still at Versailles, and, that it might be read to the best advantage, he entrusted the loose leaves of his MS. to a copyist. It is not known by what means this craftsman was tempted to betray his employer, but the crime was facilitated by Fénelon's exile; weariness and anxiety had probably driven all thought of *Télémaque* from his mind, and assuredly it was not by his intention that, at the very moment of his disgrace, it was launched upon the literary world of Paris. Even if he had ever intended its publication, which seems improbable, it is certain that he would not have selected that most unpropitious occasion. The book is charming in its way, and Fénelon's fine literary instinct must have assured him of its quality; but it was utterly out of keeping with the attitude of submission and reserve which he assumed before the world. He had reached the tragic crisis of his life, and it was a spiteful degree of fate that public attention should be distracted from sorrow at his misfortunes by admiration for his command of style and graces of imagination.

No mistaken zeal of friendship was, in this case, responsible. The book came to light somewhat mysteriously, but there is little doubt that the copyist was the transgressor. It was distributed in MS. first, and afterwards printed, but Fénelon did not authorise any edition. The first evidence of its publicity is in March 1699, when Aubouin, a librarian in Paris, wrote thus to a servant at Cambrai: "A MS. of Monseigneur is circulated called 'The Education of a Prince, or the Adventures of Telemachus.' It causes much excitement; they say no finer work was ever printed."[1] It has stood the test of two centuries of existence, and the varying phases of taste during that period have hardly lessened its popularity: it has been translated into many languages, and made the name of Fénelon familiar to thousands whom he could not otherwise have touched; nevertheless, he may well

[1] *Correspondance de Fénelon*, x. 591.

have looked back on its composition as the most ill-fated labour of his life. The King was already incensed because his ruin had not proved more complete. Being shrewd enough to realise that, but for fear of the royal wrath, Fénelon would still be openly applauded by the general voice, he had been ready to read defiance in his silence, rebellion in his expressions of submission, and treason in the display of any qualities that made him worthy of esteem; and when *Télémaque* came under his notice he construed it into a satire on the existing government. His resentment was thus inflamed anew, and Bossuet and his allies made every effort to increase it. If there had ever been any hope that the King would relent and recall Fénelon from exile, it was quenched when *Télémaque* was put into his hands; he was a tyrant, and therefore sensitive to reflections upon tyranny, and it must be admitted that the pages of *Télémaque* bristle with such reflections.

"I wish Monseigneur de Cambrai had made his Mentor a little less instructive," wrote Boileau the year that it became public property, "and that the moral ran through the book somewhat less obtrusively and more ingeniously. Homer is more instructive, but his teaching is not precept, but is given rather in the action of the story than in the conversations. Ulysses teaches us more what we should do by what he does than by all which he and Minerva say."[1]

This would, in all probability, be the criticism of the average reader, for the charm of the unusual and poetic diction hardly softens the didactic expression of the

[1] *Œuvres de Boileau*, iv.

writer's theories upon government; his responsibility in training the future ruler of a great nation looms large on every page, but only a morbid sensitiveness could have read satirical intention into his general and somewhat trite conclusions. He seems to have accepted this interpretation — the completion of his ruin — in hopeless silence, and Voltaire [1] perpetuates it, but ten years later Fénelon unburdened his mind upon the subject, and his testimony puts the matter beyond doubt :—

"As for *Télémaque*, it is a fable formed on the plan of heroic verse such as Homer or Virgil's, wherein I have inserted the chief lessons profitable to a prince born to the throne. I wrote it at a time when I was overwhelmed by evidence of the confidence and kindness of the King. I should have shown myself to be not only the most ungrateful but the most reckless of men if I had attempted to take satirical and insolent examples; I shrink from the very thought of such a thing. Certainly in these *Aventures* I have set forth the essential truths and possible pitfalls of sovereign power, but I have not emphasised any so as to point to any individual character. The more you read the book the more you will see that I wished to be outspoken without being personal. Moreover, the published version is not the same as the original." [2]

"Not only the most ungrateful but the most reckless" —that argument alone confutes the accusation. When *Télémaque* was written, Fénelon was in office at the Court, and his good sense would have assured him that he could

---

[1] *Louis XIV.*, ch. xxxii.
[2] *Correspondance de Fénelon*, iii. 177, to Père le Tellier, 1709.

serve no worthy purpose by a covert attack on sovereign power. Even had there been no consideration of honour to prevent such treason while he held his place, every evidence is in favour of his innocence; but it may be that he was careless in utilising his observations of the life around him, and his knowledge of the general condition of the kingdom, when he wanted illustrations to depict the evils of despotism and serve as a warning to the child who, in a golden future, might have power to change his Utopian dreams into reality.

"A king should have no advantage over others, except what is necessary either to help him in his arduous duties or to exact from the people the respect due to the representative of law and order. Moreover, the king should be more sober, less prone to indolence, freer from arrogance and pride than others. He must not have a larger share of riches and pleasures, but of wisdom, of virtue, and of renown. He must be the defender of his country and the leader of his armies abroad, and at home the ruler of the people, who wins them goodness and wisdom and happiness. The gods did not make him a king for himself, but that he might belong to the people; all his time, all his care, all his love is due to the people, and he is only worthy of royalty inasmuch as he forgets himself to devote himself to the public good."[1] This is a typical passage, and it is incredible that it could have been intended for general reading by any subject of Louis XIV.: it was an ideal of monarchy—an impossible ideal, no doubt, but one by which the young prince might have profited, and over which the Great

[1] *Télémaque*, liv. v.

King must have fumed in impotent wrath, seeing how surely such a picture must shadow his own attitude as a model sovereign. In truth, the kingliness to which Télémaque—and, incidentally, the Duke of Burgundy—is exhorted to aspire was not the kingliness assumed by Louis. The contrast betwixt the royalty of Fénelon's imagination and that which Versailles exhibited is almost ludicrous: to have drawn it intentionally would have been both reckless and ungrateful. Fénelon was neither, and the incident was another unmerited misfortune. Nevertheless, *Télémaque* gains in interest if it be read in connection with contemporary history; the attitude of the tutor towards his pupil becomes clearer, and the result of the teaching of Mentor is traceable in the after-career of the ill-fated Duke of Burgundy. "You need a man who loves you and the truth only; who loves you better than you are able to love yourself; who tells you the truth whether you will or no; who breaks down every barrier. Remember that a prince is but too fortunate when one man of such a temper is born in his reign; that there is nothing more precious in his dominion; that he can dread no heavier penalty from the gods than to lose such a man should he show himself unworthy by not knowing how to profit by him."[1]

"When kings allow themselves to recognise no law but their own sovereign will, and put no curb upon their passions, they can do what they please; but by doing as they please they undermine the foundations of their power: they have absolute laws no longer; nor

[1] *Télémaque*, liv. xi.

traditions of government; every one will compete to flatter them; they will not have a people; there will be none but slaves remaining to them, and these will grow fewer daily."[1]

"An individual may lead a quiet, pleasant life without dishonour. A king cannot honourably choose a soft and idle lot instead of the arduous toils of government: he is bound to all whom he governs; he can never belong to himself; his smallest failings are of infinite consequence because they result in misfortune on the people which may be prolonged for centuries; he must reprove the audacity of the wicked, uphold innocence, put down slander. It is not enough for him to do no harm."[2]

Such, in brief, is the teaching conveyed by the story of *Télémaque;* the teaching of a bold and conscientious man, who, in endeavouring to put himself in his pupil's place, had realised the worst temptations that the future held for him, and was strong enough not to be blinded by the delusive grandeur which defended the King from criticism. Truly, "a prince is fortunate when one man of such a temper is born in his reign," and the duke was wise enough to understand his good fortune though the gods denied him the full opportunity of profiting. There are also touches more intimate and personal than these somewhat didactic generalities, and, in spite of the gaps caused by the ruthless destruction of Fénelon's letters to his pupil, enough has been preserved to show that the spirit of his teaching never changed, that he never deviated from the principles he strove to impress on those childish

[1] *Télémaque,* liv. xvii.   [2] *Ibid.,* liv. xiv.

ears, and through the prince we come to nearer knowledge of him than by any other means. There are details of his life at Cambrai sufficient to admit us to a certain intimacy. We may see his inspired power of sympathy in his letters of direction, and his generous nature in his intercourse with his own family; but in each succeeding position he is still the priest *santissimo, piissimo, dottissimo*. Only in contact with the Dauphin do we discover the other side of his character—the spirit that he drew from a line of chivalrous fighting ancestors, the warm human instinct which may be lacking in the scholar and the saint. "Go," he writes in the character of Mentor, "into the greatest peril whenever it seems well that you should do so. It is more dishonourable for a prince to avoid danger in battle than never to go to the wars. The courage of those who command must be irreproachable. A leader or a king may be essential to a people, but it is yet more necessary that his valour should be above suspicion. Remember that he who commands must be the model for the rest; the whole army should be animated by his example. Fear no dangers, then, O Télémaque, and fall in battle rather than bear a doubt upon your courage. The flatterers who are most eager to withhold you from risking danger when the occasion calls for it will be the first to whisper that you are faint-hearted if they find it easy to restrain you."[1]

The life of the child to whom this exhortation was addressed was especially precious to Fénelon, and it was a life that was likely to come near to the dangers of

[1] *Télémaque*, liv. x.

battle. As a priest he would have been justified in striking a more peaceful note, but he loved his charge too well to rest content with anything short of his ideal of chivalrous manliness; for his sake he looked at life from the level of a man of the world rather than from the elevation of the devotee. He would have him a valiant soldier and a ruler equipped with the wisdom which must be learnt rather than taught, even though in the learning there might be risks whereat the simple-minded stand aghast. "How can one hope to govern men without knowing them? And how can one know them if one never lives with them? To see them publicly only when the talk on every side is artificial is not to live with them: that is a question of seeing them individually, of discovering the secret springs of their being in the deepest recesses of their hearts, of sounding them on every side, of searching for their motives."[1]

M. de Bourgogne might have come by strange knowledge in pursuing such injunctions, for the motives governing action will ill bear scrutiny, and in that age of intrigue and immorality there was many a dark mystery not far below the surface. But Fénelon knew what he was doing; he had proved a stern and rigorous confessor, and by that office had learnt to understand the world and the weakness and corruption that underlay the gloss of graceful manners and light flattery, and he knew the prince also, and was assured that for him knowledge did not involve participation, but was a necessary part of his apprenticeship in the art of governing. It

[1] *Télémaque*, liv. xviii.

is by understanding Fénelon and the strength of his influence that we obtain some light upon the prince's attitude towards his environment; in any picture of the time he stands apart from the throng that cluster round the throne—a solitary figure struggling perpetually to fit himself for a destiny he was never to fulfil—and those who lived near to him in manhood had little knowledge of him. But it seems evident that the maxims of *Télémaque* had sunk deeply into his mind, and undoubtedly Fénelon intended him to identify himself with the hero of his story. St. Simon's description of the prince has been already quoted, and it is thus that Télémaque is portrayed: "He looked upon himself as being of a different nature from other men; it seemed to him that the gods put other people in the world only to please him, to serve him, to anticipate his wishes, and to yield all things to him as to a god. In his opinion the honour of serving him was a sufficient recompense for those who served. Nothing that he desired must be impossible, and the slightest delay ruffled his quick temper. Those who saw him thus as he was by nature would have believed that he was incapable of loving any one but himself, that he was oblivious of everything but his own vainglory and his own pleasures."[1]

The two are identical, and no less severe and rigorous a view of life was inculcated on the King's grandson than on the son of Ulysses. For this reason the historical value of *Télémaque* is as great as its artistic charm, and in spite of its direful effect on the fortunes of its author, its publication cannot be regretted. The resentment that

[1] *Télémaque*, liv. xiii.

it aroused in the breast of the King may be justly attributed to Bossuet; he remained persistently inimical to Fénelon; his nominal success at the Vatican left him unsatisfied, and, knowing the King's indignation to be already kindled, he fostered it till it became implacable.

The more he injured him, the more Bossuet seems to have hated Fénelon: never has history shown a more striking example of the power of jealousy. There is much that is venerable in the Bishop of Meaux; such a reputation as his is not won lightly. He was a man of deep learning, and his influence on the King and on the Court —gay and frivolous as it was when he became tutor to the Dauphin—effected deep and radical reforms. It is all the more extraordinary to trace so much of his own conduct to the pettiest of human passions. With such intellectual power as his, ambition was almost a necessary shortcoming. Fénelon himself was not free from the same weakness, he coveted a cardinal's hat as eagerly, but it would not have cost him a pang to see that dignity conferred upon his friend, while there is little doubt that the root of Bossuet's enmity lay in the dread that one whom he had patronised and instructed would reach an elevation to which he aspired in vain. His plebeian birth was, in fact, the bar that divided him from the goal of his desires, and gave Fénelon so great an advantage over him: there can be no disability more galling to a man of strong character and intellect, and as life wore on he did not learn philosophy.

The diary of the Abbé Ledieu reveals the malignancy of his temper in those later years. Ledieu was one of those uncompromising admirers who are the scourge of the great; his admiration was wholesale, he had no capacity for discrimination, and his daily chronicle of words and actions is not calculated to increase the reputation of his hero in the eyes of succeeding generations. Few lives will bear so minute a scrutiny, and, on the whole, the bishop comes through the ordeal with credit; he suffers chiefly where he is concerned with Fénelon, for the naïve candour of the good abbé leaves no room for doubt of the rancorous feeling cherished by his patron. He could not tolerate a word of admiration for the writings or the conduct of his rival; he would not admit that there was merit to be found in *Télémaque*: it was too poetic and effeminate in diction, too exaggerated in its descriptions, while the number of love-scenes and the avowed passion of Calypso for the hero made it unprofitable reading for the prince and unworthy the pen of a Christian and a priest. Also the latter portion of the work contained a covert censure, not only on the Government, but on the King himself. Such were the great man's strictures on the unpretending volume over which the world was buzzing. He delivered himself of them in the privacy of his own household, where there were none bold enough to take up the cudgels for the exiled author; but a natural query rose to the lips even of submissive listeners: "Why should such a book be published, and how could it benefit Monseigneur de Cambrai?"

Bossuet's reply is characteristic, and reveals the bitterness that rankled in his breast: "It is a scheme of his friends," he said, "to add to his popular reputation as the best writer the honour of being unique in possessing the courage to tell the truth." [1]

He was conscious that he had squandered his own waning powers on a controversy which had added no lustre to his reputation nor brought him nearer to the goal of his desires; too late also he realised that it was impossible to ruin such a man as Fénelon in the eyes of the thousands who had learnt to love him. He might be banished from the Vatican and from Versailles; he might be silenced by the Pope and disgraced by the King, but he was cherished none the less in the hearts of the people. The effect of the long contest was, in truth, more tragic at Meaux and Germigny than at Cambrai, for Fénelon was dignified in his submission, while Bossuet struggled to trade upon his superficial triumph, and struggled vainly.

"It had been evident to me for the last ten or twelve days," writes his ingenuous satellite, "that our bishop pays his court to the English. He attends the King's Mass in the morning, and his dinner, and sometimes waits on the Queen about supper-time. If he has an eye on a cardinal's hat by the King's interest, it is still a secret. I think one may suspect it, however; perhaps Cardinal de Noailles is in the scheme, for he loves Monseigneur de Meaux dearly, and admires him very much, especially since the happy outcome of the Cambrai affair, for which the cardinal receives the credit, while Monseigneur de Meaux had all the trouble. It may be that Monseigneur de Paris could stir Mme. de Maintenon, she having felt such relief at being free of the Cambrai

[1] *Journal de l'Abbé Ledieu*, vol. ii.

intrigues, and knowing better than any one that that success was due as much to the wisdom as to the learning of our bishop."[1]

In the ardour of his admiration Ledieu was blind to the shadow he was casting on the greatness of his master. Old age and disease had already taken hold on Bossuet, but he had yielded to the unworthy passion which was ruling him while his moral and intellectual powers were at their fullest ripeness. He might have been more reticent in the prime of manhood, but not more temperate; ten years earlier he would not have betrayed himself, but he would have hated just as fiercely.

The most scandalous episode of the controversy was the publication of Bossuet's *Relation sur la Quietism*, but Ledieu records another incident, less known, but hardly less disgraceful. There is frequent reference to the Abbé Bossuet in the letters of de Chanterac from Rome; he was the representative of the opposing side, and therefore not likely to find favourable mention, but de Chanterac regarded him with more friendly eyes than Ledieu. The journal of the latter has no word in his favour; it paints him in the darkest colours, portraying his habitual greed and self-indulgence, and hinting freely at graver vices. It is only incidentally that he brings to light the story of the Abbé Phélippeaux. During his stay in Rome the younger Bossuet made Phélippeaux the partner of his toils and pleasures, but the terms of their friendship were but little to the credit of either,[2]

---

[1] *Ledieu*, vol. ii.
[2] See Abbé Bossuet to his uncle, February 1699, *Œuvres de Bossuet*, xlii.

and it is remarkable that the bishop should ever have admitted Phélippeaux among his associates at Meaux. A love of flattery—characteristic of old age—is the probable explanation, and Phélippeaux proved himself a dexterous courtier, availing himself of the quiet and security of the Episcopal household to write an account of the late proceedings at the Vatican, which he believed likely to commend him to the favour of his patron. He gauged the malignancy of Bossuet's temper only too justly. When, thirty-one years later, the pamphlet was published, it was seized by the police and burned by the common hangman. It depicts the worst scenes in the miserable controversy it commemorates, and the tone of unmeasured adulation towards the Bishop of Meaux is varied by scurrilous calumnies on Fénelon and Mme. Guyon. Nevertheless, Bossuet listened to it calmly, and continued to hold the writer in an honourable position in his household, and Ledieu records the affair without any perception of its importance to future generations who would fain form a just estimate of his master's character.

It was read aloud to beguile some autumn evenings in the year 1701 to a circle composed of the bishop and the most intimate of his following, who, apparently, were an appreciative audience. "It is a sort of journal," says Ledieu, "from the year 1696, when the doctor (Phélippeaux) went from Paris to Rome, to the death of Innocent XII., and on to the end of 1700." It gave a record of Roman affairs and contemporary doings in Paris, "making a very agreeable variety," as Ledieu quaintly expresses it. No wonder that the book was a source of entertainment to adherents of the winning side, and that they welcomed approval from the bishop which encouraged the author to proceed. To the old man himself it was invigorating to see so skilful an attack on Fénelon by another hand than his, and his satisfaction brought him back to a theme of conversation which had ceased to be a favourite one. "He told us," to quote Lediue again, "that it had been the original intention of Mme. de Maintenon to save Monseigneur de Cambrai; ... she charged him (Bossuet) to do so at the very first, and, with the utmost secrecy, he worked for this object from September 1693, having it solely in his hands until the time of the Thirty-four Articles (of Issy) in March 1695. Later, Mme. de Maintenon discarded Fénelon entirely, and desired Monseigneur de Meaux to direct his labours to the refutation of the new Quietism."[1]

Thus, on fresh testimony, we find Mme. de Maintenon weaving the destinies of men whose character and conduct should have raised them beyond her reach, and instigating a prelate, fully competent without assistance to shield the Church from all encroachment, to throw down the gauntlet and enter on that fatal conflict. The combative spirit was latent in Bossuet, or he would not have responded so readily to the call she made upon him. It would seem that he and she acted and reacted on each other disastrously, sharing, and yet dissembling, the same mingled sentiments, but in her, ambition had the harder conquest, for she, in condemning Fénelon, was false to her faith, while Bossuet only denied the claim of friendship.

[1] *Lediue*, vol. ii.

Once fairly started on reminiscences, Bossuet, habitually careful and reserved, became almost garrulous; he did not shrink from admitting that he tried to poison the King's mind against Fénelon. Ledieu wrote with his patron's voice still ringing in his ears, and is not to be doubted: "After the publication of the *Maximes* of Monseigneur de Cambrai there were some murmurs of opposition to it, but the King remained uncertain and irresolute as to what course he should take, and it was he (Monseigneur de Meaux) who decided his Majesty to demand and insist upon the condemnation of the book, having explained to him in detail all the false principles of the work and the results which were to be feared."[1]

This statement gives another reason for the ardour with which Bossuet pursued his victim; his own reputation hung in the scale against that of the accused, and every breath of passing encouragement which cheered the little company at Cambrai inspired the Bishop of Meaux and his adherents to renewed endeavour. De Chanterac, who, to judge by contemporary accounts, was precise and correct in his information, wrote to de Langeron at Cambrai early in 1698 as follows:—

"Some people who are in close correspondence with Paris and Versailles have received letters saying that the Court is changing greatly towards Monseigneur de Cambrai, and that the King said to Monseigneur de Meaux that the matter of his book was not going as he, Monseigneur de Meaux, had expected; that many wise people approved of it; moreover, that the examiners

[1] *Ledieu*, vol. ii.

were divided, and that half, and the most important half, were sure that it could never be condemned."[1]

The restoration of Fénelon to favour and possibility of advancement would have been intolerable to Bossuet; but that he himself should at the same time be proved a bad adviser, and taunted by the King for his discredited accusations, was a consummation too outrageous to be even contemplated. Compared with that alternative, his triumph, though there was something lacking in it, was a theme for unrestrained rejoicing.

The first reading of Phélippeaux' book occupied two evenings, and the listeners were led through varied scenes and placed in distorted intimacy with many contrasting types of human nature. He set forth the "intrigues and secret practices" of Fénelon's adherents in Rome, "and the tricks of the Society of Jesuits, from the superior to the humblest unit among them, at the French Court and in Paris, with all their outward compliance and humility, are so aptly unmasked and so well introduced amid so many doings and doctrines that they make the narrative a very curious one."

The Abbé Bossuet and his companion must have had a degraded view of Roman life and society, to judge by de Chanterac's description of their proceedings, and Phélippeaux' book was rather curious than improving; but it is easy to understand how his audience, in the security of their success, gave amused attention to his account of the last efforts of Cardinal de Bouillon and the Jesuits to save the *Maximes* and its author from disgrace, until, hope failing them, they suddenly withdrew

Correspondance de Fénelon, viii. 375.

support and left him to his fate; of the hesitations of the Pope (his rectitude being, of necessity, much insisted on), the firmness of the King, the manœuvres of the cardinals whom Cardinal de Bouillon had won over, and all those fruitless schemes and efforts of the losing side which the younger Bossuet had collected and exaggerated for the delectation of himself and his ally. It is not the intrinsic merit of the narrative that preserves it from oblivion, but the observations that it suggested to the bishop. Whatever may have been the original intention of the writer, the work degenerated into a *chronique scandaleuse* of the most objectionable type. "It is, in fact, so outspoken," remarks the guileless Ledieu, "that there would be neither prudence, wisdom, nor security, in making it public. Not only are the Jesuits and Cardinal de Bouillon and all those who shielded the heresy shown in their true colours, but the behaviour of the Court of France is frankly described also. One may see Mme. de Maintenon with all her devotion to M. l'Abbé de Fénelon and her care for his advancement and the like. MM. de Beauvilliers, de Chevreuse, their wives, their relatives, their friends, and all the people concerned in the matter appear upon the scene entirely unmasked; neither is the Court of Rome neglected: it is indeed such a collection of invidious truths as might overwhelm their chronicler."

Bossuet, having no dislike to invidious truths which did not touch him personally, considered that the book might with advantage be given to the public at some future day. This was his verdict after having heard it a second time with ample leisure to reflect upon it, and he made only one criticism, advising the removal of a detailed description of Fénelon's secret motives and ambitions before he came to Court. Apparently Phélippeaux represented him as coveting the office which he afterwards obtained, from his earliest youth, and scheming deeply to obtain it, paying assiduous court to the Bishop himself, and striving to divert him from any leaning in the same direction by reminders of the claim made by the Church on his full abilities and time. Such a picture of Fénelon is a little difficult to reconcile with the conception that others formed of him, even though Phélippeaux urges that he obtained these intimate details from his own lips when they were fellow-guests at Germigny before his appointment to the Court. Bossuet's memory, however, refused to furnish any corroborative evidence, and he condemned the passage.

Having thus detected the chronicler in one falsehood, it is astonishing that he, an honest man, should have let his other statements pass unchallenged; but his sight had become distorted irremediably and he could no longer regard anything that had reference to Fénelon with justice. Having reluctantly acquitted him on one false charge he proceeded to make another of far graver import. His method is best given in the words of one who actually listened to his voice:

"From that we entered upon M. l'Abbé de Fénelon, whom Monseigneur de Meaux pronounced to have been a complete hypocrite all his life; having from the first, in dealing with him, used finesse and dissimulation to obtain what he desired, which he himself had not detected, crediting him with sincerity equal to his own. But he added that the business of his book had shown what he really was, for he had resorted to every sort of subterfuge in his defence, denying the most assured and evident truths and matters of fact to such a point that even his old friends, Cardinal de Noailles and Monseigneur de Chartres, became convinced of the deceitfulness of his disposition."

In all likelihood Bossuet had brought himself to this conviction. Unless he did believe Fénelon to be the cunning strategist he represented him, his conduct towards him is quite at variance with his character for probity. But, having once persuaded himself that he fought in a righteous cause, and that his anger was sinless, he allowed no further misgiving to weaken his attack, and no method seemed to him to be unlawful. This is the only explanation of his position regarding Phélippeaux, for not only did he approve the scandalous chronicle of his dependant, but he also sanctioned a scheme for its publication after the death of the writer. The fact that Phélippeaux was a younger man than Fénelon conveys an idea of the iniquity of the suggestion. The former was to be preserved from possible inconvenience during his lifetime, while the reputation of the latter was to be condemned to obloquy when neither he, nor any of those close friends who could have cleared him by their personal knowledge, were left to confront the slanders of a dishonourable enemy. That he was saved from such a fate was due to the tardy justice of the public. It is impossible to exonerate Bossuet; and Ledieu—inspired by an honest spirit of adulation—has injured his master's memory more deeply than the bitterest of his opponents.

CHAPTER VII

FÉNELON AND THE JANSENISTS

IT is impossible to form a just estimate of Fénelon without considering the conflicting religious influences through which he had to steer his course, and to what extent they left their mark upon the national character. The struggle of the Huguenots was as important politically as ecclesiastically; they have, therefore, a prominent place in history, and Fénelon's position with regard to them is clearly defined by the record of his mission in Saintonge, a record which even his enemies found it difficult to criticise. But when the eighteenth century began, the Huguenot faction had ceased to take the foremost place as a target for ecclesiastical agitators. They had been ousted for a time by the Quietists, who were of no political importance; and when, with the close of the century, the triumph of court intrigue and private animosity was proclaimed through Europe and Fénelon's book condemned, the militant instinct which animated so many defenders of the Church was free to concentrate itself upon a new crusade.

The fall of Molinos is attributed to the Jesuits; but in the Quietist controversy their influence was not paramount. Many of them were friendly towards Fénelon; Cardinal de Bouillon had supported him until he considered his defeat inevitable, and Père La Chaise had feared his hold on Mme. de Maintenon more than his doctrine. It was otherwise, however, with the next conflict that stirred the ecclesiastical world : there can be no doubt of the attitude of the Jesuits towards Port Royal and the Jansenists. Their hatred was no new sentiment; it was always smouldering, always liable to burst into devouring flames. The century during which Port Royal held its place as a national institution was one of great importance to the national life; a century during which new thoughts and new ideals broke through the narrow limits of the old religious slavery, and men woke to a desire to think for themselves, and claim a heritage of hope that did not depend on the favour of the priest. Such novelties bring energy and power in their wake, and Port Royal may justly claim a share in the glories of that age of progress.

The name of Port Royal has become synonymous with Jansenism, but the actual convent of Port Royal des Champs was founded in the thirteenth century and afterwards came under the Benedictine rule. Its real life, however, did not animate it till Jacqueline Arnauld, better known as Mère Angelique, became Abbess there; but it was owing to her that the lax and often disgraceful customs of her own and other convents were abolished, and the true spirit of conventual discipline enforced. Her plea for a purer life won her the friendship of St. Francis de Sales, himself the keenest of monastic reformers, of Mme. de Chantal,[1] a woman celebrated for her saintly life, of Vincent de Paul and of de Hauranne,

[1] The grandmother of Mme. de Sevigné.

Abbot of Saint-Cyran. The last named merged himself so completely in loyalty to Port Royal that he has no separate place in history; but it was owing to him that the doctrine of his friend, the Flemish scholar Jansenius, became an inseparable part of the faith of the Port Royalists, and in 1636 he was appointed the spiritual director of the Community. From this appointment may be dated the greatest fame and the eventual ruin of the institution. As in all religious controversy many elements besides religion were involved. Jansenius was inimical to Richelieu. Richelieu was all-powerful, and, therefore, Jansenius himself being out of reach, his friend became the sufferer. His fate was somewhat similar but yet a harder one than that of Fénelon, for he was arraigned with as little reason, and was actually imprisoned for five years. When, on the death of Richelieu, he was released, his misfortunes had won him a band of devoted followers, and his celebrity a strong force of determined enemies; from that moment he was the recognised leader of every Port Royalist recluse—that is to say, of those men who had resorted to Port Royal des Champs (from whence the convent had removed to Paris) to seek strength in prayer and meditation against the temptations of their life in the world.

It was only when Richelieu died that the full strength of the Jansenist party became evident. Petty persecution had sown the seed of rebellion among them, and the animosity of the Jesuits was ever ready to show itself. St. Cyran was a natural object for hatred, for his secret influence in Paris was greater than that of any member of the famous College, and he was also avowedly the friend of Berulle, founder of the Oratorians, an order abhorred by the Jesuit powers.

Ecclesiastical power as represented by Richelieu had been almost limitless while Louis XIII. filled the throne; it was hardly less when Mazarin replaced him under the new King, and Mazarin was as much a Jesuit at heart as Richelieu. Thus royal and Jesuit interests were merged, and revolt against Jesuit influence came near akin to treason. It was inevitable, therefore, that when the spirit of anarchy was abroad the Jansenists should range themselves in opposition to the Crown; but such a position was fatal to a party bound together only by agreement on points of doctrine. They were the tools of men more subtle than themselves, men who were as reckless as they were unscrupulous, and thus they became so inextricably involved in the Fronde Rebellion that the stigma of the King's displeasure could never be erased. It was their fate to be injured by their friends. De Retz favoured them, and they did not escape a share in his well-merited dishonour, but it is unlikely that he had any better reason for his favour than spite against Mazarin; his history gives small ground for a belief that the reflections of Jansenius and St. Cyran awoke a responsive echo in his breast. It was quite another type of man that was ready to risk life and sacrifice liberty for the fruit of those reflections—it was to the thinker they appealed, to those to whom religion was the most important element in human life; and the immense stir caused by the successive controversies during the seventeenth century testifies to the numbers who may be thus described.

It is difficult to summarise briefly the heads of the

FÉNELON AND THE JANSENISTS 183

Jansenist doctrine.¹ It was founded on the works of St. Augustine, to which Jansenius and St. Cyran had dedicated five years of study and meditation. Jansenius in the course of his life read, according to his own statement, all the writings of St. Augustine ten times, and the treatises on the Pelagians thirty times. He appealed to St. Augustine for authority as the Reformers appealed to the Bible. He rebelled against the theological monopoly claimed by a small section of learned priests, and his controversy with the Jesuits was in some degree a replica of the original dispute between Augustine and Pelagius, founded on the question, "How is Redemption effected?"

Two centuries of thought have resulted in acceptance of the human limitations that make that question absolutely unanswerable, but its fascination for these earlier students seems to have been inexhaustible. To use the cant phrase with which all are familiar, Augustine believed salvation to be the work of grace, effected only by the inspiration of the Holy Spirit. Pelagius held that all alike can of their own free will turn to God and claim redemption.² Molina, who was originally a Jesuit, attempted to combine the two theories in his treatise, "The Compatibility of Free-will with the Gifts of Grace"; but they seem to have been incompatible, and the Jesuits

[1] True Jansenism consists in saying that after the fall of Adam man found himself between two opposing attractions, one of heaven towards virtue, the other of earth towards vice, so that it is *necessary* that at each moment the will should follow whichever of these attractions proves the stronger (*Œuvres de Fénelon*, xviii.).

[2] Some clue to these differing doctrines may be found in the lives of the disputants. Augustine was converted after a life of sin. Pelagius had a clear record from his youth up.

would not allow their rivals to preach a doctrine which, if it had no other flaw, was so evidently destructive to the supreme spiritual power of the priests. Fénelon found other reasons for claiming the necessity of free will, and his conclusion of the whole matter appeals to the natural instincts of average humanity. Briefly it was this: Take away free will, and you take away all vice, all virtue, and all merit.

Nevertheless, Jansenius drew something very like a denial of free will from St. Augustine. The elect, according to him, were saved without any choice of their own, by the choice of God; all might have the power to turn to God, but only the chosen had the will to do so. It is not necessary to attempt to trace the subtleties of this theory further. Jansenius spent his life in study and meditation on it, and two years after his death, in 1640, his great work, "The Augustinus, or, The Doctrine of St. Augustine," was published at Louvain. It threw down the gauntlet for Jansenism, and the conflict raged fiercely. Though the Port Royalists were many of them of earnest purpose and devoted life, the balance of reason, of power, even perhaps of saintliness (for Vincent de Paul opposed them, and Francis de Sales, who might have aided them, was dead), was against their triumph, and a papal bull in May 1653 condemned their doctrine. St. Augustine himself, in his eagerness to reveal mysteries which have been hidden from the eyes of men, loses himself in a maze of inconsistent speculations. The Jansenists, appealing to him for authority, exaggerated his mistakes and were betrayed into professions which were declared to be heretical. The difficulty, as in the subsequent case of Fénelon's *Maximes*, was that the saints acknowledged by the Roman Catholic Church had frequently given utterance to such ambiguous opinions that it was hard to separate them from the condemnation pronounced upon their over-zealous followers—a consideration which only increased the wrath of the faithful against the offenders.

From first to last the influence of the Throne was definitely against the Jansenists; and this would have been the case even if they had not been connected with the insurgents of the Fronde, for Louis XIV. was consistently opposed to any attempt at independent thought, and an endeavour after spiritual freedom was in truth the source and inspiration of their creed. He and Mazarin united in ardent support of the papal bull, the fiat of the learned doctors of the Sorbonne went out against the writings of Jansenius; even the University of Louvain, the birthplace of his doctrine, subscribed to his condemnation, and it seemed that the faction of Port Royal must be either crushed out of existence or converted to accepted orthodoxy. But if they were to die they were determined to die hard. Among the Port Royalists there were names which have an individual place in the honourable records of their country, and persecution aroused in them that spirit of resistance which had already made the Huguenots so dangerous to the national peace.

Antoine Arnauld, the brother of Mère Angelique, was a celebrated scholar and a doctor of the Sorbonne. De Saçi, less celebrated but no less learned, translated the Bible in the version in general use. Nicole, Tillemont, and Racine were faithful sons to the community. Boileau was ready to risk his liberty for its defence; and Pascal's "Provincial Letters" bear witness still to his loyalty. It claimed protectors also among those whose greatness was not due only to their intellectual power. Mme. de Longueville and her brothers the Duc d'Enghien and the Prince de Conti are the most noticeable of these. There was the Duc de Luynes also, the recipient of Arnauld's celebrated "Letters to a Duke and Peer of France"; but the King on one occasion stated openly that "those who go to Port Royal do not come to Marly," and therefore an avowal of Jansenism made serious demands on the self-devotion of a courtier. In the case of Racine the conflict of interest was particularly cruel; for he seems to have had an honest personal affection for the King, and was held in high esteem by Mme. de Maintenon. As in other notable instances, this last advantage was his ruin. When suspicions of Jansenist heresy were rife at Court, she betrayed him to make her own position more secure. It was her intention to do her utmost to reinstate him, but he died, heartbroken at the loss of a favour which he had valued far too deeply, before she could accomplish her purpose.

"I know that in the King's mind a Jansenist is simply an intriguer and a rebel to the Church,"[1] he wrote to her when his disgrace fell upon him; and no one familiar with the royal attitude towards the Arnauld faction could question the accuracy of his judgment. There must have been strong personal influence in addition to the strength of their convictions to bind

[1] *Œuvres de Racine*, vol. v., March 4, 1698.

FÉNELON AND THE JANSENISTS 187

them together in a unity of resistance which endured through three generations. The heads of the community needed higher inspiration than the political partisanship of which they were constantly accused, and their tenacity, as each new decade only brought them fresh misfortunes, testifies that their revolt was rather against the tyranny which the King sought to exercise over the brains and spirits of his subjects than against a despotism that merely touched their bodies.

While the attention of the Church was concentrated on the Quietism controversy the Jansenists had a period of repose. Pascal and Arnauld were dead, and it seemed as if the survivors of the party were not likely again to become a cause of danger. The situation of the convent of Port Royal in the Hôtel de Clugni in the Faubourg St. Jacques, and the proximity of Port Royal des Champs, brought both especially under the eye of the Archbishop of Paris. De Harlai was never troubled by his theological convictions; he was ready to obey the King's commands and carry out a system of unrelenting persecution against any sect which had the misfortune to excite the King's displeasure, and it is recorded of him that he pronounced the harshest sentences with a smiling courtesy, which showed that he at least bore no ill-will towards his victims. Possibly he lived in anticipation of a sudden swing of the pendulum, and judged it best to bid for the favour of all parties. Nevertheless, despite his dexterous diplomacy, he died without the cardinal's hat which was the goal of his ambition. De Noailles, who followed him, was more fortunate in this respect, for he was made a cardinal ten years after his appointment to the see of Paris; but he owed that distinction, so far as common rumour may be trusted, to the intervention of Mme. de Maintenon, and he failed signally in the far-sighted judgment which had protected his courtly but notorious predecessor.

De Noailles holds a prominent place among the group of contemporaries who were closely in touch with Fénelon. They were both favoured friends of Mme. de Maintenon, and during Fénelon's years at Versailles there was mutual friendliness between them. But the conduct of de Noailles regarding *Les Maximes* made further confidence impossible; his vacillation was worse than the open enmity of Bossuet, and he forfeited Fénelon's regard for ever. The injury inflicted was not one to be forgotten, and the memory of it rankled. It is, therefore, possible that Fénelon's subsequent antagonism, when the Cardinal's own orthodoxy was called in question, was, perhaps unconsciously, the more determined by reason of personal resentment. He had suffered much at the hands of those who professed to be his friends, and he was a man of strong human passions, latent in him till the day of his death in spite of long years of self-repression. Nor did he ever approach the perfection of charity, for he was an old man when de Noailles forfeited the royal favour, and it is evident that he exulted in his downfall. But at least his antagonism was undisguised; and it should be remembered that the particular form of heresy with which the Cardinal was charged was one which Fénelon had always held in abhorrence.

FÉNELON AND THE JANSENISTS 189

The controversy over the *Augustinus* had long been laid to rest, but it was revived in a somewhat varied form by the *Théologie* of Père Habert and the *Réflexions Morales*[1] of Pasquier Quesnel, and this last was the beginning of a dispute even more sensational than that on Quietism. Quesnel was a Father of the Oratory, and therefore claimed the opposition of the Jesuits at the outset; he had so far drawn their resentment upon himself that, in 1685, six years after the publication of his book, he thought it safer to retreat to Brussels. But, though his writings seemed to most theologians to correspond with the doctrine of the Jansenists, he did not acknowledge his sympathy with them, and his book was accepted by Bossuet, while the second edition, which appeared in 1699, was revised by de Noailles, who was then Archbishop of Paris, and dedicated to him with his own permission.

When Father Souatre, Jesuit priest, as the mouthpiece of his order, attacked it, Bossuet began a vindication, and had he lived a few years longer, he and Fénelon must have once more crossed swords on the field of theological controversy; he died, however, and de Noailles was left as the principal supporter of Père Quesnel. His support was given fearlessly and openly, and his enemies had only to prove the heresy of the Oratorian to attain his ruin. The Jesuits could not brook that one who did not work in their interests should stand so high in favour at Court and at the Vatican, and they detected how deeply de Noailles had

[1] *Abbregé de la Morale de l'Évangile, des Épîtres de S. Paul, des Épître Canoniques et l'Apocalypse, ou Chrétienne sur la Texte de les Livres sacrez:* à Paris en 1693-1694.

compromised himself by his approval of Quesnel. The death of La Chaise in 1708 and the succession of Le Tellier to his office as Confessor to the King, gave their scheme the impetus it needed, for Le Tellier was a Jesuit of the most dangerous type, crafty enough to know when wisdom demanded silence, but daring in stratagem when the propitious moment offered itself.

A few years earlier one of the Jansenist faction had hastened the approach of ruin by compiling a pamphlet known as the *Cas de Conscience*, which set forth an intricate difficulty of conformity with the papal bull against the *Augustinus*, and was published with the opinions of forty doctors of the Sorbonne appended. It called forth all the dormant antagonism towards the Port Royalists, and its author, Père Eustace, himself confessor to the convent of Port Royal, was responsible for the last papal bull destined to be launched against the community. But he only effected a little sooner what must of necessity have come as the years passed, for the Jansenists' claim of liberty of judgment was as impossible to reconcile with the passive obedience required by authority as that of the Huguenots themselves.

In 1709 the final blow fell on Port Royal. By order of the Archbishop of Paris all members of the Community who would not subscribe to a profession of faith which denied them any vestige of that liberty for which they had struggled so long, were expelled, and many of them condemned to imprisonment.

In this case de Noailles yielded to expediency, and allowed himself to be the tool of the King and the

FÉNELON AND THE JANSENISTS 191

Jesuits; but he would have done better to have saved his honour, for by disloyalty to a party with whom he had so much sympathy, he only succeeded in postponing his own downfall. A man whom the Jesuits marked as a victim had little hope of escape; they were confident enough to be patient, and they seldom waited in vain. The *Réflexions Morales* of Pasquier Quesnel gave them a basis from whence to direct their attack on Cardinal de Noailles, and the movement was dexterously organised. The Bishops of Luçon and Rochelle compiled a *mandement* condemning the *Réflexions Morales*, and warning the faithful against its perusal. This was placarded at every street corner in Paris, and even on the gate of the Archiepiscopal Palace. The doctrine contained in the *Réflexions Morales* is almost identical with that of Jansenius; but such a proceeding was an open insult to the Cardinal (although the Bishops declared that they intended no reflection upon him), and his first method of retaliation was the expulsion of two nephews of the Bishops from the College of Saint-Sulpice, of which he was the head by reason of his office. The Bishops retorted by a letter to the King, which is in itself a masterpiece; for without bringing any direct charge against the Cardinal, they contrived to leave the impression that he was an open supporter of acknowledged heresy. They had a strong plea for their condemnation of Quesnel in the fact that Godet Desmarais had suppressed the *Réflexions* in the diocese of Chartres just before his death, and Desmarais' place in the esteem of the King and Mme. de Maintenon was unassailable.

"Must a book be left in the hands of the faithful

which corrupts their faith," they demanded, "which suggests and encourages distrust of all established authority in every community where it is admitted? Should this book be left in the hands of the faithful because my Lord Cardinal was taken by surprise and thought it orthodox? What have we to fear in addressing the most religious of princes, the truest lover of the Church?"[1]

Thus, with their righteous indignation adroitly tempered with the flattery to which Louis was most susceptible, they made their appeal. They were venturing on dangerous ground, for de Noailles was no new comer at Court; his intimacy with Mme. de Maintenon had endured for twenty years, and he had been fortunate enough to retain the favour of the King besides. The veneration in which the memory of Bossuet was held was an additional support, for the veteran theologian was supposed to have held the same opinion of Quesnel; and if La Chaise had still controlled the conscience of the King, the movement would never have had force sufficient to attack so well-defended a position. But Le Tellier was its mainspring. No man in the kingdom, probably, held so much power as the Jesuit Confessor of the King in his later years, and the immensity of what he accomplished in this instance is only the more striking, because there was a moment when even he, secure as he believed himself, stood on the brink of failure and consequent disgrace.

The King's treatment of the Cardinal was in striking contrast with that which he accorded to Fénelon fifteen years earlier; he invited him to justify himself against the accusations of the Jesuits, and simultaneously the

[1] *Correspondance de Fénelon*, vol. iii. 207.

Chapter of Paris, jealous for the honour of their archbishop, besought him to confute the insulting charges. To comply with both demands he published a *mandement*, as militant as any of those in the Bossuet and Fénelon struggle, denouncing the bishops as assailants of the faith and doctrine of St. Augustine, and forbidding the faithful in his diocese to possess or to peruse their ordinances or pastoral instructions. It was characteristic of de Noailles to be bold at the wrong moment, and to waver when the occasion demanded resolution; in this instance his audacity was displeasing to the King, who had expected an explanation and defence addressed to himself, and he was playing into the dexterous hands of Le Tellier. It was at this crisis, when, once more, one of the princes of the Church stood arraigned on a charge of ecclesiastical treason, that Fénelon appeared again upon the scene, ranged on the side of authority, yet with the deep conviction that in choosing it he chose the side of truth.

It was not, of course, a bodily appearance at Court, or at the Vatican; but his pen was powerful enough to bring him as a living presence among the combatants, and what he wrote was animated by an intensity of feeling which must have had a deeper source than mere personal rancour. Before the cardinal's *mandement*, he had written to Le Tellier urging upon him the terrible danger of the doctrine of Quesnel and Habert, a danger infinitely more to be dreaded on account of its subtlety than open and decided Jansenism. As he viewed it, it was indeed subversive of all morality. Quietism in its darkest aspect had not appeared so black—he summarised it as the belief that all human desires were directed by the will of God, and therefore to be obeyed; and he expressed his intention of entering the lists once more in defence of the true faith if the Cardinal were suffered to make such an assault upon it as his forthcoming *mandement* threatened. It was his desire that the King should see his letter, and Le Tellier showed it to him. Conflicting currents of feeling swayed the royal influence during that controversy, and at that moment they set against the Cardinal. A gracious message from Versailles found its way to Cambrai, the first since Fénelon's appointment, leaving him full liberty in general to do what he would in support of pure doctrine, and in particular encouraging him to prepare a reply to the Cardinal with promptitude. It seemed that the ruin wrought by his eagerness to proclaim the truth was about to be repaired by the same means; but the tide turned suddenly, and just when Fénelon had finished the work that was to refute the dangerous teaching of de Noailles, he received another message from the King withdrawing the sanction he had extended to his suggested onslaught, and binding him to silence.

It was a cruel blow, so sharp that it could not be accepted without remonstrance. The pamphlet was already in the hands of the printers, and its author had gloried in the thought that he was once more to be known among his fellows as the defender of the Church he loved, but was supposed to have attacked. Fancying that a recollection of his old injuries at the hand of de Noailles might have moved the King to this unexpected course, he made a desperate appeal to Le Tellier.

FÉNELON AND THE JANSENISTS 195

"CAMBRAI, *May* 8, 1711.

"If the King thinks I am moved by passion, or that I am mistaken in the doctrine, I implore him to name four or five bishops, sincerely anti-Jansenist, pious, gentle, moderate, but without ambition or worldly calculation. I will consult with them with the utmost secrecy. They shall report to his Majesty. I will do nothing without consulting them; and I dare be certain that they will see how I deprecate all extreme measures, how I love peace, and how sincerely I mistrust my own feeble understanding.

"M. le Cardinal de Noailles, who is so sharp against his Episcopal colleagues, and rebukes them so freely, has nothing but indulgence for Père Quesnel."[1]

One of the most galling disabilities of exile was an ignorance of the progress of events, which caused Fénelon to expend his strength in useless effort. In the present case, had he had full information of the progress of affairs, he would have been able to foretell the obduracy of the King. Events had, in fact, taken a most unexpected turn, which, had he availed himself of it prudently, would have changed the very precarious position of de Noailles to one of absolute security. By some chance which is involved in mystery, some letters fell into his hands, written by one Jesuit, the Abbé Bochart de Saron, to another, which described the original scheme of attack upon the Cardinal through Quesnel, as concerted between Le Tellier and other prominent members of the community. So skilfully had the scheme been conceived

[1] *Correspondance de Fénelon*, vol. iii. 212.

that the actual result accorded with that on which they speculated, and it was easy for the cardinal to insinuate that they had used the King and Mme. de Maintenon as their tools.

"The Jansenists, the Jesuits, M. le Cardinal de Noailles, M. de Cambrai, and several bishops, are making a great fuss," wrote Mme. de Maintenon. "If you wish to know my opinion on the subject, I tell you that they are all in the wrong. M. le Cardinal has asked leave to come here on Wednesday, to make his plea in form. I greatly fear the audience will only anger both parties." [1]

So great was the triumph and elation of the Cardinal that it turned his head. A single reverse did not shake the power of the Jesuits more than temporarily, but he, remembering that they had not saved Fénelon, believed that they had not sufficient strength or determination to ruin him. As Archbishop of Paris, it was his office to issue licences annually to preachers and confessors, and he made use of his power to deny the right to receive confession to twenty Jesuits who presented themselves, only extending it conditionally to Le Tellier. Once again he played into the hands of his enemies. There was an outcry throughout Paris which found an echo at Versailles. The prejudices of a lifetime in such a mind as the King's could not be routed in a moment even by such a revelation as that of the intrigue against the Cardinal, and Le Tellier, though his post might be insecure, was still at Court, and knew how to turn every whisper to the best account to save his party.

"It is my fate to die by these bishops," wrote Mme.

[1] To M. le Duc de Noailles, Marly, April 27, 1711.

FÉNELON AND THE JANSENISTS 197

de Maintenon in despair. "You know what M. de Cambrai made me suffer: it is much worse to be at odds with one's own archbishop."[1]

Certainly her position and that of the King deserved commiseration; they could have pursued their course so confidently along the narrow path of bigotry, crushing all who showed any inclination to diverge from it, and happy in the conviction that all other routes but theirs led to inevitable damnation, but for the fact that just those companions whom they chose as guides or fellow-travellers, again and again deserted them and rushed headlong down forbidden byways towards destruction. The King was old, and had been shaken by national disasters; the firmness he brought to bear on other similar controversies was lacking in this instance, either from general weakness or by reason of his friendship for de Noailles. Had it been possible, he would have retained Le Tellier and countenanced the Cardinal at the same time. But it was not possible; on both sides the enmity was so declared that complete surrender from one or other of the combatants seemed the only conclusion. The King turned to his grandson for assistance in his difficulty. The young Dauphin had not been a success on the battlefield, but it was hoped that he might shine as a peacemaker; in many ways he was eminently fitted for the office assigned to him, for he had given even more study to religion than to politics, and his intimacy with Fénelon taught him to know the minds of the leaders of the Church as other princes could not do. He summoned a council of men who stood high in repu-

[1] To the Bishop of Chartres, July 1711.

tation for firmness and moderation, and made it his aim to obtain concessions from both parties. Le Tellier seems to have aided him in persuading the bishops, on whom fell the onus of the controversy, to make a conciliatory advance towards the Cardinal, representing that by so doing they would please the King, and so serve the cause of their party, although at the cost of personal humiliation; but the reckless step of de Noailles in withholding the licences of the Jesuits made any moderate or peaceful settlement impossible. Moreover, the bishops would only consent to humble themselves if he withdrew his *mandement*, and, with the obstinacy of weakness, he would not yield an inch of the position of defiance he had adopted.

The offending books were already under consideration at Rome, and Fénelon, who watched the controversy with the utmost eagerness, could obtain more intimate information regarding proceedings at the Vatican than of what took place in Paris. A letter from Père Daubenton,[1] his correspondent there, gives a curious picture that recalls the expedients of Phélippeaux and the Abbé Bossuet in a struggle which had become only a vague remembrance to all but a very few, and commemorates once more the absolute unscrupulousness regarding the means to a desired end, that characterised ecclesiastics of the highest reputation.

"ROME, *October* 23, 1711.

"There is a very dangerous man called Roslet here, the agent of Cardinal de Noailles. He scatters a thousand

[1] Representative of the French interest in the College of Jesuits at Rome.

falsehoods with the utmost audacity in support of de Quesnel's book. For instance, that the Dauphin has openly declared himself on that side; that the bishops gave the letters to Cardinal de Noailles; that they will alter their *mandement* to the will of the cardinal, while he confirms his. He adds, which is a notable lie, that he knows all this from the cardinal. All the Jansenists assemble at Père Roslet's."[1]

But, by one of those curious paradoxes that, in spite of all entanglement wrought by corruption and intrigue, reveal the character which is the mainspring of all controversy, it was because de Noailles had so scrupulous a conscience that he ruined his career, and brought disaster and anarchy to the Church of France, which was prolonged and extended until the Church of France ceased to exist. The spirit of revolution had breathed on the Jansenists, though they themselves were unconscious of the magic that inspired them to risk all to claim the right of independent thought. Mazarin was not so much deceived as he is sometimes represented to have been, when he attributed to them a share in the guilt of the riots of the Fronde. That spirit had been nurtured at Port Royal; but, when Port Royal vanished, it was diffused throughout the people. Quesnel and Habert were its interpreters, and it would have been as judicious of the King to applaud the proceedings of d'Enghien or de Conti, as it was for de Noailles, cardinal and archbishop, to stamp the works of Quesnel with the seal of his approval. Nevertheless, disastrous as his honesty

[1] *Correspondance de Fénelon*, vol. iii. 249.

might be to himself and to all concerned with him, he was honest in intention. He had not connected Quesnel with Jansenism, and when that connection was suggested to him it was done in such a way that his resentment blinded him. Inherent obstinacy strengthened resentment, and he believed that his recklessness proved his self-devotion, and was demanded of him by his conscience. " His Majesty will no doubt be displeased; but in order to gratify my sovereign I have no right to offend God." [1] Such was his attitude towards all reasoning and rebuke, displaying a self-righteousness which was galling even to his friends, but especially offensive to a king who professed that his highest gratification was to serve and protect the Church.

And having plunged the Church into a conflict, beside which the Quietism difficulty must have seemed little more than a friendly argument, when a little prudence and generosity might have saved her, de Noailles failed even to save his dignity. Like Fénelon, he vowed that he would abide by the decision of the Church, even while he was supporting his original opinion; but before the decision came he had admitted his mistake, and yet could not accept the papal Bull without haggling and questioning, which was as destructive to his own authority as to that of the Pope. In his various attitudes he occupied the attention of the Church for five years, and when self-reproach at length overwhelmed him, the aspect of affairs in his native country had altered signally. The King and three generations of those who should have succeeded to his crown were dead. Nothing which wise men had pre-

[1] To Mme. de Maintenon, Aug. 20, 1711.

FÉNELON AND THE JANSENISTS

dicted for the future had come to pass. Fénelon, whom many had regarded as a dangerous influence looming before them, had ceased to be a source alike of consolation or of danger. The little society at Cambrai was scattered, and the two great nobles who had ever remained its faithful friends were only memories at the Court which they had graced. Yet to Fénelon, though he did not live to see the end, the matter had been vital. He had never perhaps felt his exile and disgrace so keenly. His talents fitted him for the field of controversy, and in this instance his feelings were so deeply stirred that he was eager to bear his part; but the King's animosity was unchanging, and the service that such support might render to the Church had no weight against it.

Nevertheless, though he could not represent the side of orthodoxy and obedience, Fénelon continued to do loyal service. His enemies were ready to declare that he attempted to trade upon the mistakes of his former friends for his own advancement, and for the joy of triumph, but facts to some degree exonerate him. Ever since he had attained to calm and exile, at one and the same time, he had been indefatigable in opposition to everything savouring of Jansenism. "This contest is concerned not only with the condemned doctrine of Jansenius' book: it concerns a dogma which in practice saps the foundation of all authority in the Church, and leaves no true resource against any heresies which may arise to the end of time."[1] Such had been his verdict at

[1] Preface to the *Instruction Pastorale* against "*Cas de Conscience*" (*Œuvres de Fénelon*, vol. viii.).

the time of the "*Cas de Conscience*," and to the end of his life he maintained it in relation to the repeated challenges of the Jansenists, declared or veiled. For him it was no party cry; his private letters breathe the same spirit of indignation as the successive *mandements* he launched upon his diocese, and it survived even when the death of the Dauphin had detached his hold on other human interests. Then, indeed, he added to his old ardour the belief that it was his duty to defend the prince's memory from what he esteemed a very awful accusation. De Noailles, or more probably his supporters, had taken advantage of the prince's effort at diplomacy to charge him with a leaning to their party, declaring that he had embodied it in a *Memoire*, written but not published. The King was known to have destroyed many of his grandson's papers, and it was likely that this would have been among them; but in this case fortune favoured the Jesuits. The King, hearing the insinuation, caused the real *Memoire* to be printed, and confuted all the assertions of the offenders. At the same time he gave permission to the bishops to go to Rome and lay their difficulties and defence before the Pope, for it was evident that the time was past for any settlement by mutual agreement.

The first instinct of the bishops was to appeal to Fénelon for advice. He was broken in health and spirits by the national misfortune, which had had such overwhelming individual bitterness for him, but he threw off private cares that he might put himself in their place and help them to the best of his ability. All his letters to them are temperate, yet they are comprehensive; it was plain that he had reviewed the situation carefully, and he advised them to avail themselves of the King's permission. It was a favour which he had coveted most ardently when his own cause was fought, and the fact of its denial had signified that the King's interest was against him; he could deduce the contrary, therefore, in the present case, and confidently do all in his power to calm the misgivings of the bishops.

He was not deceived. The tide of Court favour had gradually set against the Cardinal, and his own unreasonable conduct was responsible; he had been secure of his position for so long that he thought its foundations were immovable, but intrigue and uncompromising bigotry were sweeping them away. The King had strong personal liking and respect for him, or his favour would not have survived the repeated reflections on his orthodoxy for so long; Fénelon, under the same circumstances, must have fallen ten years earlier, and it is curious to note how even the King's intolerance was governed by his caprices. The Chancellor d'Aguesseau, who watched the affairs of Church and State with discriminating attention, gives a strange instance of the indulgence given to de Noailles on an earlier occasion: "The Cardinal had made a list of bishops for a commission on the Bull, which included two under suspicion—de Rouen and de Montpellier. He (the King) observed: 'How, Monsieur, you place the Archbishop of Rouen at the head of the commission, and the Bishop of Montpellier is one of the committee! Here is a commission that will not alarm the Jansenists very much!' The Cardinal was about to reply with some observation touching the Bishop of Montpellier, when the King continued, 'If I was speaking to any one but you, I should formally forbid him to put such a person on such a commission, but I am convinced that it is enough for you to know that it would not please me, to think no more of it!'"[1]

Such rashness would have been enough to ruin even Bossuet, and the man who could indulge it with impunity was perhaps justified in thinking himself exempt from any danger. He had no lack of warning, but his original triumph in the discovery of the Jesuit intrigue had seemed to him conclusive, it had saved him at a perilous moment, and he was tempted to think it a direct interposition of Providence in his favour. In the event it proved the saving of the Jesuits, for it robbed him of every vestige of common sense remaining to him. Mme. de Maintenon did not turn on him as she had done on Fénelon, or desert him as she had deserted Racine in the hour of danger; but fidelity was not her foremost characteristic, and, in the end, she lost patience with him. Her letters prove how deeply she was interested in his concerns, and her readiness to help him when occasion served; such a one as the following shows her, perhaps, at her best, as a woman of rare good sense, far-seeing and observant. It was written to M. le Duc de Noailles, who was enabled to retain her regard unshaken till her death.

"SAINT-CYR, *November* 15, 1712."

"Cannot you make another attempt, my dear duke, to prevail on M. le Cardinal to receive the advances of the Jesuits? Can he honestly imagine that the world will wonder at his having this indulgence for the King? 'He follows his conscience!' says he. This is revenge rather

[1] *Memoires Historiques sur les Affaires de l'Eglise de France*, 1697-1710.

than punishment. But, if it be the latter, the length of the punishment might, it seems to me, be sacrificed to his master, his patron, and a prince who alone supports religion. Let us be candid, Monsieur: we shall see a great explosion if we do not see a truce. I know the King. Time increases his anger. I have told you so many times. The King detests these quarrels; he desires the end of this one eagerly. It rests only with your uncle to end it to his own advantage. He will have shown the Jesuits the harm that he could do them, and the King what he was prepared to sacrifice to him.

"I cannot make up my mind to seeing the name of de Noailles on the eve of disgrace."

She herself was not accused of Jansenist tendencies, and her conscience did not reproach her as it had done on the score of Quietism; she was, therefore, able to hear both sides impartially, and admitted many among the number of her correspondents whom the King would not have admitted to Marly. But she grew weary of it; she was loyal to Rome as befitted the consort of Louis XIV., and when the Pope had decided a matter, she considered that it admitted of no further question; moreover, she had a habit of regarding the theological difficulties of her friends as personal grievances to herself, and the captious tone which she had used regarding Fénelon crept at length into her comments on de Noailles. Once more she wrote to his kinsman.

"*August* 4, 1714.

"All the negotiations have fallen through: it is time, my dear duke, that you should let the King know how much you disapprove the conduct of M. le Cardinal de Noailles. Otherwise you may find yourself involved in his disgrace. . . . If M. *votre oncle* continues to prefer the interests of Père Quesnel to those of his family, it is not right that I should be sacrificed for him, or that he should drag you into his downfall."

It was time, indeed, that the Cardinal should make submission. His case was not so hard as Fénelon's, he did not need to proscribe the book which was the outcome of his deepest meditations, of his most spiritual thought; he was only required to withdraw his approval of the writings of another man, a proceeding which he had not found difficult in the case of the *Maximes*. The Bull *Unigenitus* condemning the propositions of Quesnel was given by the Pope in 1713; it was the second levelled at Père Quesnel, for the Jesuits had obtained his condemnation in 1708, but this had been evaded as infringing the privileges of the Gallican Church. King and Pope were now in accord, however, and the King, instead of waiting for a full convocation, in his impatience to be done with the business summoned forty-nine bishops, who happened to be able to obey at once, to meet at the Archiepiscopal Palace to choose a commission among themselves to study the Bull and agree on the best means to further its acceptance. At the beginning of the following year the deliberations of the commission were concluded, and they were agreed that the occasion demanded complete submission to the Holy See, and acceptance without reservations of the Bull *Unigenitus*.

The question presented to de Noailles could no

FÉNELON AND THE JANSENISTS

longer be evaded; the decision of the Pope pronounced his judgment to have been an error, and, as a cardinal of the Roman Church, he was bound to acknowledge Papal authority; nevertheless, by so doing he would have been denying his convictions, and professing a belief which he did not hold. To Protestant minds such a condition seems an almost necessary part of the Roman creed, but to all alike the course chosen by de Noailles was indisputably wrong. He would not confess that his independent judgment unfitted him to hold high office in the Church, neither did he submit as Fénelon, believing disloyalty the greater evil, had done in similar straits, but he temporised, urging objections in detail, and gradually winning others to join him in his opposition. By so doing he was causing a division in the Church of France which undermined her strength until she had no power to resist the assaults of those who were the enemies of law and order, and was engulfed in the ruin of the monarchy. Beside the immensity of this result, the misfortunes which he brought upon himself and the weakness of the expedients to which he resorted have small significance. Fénelon, to whom the interest of Church and State were, undoubtedly, of more importance than any personal sentiment, was in despair. Being denied active participation in the struggle, he was the better able to observe it, and he did not scruple to give words to his conclusions.

"The King, pious, and zealous for the truth, silences truth itself for love of peace."[1] Such was his verdict on the favour shown the Cardinal, in a letter which he hoped

[1] To Le Tellier, *Correspondance de Fénelon*, iv. 297.

that the King might read. He realised none the less how much the unpopularity of the Jesuits had to answer for, even if he did not acknowledge that they had abused the enormous power they had won. It is strange to find one who was the friend of Le Tellier, and had once relied on the protection of Cardinal de Bouillon, displaying such insight towards the popular mind, as is conveyed by the following: "So far does passion go, that hatred of the Jesuits becomes a decisive reason for loving the Jansenists in spite of the thunders of the Church. If the Jesuits became Jansenists, their perversion would convert numbers of their enemies. The party cry is: that the Church is no longer to be listened to, because it is directed by the Jesuits instead of the Holy Spirit."[1]

It cannot be doubted that Fénelon was stating the exact truth of the situation, seeing it with the clearness of view impossible to those directly involved. The anti-Jesuit party was as strong at Court as among the commonalty, and the triumphs of Le Tellier seemed only to lend new zest to the eagerness with which he was opposed. No wonder that loving and loyal sons of the Church regarded her position with dismay, hardly daring to look onwards to the promise of the coming years. Fénelon was failing in health, and weary with many sorrows, yet the crisis inspired his pen anew, and was the occasion of a production which was the last and the most felicitous of all his controversial writings. In the days of Quietism Bossuet bore away the palm of popularity by his scurrilous *Relation*; in the present case Fénelon won a like honour by fair means. To all but a

[1] Preface to *Instruction Pastorale*, 1714, *Œuvres de Fénelon*, xv.

very few the interest of the strife betwixt Jesuits and Jansenists is long since dead, and the voluminous compositions on the subject unworthy of attention. Nevertheless the *Instruction Pastorale* on the Bull *Unigenitus*,[1] composed by Fénelon, may still be read with pleasure by many who have no concern with theological intricacies; the lightness of touch, which was the charm of his earlier writings, is here combined with the vigour with which his subject had inspired him. The volume is a masterpiece, and, appearing as it did so soon before his death, its celebrity was enhanced by regret at the loss of so great a power for good.

Ten years earlier, in a published letter to a bishop concerning the *Cas de Conscience*[2] before mentioned and the papal decree thereon, he had evolved a method of expression which arrested popular attention: it was the method of dialogue, conveying the specious arguments urged by the offending party and the convincing manner of confuting them. In his last *Instruction*, which was to arm his flock against the seductions of the newest heresy, he adopted this form once more; the exhaustive discussion which fills the volume taking place between the writer and two imaginary characters, Frémont, a Jansenist, and Perault, whom he represented as having been convinced of the errors of Jansenius six months earlier. Such is the dramatic power that characterises the work that it is difficult to remember that the confusion of Frémont is a foregone conclusion, and, as representing the weaker side, the reader is apt to wish that he may triumph. In the end his arguments fail him,

[1] *Œuvres de Fénelon*, xv.   [2] *Ibid.* xiii.

and he retires abruptly from the scene, having displayed a tenacity in face of apparently incontrovertible reasoning worthy of Cardinal de Noailles himself.

The novelty of this treatment of a subject, which was necessarily somewhat repellant to the lay mind, gave the work great notoriety and consequent possibilities of far-reaching influence. It was issued before the death of Fénelon, and he was overwhelmed with testimonies of admiration from all quarters; it was a gleam of sunshine on his closing days. But the storm that was gathering on the Church of France made him incapable of rejoicing in any personal success, and those who mourned him most deeply must have found comfort in the thought of the pain he had escaped. In a letter to Le Tellier a month or two before his death, he disclaims any personal resentment against the Cardinal. "God is my witness that my heart is in no wise changed towards him; that I respect him in all good faith." He recognised the sincerity of that claim of conscience with which de Noailles justifies himself, to himself at any rate, but their view of loyalty differed widely. "We are but the ministers of Christ," wrote Fénelon, " to prefer God to ourselves, the Catholic faith to our pledges, and the decision of the Church to all our prejudices. Our glory is to be free of these, and yield with humility what the Church requires of us."[1]

That is the creed of a consistent member of the Roman Church; in departing from it the Cardinal was joining the enemies of Rome. In practice he was a rebel, but he missed all that can give rebellion dignity; he was reckless, but his recklessness came at the wrong moment,

---

[1] *Correspondance de Fénelon*, iv. 389, May 1714.

FÉNELON AND THE JANSENISTS

and was not glorified with the spirit of self-devotion. His ineptitude as the leader of a party is without parallel, yet the most determined and convinced reformer could not have brought greater confusion on the Church. It is difficult to conceive the motive for his perpetual inconsistencies : he pledged himself to support Quesnel, and if he had been faithful in defiance of the thunders of the Church, his courage would be worthy of admiration ; but in the *mandement* which challenged the papal decision he condemned the book of *Réflexions Morales*, for which he had fought so long, as comprehensively as the Pope himself.

He maintained his opposition to Rome while the King lived, though his deposition and the irrevocable disgrace of himself and his adherents seemed imminent. When the King died a swing of the pendulum restored him to more than all his former dignities. But he was only dangerous in opposition ; without the spur of real or fancied persecution his militant spirit subsided into inertion, and, before his death, having brought such discord on the Gallican Church that she was never destined to find peace again, he became as submissive to the authority of Rome as Fénelon himself. A hackneyed phrase describes Charles I. as a good man but a bad king ; even so may it be said of de Noailles that he was a good man but a bad archbishop. But as the one has been shown to be a contradiction in terms so must also be the other. He was as false to himself as to others, and treason is no less dangerous because the traitor is well-intentioned.

PART II
FÉNELON IN EXILE

CHAPTER I

THE FAMILIAR FRIENDS OF FÉNELON

IT is undeniable that controversy claimed a share of Fénelon's energy and thought which could have been better employed in other directions. That controversy was the spirit of the times makes it no less deplorable; but a portrait is not a true one if the blemishes are painted out, and if Fénelon seem less worthy because his life bears the impress of the influences that touched it, it has been necessary, nevertheless, to show him as he is portrayed by his contemporaries. Warfare between nations can be represented to have advantages in inspiring the spirit of self-sacrifice and gallantry, but it would need a skilful advocate to depict the benefit resulting from conflict in the Church. As in the Quietism trial, so in the charge against the Jansenists, the best protectors of the Church appeared to be the men who could hit the hardest, and those who should have been an example became a laughing-stock.

No more melancholy spectacle could be displayed to lovers of their country and their Church. The short-sightedness which permitted such lowering of their dignity is a curious study for future generations, and the most absolute lawlessness was the final result evoked by the clash of Inquiry and Authority. There were many who watched with eager interest and were not slow to record their observations, for the nineteenth century itself is less prolific in reminiscences than the seventeenth; but one who had every opportunity of judging has so laid bare the root of the evil of religious controversy, as it was waged within the Roman Church, that nothing remains to be added to his conclusions. The Chancellor d'Aguesseau was given exceptional chances of insight by his office and by the royal confidence; he was gifted by nature with the qualities which enabled him to profit. He was shrewd and far-seeing, one who could scrutinise intently, even laboriously, realising that, as the movement of the straws tells the direction of the wind, so the most trifling incidents predict the issue of a crisis. Having observed and reflected, d'Aguesseau was competent to summarise the result with fairness, although from the point of view of a loyal supporter of the Church; and it will be seen that, had the ecclesiastical authorities agreed with him and quashed the war of pamphlets, the religious atmosphere would have been far less exciting, half the works of the prominent theologians remained unwritten, and some of the writers, possibly to the benefit of mankind, have never emerged from obscurity. "When a question is still undecided by the Church there can be nothing more dangerous, especially when passions have become heated on the subject of the question, than to permit it to be supported and attacked; the danger is equal on either side. Because, as the Church has not defined the precise limits of such a doctrine, and as there is hardly any truth which is regarded from the same point of view by differing understandings, each mixes up his own prejudices, predilections, and interests, so that it often happens that, on one side, one who supports permits too large a limit; and on the other, he who attacks it wishes to confine it within too narrow bounds; and, because there is not yet any authority to arrest and unite such temperaments, each one makes up a system according to his own fancy, and, charging every opinion that differs from his as heresy, disturbs the peace of the Church in attempting to forestall decisions which he ought to await respectfully."[1]

Those who were most eager for the fray were quite ready to adopt this view as applied to others: "What becomes of the great diocese for which you are responsible," wrote de Noailles to Fénelon, when the *Maximes* were the question of the day; "it is doubtless requiring all your efforts while you give all your labour to the defence of your book."[2] The question from an impartial spectator would have been a just one, from the Archbishop of Paris, the future champion of Quesnel and Habert, it was merely an impertinence; yet, had he deigned to answer, Fénelon might have proved that if his thoughts were at Rome, if his heart and soul were filled with the desire that those beliefs, which were his dearest support and consolation, might not be pronounced to be inimical to the orthodox faith, yet he was none the less at the service of his flock.

There was a dual, nay, a triple self, in Fénelon: it is a phenomenon common enough in human nature, and it is perhaps responsible for the absolutely contradictory testimonies of historians in all ages. It has been a

---

[1] *Mémoires sur les Disputes de Théologie : Œuvres d'Aguesseau*, vol. viii.
[2] *Œuvres de Fénelon*, vol. vi.

constant endeavour of the student to classify and label each actor in the drama of the world's history as belonging to a particular type; the patriot and the self-seeker, the champion of truth and the intriguer, the hero and the coward, each has his separate pigeon-hole, and some, in the strange jumble of individual opinion, may find themselves in curious company. Yet, in truth, this human nature, even as it is shown to us, darkly and incompletely, through the veil of chronicle and tradition, cannot be so classified. These men of mark were men of a thousand varying moods, many of them, doubtless, with a fixed aim to serve as the loadstar of their life, but dependent, nevertheless, on chances of environment and influence; aiming high at one moment, falling unaccountably the next—men many-sided, with interests and motives of which the world knows nothing, and, because they were men and like to ourselves in all things but for that touch of genius that gives them immortality, not to be ticketed as pure and noble, or corrupt and vile, but as complex and mysterious beings in the best of whom evil was sometimes dominant, while in the worst it is likely there were finer traits than those which are recorded.

It would be false to say that Fénelon's character remained unaffected by the evil passions at work within the Church; the spirit of resentment took hold upon him in spite of all his protestations to the contrary, and he showed no eagerness to shelter others in storms such as had broken over him. But, if he was bitter towards those who injured him, he did not let the downfall of his hopes warp his general outlook upon life, or harden him in relation with his fellow-men; neither did he seek the consolation of the student, to the exclusion of the world that proved itself unworthy of him, as many an earnest thinker has done before and since. It was not, indeed, till the door of further advancement was closed that he gave proof of the purity and singleness of purpose that distinguished him, and threw himself into duties, which he believed he held in trust for an Authority higher than the Pope, with an energy that must have been astounding to a people accustomed to the slackness and indifference of his predecessors. And, having followed him through those passages of controversy so important to his career and to his character, which show him with the shadow of inconsistency that the Church had forced on him, and that other shadow, darker and yet less defined, of rankling ill-will, we find that there is another aspect of him—the Fénelon who won and kept his hold on the hearts of all his stolid Flemish flock, who made his little court at Cambrai a centre of pure thought and genial wit, who, amid his manifold duties and employments, had always sympathy and counsel to give ungrudgingly to all who claimed it.

He had been appointed to his diocese in 1695. It was a great appointment, for Cambrai, though distant, lay on the important Flemish frontier to which so many thoughts were necessarily directed, and the Archbishop held ducal rank, and nominally immense revenues; it was no wonder that the young Abbé was considered a favourite of fortune, and this promotion only a stepping-stone to still greater honours. He made his first visit to Cambrai in a spirit of humorous curiosity; but, even while he smiled, he had only friendly criticisms to make on a people whose manners and opinions had nothing in common with those to which he was accustomed. "When I arrive at a convent the Superior comes to receive me in the road," he wrote to Mme. de Maintenon on his first arrival; "all strangers are received in the outer parlours without grille or fence. When I arrive I am led to the church, the choir, cloister, the sleeping-room, and finally to the refectory with my whole party. The Superior then presents me with a glass, and we drink together, she and I, to each other's health. The community also attack me, but my grand-vicare and clergy come to the rescue. All of which is done with a simplicity which would delight you. . . . Piety is no more refined than anything else; virtue is as homely as outward appearance; but the foundation is excellent. The general Flemish mediocrity results in less good and less evil than we have in France, neither virtue or vice go so far, but the average of men and women belonging to communities is higher and more innocent." [1]

There is the ring of laughter in the description; how could it be otherwise when he portrays himself, the courtly and fastidious abbé of Versailles, hobnobbing with the stout Flemish abbess in her own refectory? But it is kindly laughter. He did not realise then that this general Flemish mediocrity was to be the setting of his future life; such a prospect would have seemed to portend the waste of the capacity which God had lavished on him. But when it was certain that his lot was irrevocably cast among them, they became his children,

[1] *Correspondance de Fénelon*, vol. vii. 91, September 1695.

he set himself to understand them, to humour their weaknesses and cherish their virtues, resolutely suppressing every tendency to compare them with their fellow-subjects in Paris and the south. The rich treasures of his intellect would have been wasted on them. He may have been capable of swaying a crowded congregation in a Parisian church as Bossuet had done, of causing his name to ring through the city on occasions of national sorrow or rejoicing like his great opponent; but such opportunities were denied to him. Instead he spoke to the Flemish throng at Cambrai or at Lille out of the fulness of his heart; needing no notes or preparation, but yet sending his words home to their dull brains by force of his own strong conviction, drawing them to him because he—scholar and courtier though he was—had remembered that the greatest lessons are the simplest, that the greatest Teacher had Himself chosen the humble and the ignorant to follow Him.

Therefore, if we too turn from the Court and contemplate those quiet years at Cambrai, the King's displeasure and the papal condemnation no longer bear with them the shadow of disgrace, and the word failure cannot be admitted to the record of his history. He was archbishop, and by birth of the nobility of France. It was a time when great ecclesiastics claimed their pomp of office to the full; but Fénelon, while he ruled at Cambrai and welcomed all who came with generous hospitality, lived like an anchorite and laboured like a conscientious village priest. It was not enough that his people should know him in the cathedral pulpit or in his official journeys about the diocese; in that same literal imitation of his Master which was the clue to so many of his actions, he went himself among the peasants, speaking to them in the fields, relieving their needs, and accepting their hospitality if they were eager to welcome him at their own tables. No office of a priest was too humble for him; the sick within reach of the palace at Cambrai might claim his ministrations, and it was rarely that he deputed any of his household to fill his place in watching by the dying. There were many testimonies to such things as these; the Fénelon of Versailles and Germigny may wear a different aspect to differing critics, but the Fénelon known to the people of Cambrai had but one face—a friendly, gentle face, in which they might read never-ending sympathy, and look for smiles that were as sad as they were humorous. Nor was he content with personal service; the importance which he gave to the ecclesiastical seminary of his diocese shows the wideness of his views of his duty to the Church, devoting to it labour of which he could hardly hope to see the fruit, and from which he would reap no benefit.

The journals of the day are full of minute descriptions. It was an age that loved detail, and Fénelon's visitors did not spare him. Perhaps the most illuminating glimpse of him is that given by Ledieu, in whose *Mémoires* may sometimes be found a foretaste of the modern interview. He came to Cambrai on the strength of a vague invitation from the Archbishop, and armed with a letter from Mme. de Maisonfort to secure his welcome. He came, moreover, full of curiosity, eager to criticise, and, as the most devoted of Bossuet's disciples, disposed to condemn all that he saw and heard. He was possessed of an immense faculty of observation, and he employed it to the full, for, in the one night he remained as Fénelon's guest, he acquired an amount of information respecting the conduct of the archiepiscopal household which is most valuable as a groundwork for realisation of the life of Fénelon and his associates. He arrived at the town of Cambrai during Fénelon's absence on an official circuit, and was present at the palace on the following day when he returned thither.

Fénelon had faithful friends who shared his exile; some of these were gathered on the steps to receive him. De Beaumont had been with him on his journey, and de Langeron seems to have been absent; but de Chanterac was there, and the Abbé de Laval, and de l'Échelle, and Lefevre, guests who had come from Paris, and the two lads—the Marquis and the Abbé de Fénelon—who were being educated under their uncle's supervision. Lediéu had eyes for all; but his thoughts centred on the tall, spare figure of the Archbishop in his purple robes, the simplicity of which arrested his attention, and he hastened to make known the excuse for his intrusion. Nothing could have obliterated the claim of Mme. de Maisonfort on Fénelon, and Lediéu was, in fact, the bearer of a celebrated letter, descriptive of the last days of Bossuet. Fénelon received him graciously; he omitted nothing which the most scrupulous courtesy demanded. Nevertheless, the ingenuous chronicler conveys the fact, of which he himself was probably unconscious, that he was not a welcome visitor, and that his presence imposed a constraint upon his entertainers. If it be remembered that he was the confidential secretary of Bossuet through the years when he had worked so hard to ruin Fénelon, it is not remarkable that Ledieu was regarded somewhat dubiously. His chief motive in coming was the harmless one of curiosity, and, as his patron was dead, he was not likely to possess the power to injure the Archbishop or those connected with him if he had so desired. Nevertheless, it is not a serious imputation on Fénelon's character for candour and simplicity that he should have refrained from reference to his dead opponent, or to their cause of conflict, during the brief period of association with his guest. Ledieu was on the watch for any expression of opinion, personal or abstract, and the one question which Fénelon permitted himself regarding Bossuet—a natural desire to know who had consoled the last hours of the great divine—was tortured into an insinuation that a heavy load must have lain upon his conscience.

That is the only accusation the guest was enabled to bring against his entertainer; he dined at his table and was assigned the place of honour, being impressed by the excellence of the fare set before him, which, as he did not fail to notice, was seldom tasted by his host. Fénelon had no liking for luxury, but he loved hospitality, and had no desire that those whom he welcomed to his table should copy him in abstinence. Not only his intimate friends but his secretaries and almoners sat down with him, and conversation, in which he joined, was general—his young nephews were required to be silent, but, with that exception, all were encouraged to talk as on an equal footing. In this he departed from the custom of the day; the archiepiscopal dignity was cherished as that of royalty, and the Archbishops of Paris and of Rheims would have thought that they debased it if they associated with the simple priests of their household. Such simplicity was characteristic of Fénelon, but his enemies designated it as pandering to popularity, an accusation from which no man who seeks the happiness of his fellows can be safe.

As Ledieu was beneath his roof, he provided him with the pastime he most desired by giving him free licence to poke and pry about the premises at will. He himself had affairs to arrange, and the various officials of the household were not at liberty, but Bossuet's secretary was fully competent to pursue the exhaustive researches that he loved, unaided; and, when his investigations were over and the state and dignities of the Archbishop of Cambrai revealed to him, it is probable that his respect for Fénelon was mightily increased. From watching him at dinner he observed that his defeat rankled perpetually, that he never rose above his mortification; but it is extremely unlikely that Fénelon gave him any ground for such a statement; it was rather a tribute to a preconceived idea suggested by the talk of Bossuet, who loved to picture his fallen rival eating out his heart in despair and solitude, and Ledieu was obliged to banish that image before he quitted Cambrai. The very fact that Fénelon never asserted his own dignity seems to have increased the reverence with which he was regarded. He might easily have made their difference of condition a plea for avoiding private conversation with his visitor, who was rather in the position of an envoy from a hostile camp. Instead, he invited him to talk freely to him,

P

pacing the length of his suite of private apartments as they did so. "Ask me what questions you will," he said, "and I will answer you as simply as a child might do."[1]

This was to give Ledieu a rare chance in the matter of Quietism, as he was not slow to recognise, but he refrained from taking advantage of it, talking instead of the *Cas de Conscience*, which was then the general topic on men's lips. He was, in fact, overawed by all he saw and heard; the Fénelon who governed this great diocese with the wisdom and authority of one born to rule, and bore himself with irreproachable gentleness and self-restraint at home, was, evidently, a very different person from the exile whose name had been the constant theme for sneers and innuendo in the little society at Meaux.

Treated with the most punctilious courtesy to the moment of departure, Ledieu took his leave and went his way, a wiser man than when he came, yet not unmindful that, from first to last—notwithstanding that posthumous eulogy was a compliment seldom withheld—Fénelon had never spoken the smallest word in praise of M. de Meaux. Ledieu went back to Mme. de Maisonfort with a letter of friendly counsel and advice from Fénelon (for, though she was nominally reconciled to his enemies, the links of sympathy between them had been too real to be shattered by any outward influence), and the circle at Cambrai may have forgotten his intrusion before many days were passed, oblivious that the little secretary had noted and chronicled them all for the benefit of future generations.

[1] *Journal de l'Abbé Ledieu*, vol. iii., October 1704.

But even he, despite his indefatigable ardour of observation, could not know the real atmosphere of love and friendship that surrounded Fénelon; it would have needed years of intercourse to understand that to the full, and even then only the actors in that quiet drama of faithful service and endurance touched the true power of it. The mind of the convinced Roman Catholic would be a curious study if it were possible to penetrate its depths: the priests assembled at Cambrai were loyal to the Church or they would not have been welcome there, and nothing now remains to show how they contrived to reconcile that loyalty with the Church's condemnation on one whom they revered as they did Fénelon. For their case was a harder one than his; a man may condemn himself, may yield up his own judgment, and yet feel the ground beneath his feet as firm as heretofore, but to maintain complete reverence for another, not only as a man, but as a priest, after the thunders of the Church had been launched against his most deliberate teaching, demands a faculty for reconciling inconsistencies rarely possessed by individuals. After the great decision Fénelon's position was not altered among his friends, and it is hardly an exaggeration to say that they held him sacred, although duty demanded that they should subscribe to the papal sentence. Perhaps in this lies the highest tribute ever paid to him, distinguishing the man he was by faith and character from the ardent and bitter controversialist whom many judged by Bossuet's slanders and his own defence.

There are three figures set apart especially as the friends of Fénelon, set apart in every sense, for by their loyalty to him they forfeited all chance of royal favour, and shared not only his exile but his disgrace. Of these, one has become familiar by his position as his patron's representative at Rome. De Chanterac had proved his devotion by effectual service, but he was not the most cherished of the three. The Abbé de Beaumont, allied by blood as well as friendship, should perhaps stand first; but de Langeron had a hold on Fénelon of a kind to which the others never could aspire, and each in their several ways had his individual place, and their sympathy taught them a friendship that was superior to squabbles for precedence.

Pantaleon de Beaumont was the son of Fénelon's step-sister, Marie, and was nine years younger than his uncle; as their mutual affection was as close as their relationship, it seemed at the outset that de Beaumont's path to preferment would be direct and easy, smoothed by his favoured kinsman. He was appointed as a sub-tutor to the Duke of Burgundy in 1689, and would undoubtedly have risen in the train of Fénelon, for he was a cultivated man, who might possibly have had a claim of his own upon distinction. In the summer of 1698 he was banished from Versailles by the King, not for any individual act or expression of opinion, but because of his connection with Fénelon, a specimen of those arbitrary acts of tyranny which are difficult to realise in an enlightened age.

The sentence secured a most able colleague and assistant to the Archbishop of Cambrai; de Beaumont, or Panta, as he is called in their intimate correspondence, managed his kinsman's private business for him. He was treated almost as a son in spite of the slight difference in their ages, and was often sent as his representative when affairs at a distance required personal intervention. "*Je n'ai qu'un Panta au monde,*" wrote Fénelon, and he needed neither caution nor ceremony in addressing him. If the fancy took him, he could mingle humorous nonsense with the affairs of gravity which called for their attention. "There are five or six white rabbits beneath my window; they would make splendid rugs; but it would be a pity, for they are very pretty, and they eat like any great dignitary."[1] Thus he concluded a letter to his grand abbé, and thus, again and again, a flash of laughter breaks through the complication of his toils and deprivations. Such occasional relief from the perpetual watchfulness engendered by controversial struggles was necessary to the balance of his mind. With the Prince he needed to be serious always, for the younger Dauphin made a tragedy of daily life; and, in the numerous letters of spiritual counsel written by Fénelon, it was necessary that he should strain his powers of reflection, and bring renewed earnestness of thought and sympathy to bear on each individual correspondent. But with those three chosen companions he could laugh freely when a moment of reaction came, and his deepest thoughts, though they were the outcome of bitter pain which had found its only comfort in the voice of God, are more appealing, more helpful in the weariness of ordinary life, because Fénelon himself did not hold aloof from comradeship and laughter.

"If Panta forgets the agenda which I have given

[1] *Correspondance de Fénelon*, ii. 61, September 1702.

him," he wrote threateningly to de Langeron, when both had gone to Cambrai together, "I will give him over to the blackest vapours. He is a lost man, like 'Le Malade Imaginaire' abandoned to all the ills in *ie*."[1]

Panta was not apt to forget the commissions entrusted to him. Ledieu observed that he "never quitted Fénelon;" but the statement was incorrect, for again and again he writes from distant provinces, and, when his patron's life was near its close, he was forced to spend a period of some months in Paris. He was *grand-vicaire* to the diocese of Cambrai, a post of considerable importance (held by the celebrated Habert in Chalons when de Noailles was the bishop there), and was treated with the most absolute confidence, not only by the archbishop, but by such correspondents as de Chevreuse and de Beauvilliers, to whom exposure of their intercourse with Fénelon would have meant disgrace. The Quietism dispute had touched him vitally, but his interest did not distort his judgment, and he was able, thirty years after its ending, to summarise its leading features with the graphic touch of the born historian who can detect the mistakes of the side he favours. In his judgment the favour of the Jesuits towards Fénelon, without being pronounced enough to save him, roused the antagonism of all the faction of Port Royal, who worked ceaselessly and secretly to perpetuate his disgrace.[2] In one who had an individual part in the struggle it is unusual to find an insight into the hidden springs that moved such complicated affairs as these, and it is a matter for regret that de Beaumont, who had access to

---

[1] *Correspondance de Fénelon*, ii. 64, October 1701.
[2] *Ibid.*, xi., to M. de Fénelon.

all his uncle's papers, did not compile a final and authentic History of Quietism. He would have been better fitted for such a task than the Abbé de Chanterac, though the name of the latter is inseparably connected with the subject. De Chanterac's letters during the last years of the seventeenth century are in fact a History of Quietism, but not that calm and dispassionate history which, while the question was still fresh, would have set many doubts and difficulties to rest.

Gabriel de Chanterac also was a member of Fénelon's family, and a native of Perigord; he and his future patron were fellow-students at Saint-Sulpice, and he seems to have been worthy of the love and confidence reposed in him. Even Pirot, the partisan of Bossuet, describes him as "a peacemaker, a wise, erudite, and virtuous man." There is evidence that he was not brilliant in addition, however, for his voluminous letters from Rome, though their details contain ample entertainment for the reader, are not the production of a brain that grasps a situation readily. He labours to describe minutely, to photograph rather than to catch and convey impressions. From the self-revelation of those letters he appears over-scrupulous, lacking the dash and daring with which the true diplomatist can seize an occasional opportunity. If there ever was a hope for Fénelon in those deplorable proceedings, it rested on the skill and penetration of his representative; perhaps a virtuous Abbé Bossuet (had such an anomaly existed) might have saved him, in defiance of the King. But de Chanterac proved as inferior in wit to his opponent as he was above him in moral character, and evinced his loyalty rather than his competence during his years in Rome. Fénelon welcomed his return with joy, and thenceforth their lives were passed with so few separations that there is not much correspondence in evidence of their friendship. De Chanterac seems to have accepted the peace of their enforced retirement with relief; he had had a strange experience in those years in Rome, and, to a man who wished to hold the Catholic Church in reverence, a very difficult one. The springs of all that vast machinery of government were very prudently hidden from the faithful, but de Chanterac was brought too near to the centre of authority not to obtain some knowledge of them. He saw the cardinals sometimes without their sanctimonious dignities; he learned that some of them were men of dissolute life, and that the most powerful were not the virtuous, and he could not hide from himself the collusion betwixt the declared opinions of the worst among them and the papal decisions which his creed forced him to regard as the decisions of the Almighty. Doubtless the careful training of the Roman Catholic priest is specially designed to meet such tests as these, to impart to him a faculty of thought-selection whereby he can ignore and set aside such inconvenient knowledge or experience as proves impossible to weld into the tissue of the Roman Catholic faith. It is this training, hallowed by the magic of tradition, that has been the defence of that great and awe-inspiring Church throughout the centuries, giving her sons (by reason of that severance, that touch of mystery, which is her very fabric), a claim not only on the hearts, but on the minds of men who may be their superiors in every quality of mind and heart.

De Chanterac had a less penetrating intellect than Fénelon, but, on the other hand, he was brought more closely into contact with the most crying evils in the Church; and, as he poured forth details and gossip and affairs of import indiscriminately, in those long letters to his chief, he must have seen sometimes that the outcome of his experiences, the sum-total of all the rumours and scandals and intrigues which it was his duty to record, was blackly damaging to the dwellers in the Vatican. Latterly he made no comments; he left the facts to testify to the extinction of seemliness and honour in the high places of the Church; and, when duty no longer bound him, he gladly shook the dust of Rome from off his feet, and in the purer air which those at Cambrai were privileged to breathe, it may be that he could forget the revelations that had come to him during his three years' struggle. He had lived on friendly terms with many eminent persons in that period, and, when the scale wavered in his master's favour, received overwhelming protestation of the reverence in which Fénelon was held. But when his cause was lost there was only one among them all who did not hasten to withdraw from any semblance of familiarity; this was Cardinal Gabrielli, a man renowned for learning, and one of the examiners of the *Maximes* originally chosen by the Pope. He maintained his correspondence with de Chanterac when the abbé had returned to Cambrai, and was ready to do what might be in his power to further Fénelon's interests, and to send him tidings of affairs in Rome when he was no longer represented there.

With this exception, de Chanterac seems to have severed himself completely from all that associated him with that dark period of his patron's life. "I understand all that you have done and suffered," wrote Fénelon to him. "I can see that you have only reported a fraction of it to us; my gratitude, my confidence, my reverence and tenderness for you are limitless. Come with what speed you may that we may comfort ourselves in the bosom of the true Comforter. We will live and die with one heart and soul only."[1]

This, in the words of a Frenchman and a priest, was a description of their subsequent relations. They shared the same affections and the same interests. Hearing of the disgrace of Pantaleon de Beaumont, de Chanterac wrote from Rome urging the younger man's acceptance of two benefices from which he drew his revenues; and, in earlier days, when Fénelon, the new archbishop, full of zeal for a fresh constitution of the diocese, was reforming the seminary of priests that is so important a part of his responsibility, it was de Chanterac whom Fénelon selected as superior. "He has the wit, the piety, and the wisdom to govern it peacefully."[2] Having gained in addition the bond of a common labour, hope, and disappointment, they were united through the years of exile which demanded patience and self-renunciation, and death itself brought them a brief separation only, for de Chanterac died in the same year as Fénelon.

It may be seen, then, that these two, de Beaumont and de Chanterac, are very important figures in any picture of the life at Cambrai; but, though they were both kinsmen

---

[1] *Correspondance de Fénelon*, x. 592.   [2] *Ibid.*, v. 39.

as well as friends to Fénelon, it was reserved for one who came of another race to win and hold the deepest measure of his love. François de Langeron is, in truth, the representative friend: reflecting his chief, yet contrasting with him, opposing him sometimes, criticising, even laughing at him, and yet making him the object of a devotion that was nothing less than passionate. When Fénelon first had the opportunity of choosing coadjutors, at the time of the mission to Saintonge, it was de Langeron whose presence he desired most; he secured for him a place at Court, and was even ready to share the love of his little prince with him. There are letters as early as 1680 which prove how deeply they were in one another's confidence. De Langeron was harassed by family difficulties, and Fénelon, who believed firmly in the isolation of the priesthood, exhorts him to remember his duty to the Church, which in his service to his relatives he seems in danger of forgetting. It was the crown of their friendship that it was never shaken by mutual disagreement or reproof; and the archbishop, although his ecclesiastical rank set him beyond the range of ordinary criticism, accepts it humbly from de Langeron. "Your remonstrance gave me some little pain at the moment," he writes; "it was well it should do so, and it did not last" (from which it would appear that the abbé had criticised, and subsequently relented)—"I have never loved you so deeply. You would be falling short of your duty towards God and towards me, if you were not prepared to inflict such pain upon me whenever you think it right to oppose me. Our friendship depends on this confidence."[1]

[1] *Correspondance de Fénelon*, ii. 61.

The charm of originality and unexpectedness was among the delights of their alliance. "We will philosophise together," wrote Fénelon, anticipating the approach of long winter evenings; they were also capable of laughing together, despite that tragic sense of privation which must have been ever with them both.

The prospects of de Langeron had been only a little less brilliant than those of Fénelon; he himself possessed that gift of personal charm which, if united to strong intellectual power, places a dangerous extent of influence in the hands of a priest, and in those days, when all promotion went by favour, might have thrown open the way to measureless ambition. The Duke of Burgundy, who did not give his love and admiration very freely, was devoted to de Langeron; the abbé held the office of reader to him, was much concerned in the right development of his precocious talents, and remained with him till 1698, a year longer than Fénelon. The warmth of the messages to de Langeron in the Prince's letters to Cambrai suffice to prove his position. Apparently de Langeron was a man to be loved; his quick wits brought gaiety into the sombre atmosphere of disgrace and disappointment that might well have darkened the palace at Cambrai; he was *le petit abbé*, one of whom all spoke tenderly, even while they deferred to his resolute will, and recognised his force of personality.

His life was as pure, his standards as exalted as those of Fénelon himself, and his presence was the principal amelioration of the fate that kept the archbishop chained to his diocese. There is, however, the inevitable shadow of sorrow on the story of their friendship; he, the best loved, was the first of that little company to die; and this loss heralded a long series of bereavements which, coming in quick succession, left Fénelon heart-broken and beyond the reach of human comfort.

"I have lost the greatest happiness of my life," he wrote, three days after the death of de Langeron, "and the chief help in the work of the Church which God bestowed upon me. But one must accept the will of God. Nothing could be deeper or truer than the virtues of him who is dead. Nothing could be a greater witness of grace than was his death"—(he was writing a letter half on business, half of advice, and tries to concentrate himself upon it, but the pressure of personal suffering will not be altogether suppressed)—"O God, how much our best friends cost us! The only solace of life is friendship, and friendship turns into irreparable grief. Let us seek the Friend who does not die, in whom we shall recover all the rest."[1]

These last words were the expression of the final result of all calamity upon him; but he was the prey of all the weakness and temptation which may spring from sorrow. In life de Langeron had called out the human and sympathetic side of his temperament; in death he taught him to understand the fierce despair with which other men, less schooled to resignation, meet bereavement.

"I have resented the irreparable loss I have sustained with a violence which betrays the feebleness of my heart. Now my imagination has become somewhat dulled, and nothing remains but bitterness and a sort of inward lethargy. But the abatement of my suffering is not less

[1] *Correspondance de Fénelon*, i. 140, to the Vidame d'Amiens.

humiliating than my grief. All that I have experienced under both conditions is nothing but imagination and self-love. I acknowledge that I have wept in mourning for the friend who was the solace of my life, of whose loss I shall be perpetually conscious. I console myself, even as I allowed myself to give way, from weariness of pain and need of consolation. Imagination, arrested and disturbed by such an unexpected blow, grows reconciled and calm. Alas! everything in us is vanity, except that self-renunciation which grace effects in us. For the rest, my dear friend died with such a peaceful and simple acceptance of the end as would have delighted you. Even when his head wandered a little, his confused thoughts were all of grace, of faith, of gentleness, patience and resignation to God. I have never seen anything more lovely and edifying. I tell you all this that I may not describe my sorrow to you without giving you a share in that *joy of the faith* that St. Augustine speaks of, and which God has permitted me to experience upon this occasion. God's will is done. He has preferred the happiness of my friend to my own comfort. I should be found wanting towards God and towards my friend himself if I did not desire that which God has desired. In my most bitter suffering I offered him, whose loss I so much dreaded, to Him. I could not be more moved than I am by the kindness with which you claim a share in my grief."[1]

This letter not only represents the importance of the place in Fénelon's life filled by de Langeron, but is typical also of that spiritual dissection which was so

[1] *Correspondance de Fénelon*, v. 20.

large a part of the inner experience of earnest Catholics. It was a habit fostered by the system of direction, doubtless; but here the adviser yields to it as freely as the advised, and traces his natural grief at the loss of the closest of his friends to that insidious failing of self-love against which he warns his correspondents so constantly. In fact, his hold on life was shaken by the suddenness of the blow. "You know all I have lost in the friend who made the happiness of my life for thirty-four years. I saw him die of a fever that, during the first days, seemed more a passing inconvenience than an illness. He regarded death with such peace and resignation to the will of God as must have come from his inmost being. He obeyed like a little child, and when he dreamed a little, his dreams were holy. It all seemed to come from the Fountain-head of grace and sacrifice. The more I admired, the more I was moved, and I acknowledge that my sorrow made me very weak. Now my condition is one of gentle sadness with frequent recollections that recall my grief."[1]

This was his expression of feeling a month after the first novelty of his loss had overwhelmed him, and this expresses the subsequent condition of his mind. "You know all I have lost in the friend who made the happiness of my life for thirty-four years." Those who did in truth realise it must have been prepared for the sadness that henceforth settled down on the little company at Cambrai. The four years that remained to him were destined to be full of constantly renewed experience of suffering. "True friends make all the joy and all the

[1] *Correspondance de Fénelon*, iii. 193, to Père Lami.

bitterness of life;" that was his verdict when de Beauvilliers was taken from him, and he found himself almost the last remaining of the little circle that had been nearest to him in his days of happiness. But even when joy failed, he knew that, when he sought it, he was always secure of finding comfort, and, while any power of thought remained, he was provided with the unfailing distraction and resource of work for others. His position gave him full scope for energy in that direction. Ledieu had understood, even in the few hours that he had listened to the conversation in the household, how great was the power the archbishop wielded in his diocese. In his devotion to duty there was no room for interested motives; he rather injured than benefited himself in the King's estimation by winning the enthusiastic loyalty of his flock; but the rigour that confined him within those narrow limits was, at least, of advantage to the people, who had never known before what the influence of a high-souled priest may be. "I envy you your nearness to Monseigneur de Cambrai," wrote Mme. de Maintenon to an old pupil of Saint-Cyr, years after his disgrace. She knew that he possessed the rare capacity of throwing a sudden shaft of light upon the common detail of a life that custom has made wearisome, so that its possibilities of sacrifice and aspiration stand out as if they had not been a part of it before.

He did not waste his banishment, but, even by reason of it, managed to seek and find an opportunity. It may be that in his connection with the Court, his written pleading and rebuke was of more true effect than if he, with all his natural charm of personality, had come in direct contact with his penitents. It will be seen that, in the rare instances after his banishment where actual intercourse was possible, he suffered from the emotional phases to which women especially are liable; and in the correspondence, which at his darkest moments he was never too weary to maintain with those who needed him, he stored up treasures of comfort and inspiration, not only for them, but for successive generations of troubled human souls. It will be seen also that that long period of isolation was fruitful in deep and luminous political reflection. To him the true Christian seemed to be of necessity the true patriot as well; the man who loved God must learn by that higher love to love his country also, and must suffer when misfortune threatened or overtook her. Though the King would gladly have denied his claim to be a loyal Frenchman, he gave proof of it at the cost of considerable self-sacrifice. His revenues were large, but the calls upon his charity never ceased, especially in the years of the Netherlands warfare that came so close to him at Cambrai. The devastation resulting from the war reduced his income; nevertheless he volunteered to supply the royal troops with the grain of which they stood sorely in need, and, with a princely generosity, he would not sue for payment. He was only on the very outskirts of the kingdom at Cambrai; but, in those strenuous disastrous years he could feel the pulse of the nation beating as he could not have done in Paris. The War of the Spanish Succession was a personal thing to those upon the frontier; and, with Marlborough and Prince Eugène at hand, and the soldiers of France constantly passing through the town, the monotony of Cambrai was animated to a feverish throb of life. Then it was that Fénelon showed how far he identified himself with the interests of the King; private resentment and political disagreement were alike forgotten, he had no thought to spare from the common danger and threatening national disgrace. In the confusion there was no one to bear witness to his part in the great struggle, and he had no desire that it should win him notoriety. His letter to M. de Chamillard, Minister of War, on the subject of his gift of grain should exonerate him conclusively from any charge of interested motives:—

"My interest goes for nothing when it is a question of the King's. It is determined by the duty of a good subject: moreover, I am bound by gratitude. All I possess is due to the former goodness of his Majesty. I would give him my blood and my life even more willingly than my grain. But, monsieur, I am very far from desiring that you should have the worth of my offer estimated, or that you should do anything for me. The thing is not worthy to go so far as the King, and if you will be assured of my good intention to forward all your efforts in his service, I am sufficiently rewarded. Besides, I am, thank God, cured of all earthly hope. It is enough to have done my duty."

It should be remembered that while he was as he professed himself indefatigable in furthering the endeavours of the King's generals and ministers, he had always been against the war, which he believed to have been undertaken in a spirit of vain-glory and arrogant self-will, a spirit which the early experience of Louis XIV.

had fostered, but which was none the less disastrous to his kingdom. So far as his position permitted of remonstrance Fénelon had remonstrated, and the advantages of peace was a prominent theory in all his political effusions; nevertheless when the time came, the most pugnacious among the young French officers was not more eager for success than he.

Never, in fact, was there a more foolhardy enterprise than the war in Flanders, which made the name of Marlborough ring from end to end of Europe, and darkened the last years of life to the Great Monarch. It was undertaken without either the funds or the administration that could give hope of eventual success. France waited in vain for the advent of that military genius from among the thousands of her gallant sons who would have power to redeem the terrors of her position; and Fénelon saw the disasters, which he had foretold yet lacked the power to avert, sweep down on his unhappy country. But the rigorous sentence that made his protests useless did not prevent him from taking active part in the struggle against Flanders: not that he himself went forth like the martial bishops of an earlier time to take his share of blows in open field; his service was of a more peaceful character but no less necessary. His hospitality had ever been unfailing, and he responded now to every call upon it made by the constant passage of the troops. But that was only the lighter of the tasks he set himself. It is well that Saint-Simon, who ranged himself on the side of Bossuet and Cardinal de Noailles, should here bear testimony to the conduct of a man whom he has persistently disparaged.

"His open house and table appeared to belong to a governor of Flanders," wrote the duke, "and at the same time to a true episcopal palace; many distinguished military men and many officers on special service, ill, well, and wounded, stayed with him, served and kept as if there was one only. He was also generally present at the consultations of the doctors and surgeons, fulfilling besides the functions of the most devoted pastor to the sick and wounded. Often he went to perform the same office in the houses and hospitals where the soldiers were scattered, and always without carelessness or pettiness, and always making open-handed provision. He was, moreover, adored by all. It was true liberality, and a magnificence which was never offensive, but spent itself on officers and soldiers; which comprised a vast hospitality, and remained within the fitting limits of his position in all concerning table furniture and equipment. He was uniformly obliging and modest, hiding the help he gave when it could be hidden, which was the case in numberless instances. So gentle and charming was he in other cases that he seemed to be indebted to those to whom he gave and to need to persuade them. He was never hurried, he never flattered, but was courteous with a courtesy that included all, and yet was always proportioned with discretion, in such wise that it seemed to be concentrated on each individual, with that tact in which he especially excelled. Enthusiasm, and devotion to him was in the hearts of all the inhabitants of the Low Countries, whoever they were, and to whatever denomination they belonged."

The palace and the seminary of Cambrai became

FAMILIAR FRIENDS OF FÉNELON 245

military hospitals, and Fénelon spared nothing that could benefit body or soul of the sufferers he succoured. Such was the impression made by his extraordinary piety and self-devotion that Marlborough himself commanded that the victorious troops should regard all possessions of the Archbishop of Cambrai as sacred, and is said to have offered him a special guard for the protection of his person, a favour which neither his courage nor his patriotism allowed him to accept.

The strain and excitement thus thrust upon him by the development of national events, was in marked contrast to the future which he had foretold when the lifelong nature of his exile was first brought home to him. Then he would have any who proposed to share it be prepared "to lead a solitary, monotonous life of general inactivity." He must have "the health, the taste, and the patience for a life that is as exact and as regular as the ticking of a clock"[1]—a description which assuredly did not represent the conditions of the palace at Cambrai when Marlborough and Eugène were on the Flemish frontier. Greatly as he deplored it, that disastrous war was in fact of benefit to Fénelon: nothing, as he realised, could eradicate the King's prejudice against him, and the time for reconciliation was past, but Fénelon, who "desired to be loved," won the reverence and affection of thousands of his countrymen, and proved conclusively that, whatever calumny might say about him, he was no enemy to the King. But in spite of the opportunities of practical influence and kindness those terrible years afforded to the Archbishop of Cambrai, there was no Frenchman, of

[1] *Correspondance de Fénelon*, ii. 53 (1701).

whatever calling, who mourned the misfortunes of his country more bitterly than he. When, in 1709, Louis XIV., moved at length from his wilful arrogance by the sufferings of his people, humbled himself to sue for peace, there was not one of his subjects who awaited the issue with greater eagerness or deplored the result more deeply than did Fénelon. As the miserable months passed on, bringing with them private losses to add to the accumulated griefs that were tearing at his heart, he ceased to hope that the threatened ruin of his country would be averted. His pessimism was not an indication of shaken faith, he was resigned to the will of an all-powerful God when he was most cast down; but he believed that the iniquities of the people must have merited retribution, and only prayed that he might be allowed to die before he saw its consummation.

There are many who, while they look on men and nations as masters of their fate, will ascribe a sudden and momentous death to the intervention of the hand of God. Illogical as such a theory may appear there is much to commend it to the imagination; and men whose religion was of the vaguest kind attributed the unlooked-for rearrangement of European interests in the year 1711 to divine intervention. The histories of many countries tell the story: not France only, but Spain and England and Austria, were watching the issue of that struggle in the Netherlands with desperate anxiety, and one event changed every aspect of it. Joseph I. of Austria died, his brother, the claimant for the throne of Spain, succeeded, and in a moment it was evident that Europe held a man more to be dreaded, more to be opposed in his greed of power, than Louis XIV. Because the greatness of her greatest King was declining, and Charles VI. was recognised by general consent as more formidable, France was saved at the moment of her direst peril. There is a strange irony in the method of salvation, but to the rank and file of the suffering people it was no less welcome; and the King, hedged and protected by the tradition of past glories, could ignore the condition on which his good fortune was founded, accepting it as a tribute to his earlier record of unvarying success. In September 1711 his envoys signed the preliminary articles of the Peace of Utrecht in London; a peace which actually secured to him the prize for which he had been contending, and bound England, victorious as she was, not to attack the claims of Philip, younger of Fénelon's pupils, to his throne of Spain.

If, in his thankfulness, Fénelon was tempted to believe that prosperity might once more be dawning over France, he was not permitted to nourish the delusion long. Before the negotiations were actually complete, while moreover the Jansenist danger was darkening the outlook of the Church, he was required to face a disaster as unforeseen as it was overwhelming. In February 1712 the younger Dauphin died, and thenceforth his own fortunes and those of his country, tragic though they might be, ceased to have the same vital interest for Fénelon; he lost all zest for the duties and labours of his daily life, and the spirit of comradeship and brave endurance with which he had faced his exile gave place to that resignation which comes of irremediable sadness rather than philosophy. Thenceforth the rigorous lines of self-denial on which he had formed his daily habits became more evident, the need of food and sleep were repressed within the smallest limits that his feeble frame allowed, while he became more strenuous in calling upon all who were within his reach to turn from the evil that he saw on every side, and seek the strength which was his sole support in the sorrows and weaknesses of his latter years. There is a passage written by St. Anselm, quoted by Fénelon in an early work, which may be regarded as the postulate on which he based his final view of human life and of his own bitter experience: "Those who have renounced self . . . should God require them to suffer, will have no thought of God unworthy of His goodness. . . . For such as are offended with this saying—Lord, grant them grace so to renounce themselves that they may understand it!"

Into that thought and that supplication his so-called Quietism had resolved itself, and his chief desire for himself and others became once more the attainment of that complete reliance on the Love of God which was the basis of his doctrine when the Church silenced him.

CHAPTER II

FÉNELON THE POLITICIAN

FÉNELON was a priest, and, according to the modern meaning of the term, he was a mystic also, therefore it is natural that the great crisis in his fortunes should be attributed to his religious opinions. There is, in truth, sufficient reason for so doing. The Church had often discovered heresy in simpler and more innocent theories of belief than those propounded by the Archbishop of Cambrai, and the most distinctive feature of the age is its narrowness in all matters of religious meditation and research. Notwithstanding these self-evident facts, however, there is the possibility of another pretext for his banishment: it is possible that the master-spirit which required his condemnation from the Vatican was not that of Louis the Most Christian King and chief defender of the Church, but of Louis the despot, the self-willed autocrat of Court and kingdom, who would not brook either criticism or opposition from a subject. For Fénelon was not only a devoted priest and an ardent controversialist, but a convinced and eager politician also, and this is an aspect of him which must not be overlooked. His politics, traced to their root, sprang from religion; but they are necessary to show the man complete, loving his fellow-men with a depth and energy which made his love a purer thing than patriotism.

He would have strained every power to the utmost, and beggared himself of personal possessions to serve his country, but his love of mankind was too universal to be absolutely patriotic, and he was unvarying in condemnation of that greed of acquisition which convulsed whole nations with the sufferings of war, even though France might have reaped the glory and the gains of victory. Clearly this was not the point of view of a judicious courtier under Louis XIV., and Fénelon suffered for his independence. In course of time, no doubt, the King discovered that he was a disturbing element at Versailles. There was no direct disloyalty in his training of the Prince (a training which was generally recognised as extraordinarily successful in result); but unconsciously his attitude towards the established order of affairs must have affected his pupil, and, in those rare periods when his duties did not claim him, he was the soul of that little coterie with which the names of Mme. de Maintenon, of de Chevreuse, and of de Beauvilliers are inseparably connected. Family reasons inclined the two latter to the policy of peace; they had both married daughters of Colbert, and Colbert was the last of the succession of wise administrators and financiers who had paved the way for the glories and triumphs of the King, but who would have been utterly opposed to the daring and extravagance sanctioned by Louvois.

The King's thirst for military enterprise was insatiable, and it was the chief aim of that small conspiracy to thwart him in its gratification. Open opposition was useless in such a case, but the result of personal influence (wielded judiciously and therefore imperceptibly)

FÉNELON THE POLITICIAN

was sometimes incalculable, and for a while the chief centre of influence was dominated by Fénelon and his opinions. It was the ambition of Mme. de Maintenon, which she did not hide from her intimates, to convert the King to such a rule of private conduct as conformed to the faith that he professed. Fénelon's aspirations soared yet higher, and had far less possibility of realisation; it was his aim to reform the public life of the King, to exorcise the vainglorious spirit of ambition that had possession of him, so that the welfare of his subjects, moral and actual, should be of infinitely greater worth than his own personal aggrandisement. At some time during those years he spent at Court his eagerness to open the eyes of the King to the striking defects of his government of his kingdom induced him to employ means so reckless and audacious that without absolute proof his action appears incredible. No subject of Louis XIV. would have dared to address a candid letter to him and sign it with his name; any possible good effect of the venture would be destroyed by its initial insolence, and he who desired licence for plain speech must at least remain nameless. Fénelon accepted this necessity and wrote the truth that demanded utterance anonymously, in consequence of which the authenticity of the letter was discredited for many years, until the discovery of the original MS. placed its authorship beyond doubt. The evidence of its having ever reached the King is less conclusive, but there are references in the correspondence of Mme. de Maintenon in 1695, the probable date of its composition, which are not easily explicable otherwise.

The "Memoirs of the Marquis de Fénelon" show

that he at any rate had no vestige of doubt upon the subject, and Fénelon proved by the plainness of speech which he employed towards the Dauphin that he was capable of putting his daring project into practice. On the other hand, if he was daring he had also a faculty of discrimination, and the very boldness of the attack on such a potentate as Louis XIV. might have been expected to defeat its own ends. It is, therefore, hard to find the verdict on such conflicting testimonies, but the letter remains to add its quota for good or ill to the tale of its writer's reputation; and whether or no it accomplished any purpose at the time, it is interesting as representing a study of the Great King which differs from the familiar records of admirers or enemies.

Such detailed criticism of his character would not be pleasant reading for any man, and least of all to Louis XIV. Fénelon had learned penetration in the confessional, and could distinguish between natural defects and the result of circumstance; but to acknowledge that the original qualities were good, while alleging that their goodness had been obliterated, was to increase rather than soften the gravity of his charges. The writer was evidently deeply moved by the signs of the times which he believed that he detected. The Ministers, he declared, "speak no more of the State and its laws, but only of the King and his good pleasure."[1] The sorrows of the people who paid the price for their ruler's glory and enjoyment are constantly before him. "As if you could become great by ruining the people on whom you found your greatness" — that is the

[1] *Correspondance de Fénelon*, vol. ii., *Lettres Diverses*, 24.

burden of his appeal. "The people themselves—they who loved you so well and had such confidence in you —begin to lose their love, their confidence, even their respect. They take no more delight in your victories or your conquests; despair and bitterness have taken hold upon them. ... If, say they, the King have the heart of a father towards his people, it will be more his glory to give them bread, to let them draw breath after so much suffering, than to keep certain places on the frontier which are the reason for the war." This was not a remonstrance likely to be acceptable to a king who prided himself on nothing so much as on his victorious arms, and Fénelon dared to pass from generalities to a deliberate challenge of a war which had been a long series of successes to the French— the war in Holland that began in 1672. He was always strenuously and consistently opposed to war, and whatever may have been the imprudence of insisting on its evils when there could be no reasonable hope of convincing his hearer, there is nothing in the attempt which is out of keeping with his character. The author of *Télémaque* was capable of assuring the King that "God has placed you in the world solely for the good of your people," uncongenial as such a maxim was likely to prove to the royal mind; and in the preamble of his letter he had said that there was no misfortune he would not suffer cheerfully to impress upon the King the knowledge necessary to his welfare. It is the spirit of true patriotism, according to his conception of it, which inspired the earlier pages, and they convey the impression that they were honestly intended to reach their supposed destination. But it is otherwise with the conclusion. Passing from public affairs, Fénelon permits himself to reflect on individuals in a manner which is neither chivalrous nor honourable. He and de Harlai, Archbishop of Paris, were enemies, and de Harlai's private life was scandalous. It was true that he flattered the King and introduced every species of corruption into the administration of his diocese; it was true also that La Chaise was narrow-minded and ignorant, that he took small bribes, and would stoop to any trick that would advance his family; but Fénelon, having elected to be anonymous, had forfeited the right to personal attack, and it is impossible to reconcile his general attitude towards life with the theory that on this occasion he did deliver, or ever intended to deliver, a stab in the dark to men who were, in some degree, his rivals.

This is the strongest argument against the belief that the letter was more than a treatise on the relative conditions of the people and the King, taking a form which made it more graphic and inspiring to him in the writing. The course of events immediately ensuing seemed to denote that the opinions which it expressed had at length forced an entrance in defiance of the armoury of prejudices which protected despotism in France. The Peace of Ryswick, after long negotiations, was signed in 1697, and by its terms Louis resigned much which formerly his pride would have required him to insist upon, and he seemed to be suddenly imbued with that spirit of pacification which Fénelon in his self-appointed office of Mentor had so ardently desired for him. But if Fénelon were deluded, it was not long before he, in common with all who watched the struggle of the nations, was undeceived. The Great King's only regard for peace was as a necessary preparation for new wars, and his latest project loomed so large in his imagination that the trifling sacrifices that this treaty had demanded were unworthy of a regretful thought. He knew that Charles, the King of Spain, was dying, and he intended that his grandson should succeed him on the throne. The result of the scheme threatened at one time to ruin France, but it could never have been entertained if at the moment that the throne was vacant the Powers of Europe had been leagued together against the French, and therefore peace was necessary.

The War of the Spanish Succession did not actually touch on the private and individual life of Fénelon till near its close, though, as a Frenchman, it was throughout of infinite and terrible importance to him. His personal part in it has been already described, and his anxiety for the welfare of the Duke of Burgundy caused him to feel every reverse to the army a misfortune to himself. The vanity of the King, who could not allow his heir to fill a subordinate position, was fatal to the reputation of the Prince; palace intrigues pursued him to the field of battle; the experienced officers who should have been his support were determined that he, at least, should reap no glory from their efforts; his mistakes were exaggerated, his orders misrepresented, till at length he was recalled, to face the humiliation of being regarded as a failure in the field in days when every gentleman bore arms. Fénelon suffered with him. He had keen sympathy for his difficulties, but he made the moment an opportunity to open the Prince's eyes more fully to the faults that had occasioned his disgrace, chief among which, in Fénelon's opinion, was his inability to view life largely, to see that his environment needed tolerance, to understand what conduct was expected of him by the tradition of his rank, as well as what was due to principles of virtue and morality. The Prince seems, in fact, to have lacked that quality of imagination which would have enabled him to realise how other men regarded his scruples and exaggerations; and but for Fénelon, he might never have been brought to a knowledge of it. But in spite of the failings of his early manhood, either an honest effort to follow the exhortations of his friend or else a halo cast over his memory by his unexpected death, has caused his contemporaries to write of his last years as a time that held the promise of wise reform and quiet government for France.

It must have been a task of considerable difficulty to reconcile such veneration as the Prince cherished towards Fénelon with the respect and loyalty he owed his grandfather. The most remarkable of the Archbishop's political writings was directly addressed to the Duke, and, though it contains no open attack on King or government, the allusions are sufficiently explicit to leave no doubt that they tallied with the actual condition of the kingdom. The pamphlet in question purports to be an attempt to prepare him for his destiny (which then appeared so certain); it is "An Examination for the

Conscience of a King," in the form of thirty-eight questions, a few only of which are confined to purely religious matters, and the whole, detailed as it is, contains very little that would bear upon a private individual.

The Duke of Burgundy is said to have treasured it very highly, even while he realised that it would find no favour with his grandfather, and he had the prudence to place the actual document in the hands of M. de Beauvilliers, a fact which accounts for its preservation.[1] It is, in fact, as far as its teaching is concerned, a reproduction of the theories contained in *Télémaque*. Fénelon is no more sparing in his treatment of a royal character than was the immortal Mentor. "Nothing could be a greater calamity (for you) than to be made the master of others at an age when you are still so little master of yourself." Such is his method of deprecating the possibility that the Prince should soon succeed to his inheritance.

Louis XIV., tried by the standard which he imposes, would be found grievously wanting; yet unmistakably the life of Louis XIV. suggested the questions which he would have had that other younger Louis ask himself when his time of supremacy should come. " Have you set an evil example of criminal and unworthy love ? If you have done so, your authority is upholding infamy; you have taught all your subjects not to blush for that which is shameful, a disastrous lesson which is never forgotten. 'It were better,' said Jesus Christ, 'that a millstone were tied around thy neck and that thou wert

[1] It was published by the Marquis de Fénelon in 1734, in Paris, but suppressed. Afterwards issued in London, 1747.

thrown into the depths of the sea. . . .' I maintain that all the faults in the most private life of royalty are of infinite consequence." Bold maxims truly to commit to paper while the lover of Louise de la Vallière, of Françoise de Montespan, and many another beautiful woman of less celebrity, still held despotic power over all who dwelt in France. Doubtless, when hundreds of miles divided him for ever from the Court, Fénelon allowed his fancy to build up an ideal of what a Court should be. It was only negatively that he could use his memories of what had been, but he drew on those memories freely in his warning. The licence and frivolity of which he had been a witness (even under the sombre rule of Mme. de Maintenon) was to be prevented by the simple means of closing the palace doors against the young and beautiful. "Only women of ripe age and approved virtue should be chosen for place about the Court. Keep young women whose beauty is a snare to you and your courtiers excluded from such posts. It is more fitting that such remain in retirement in the midst of their families far from the Court. Although you are king, you should avoid all that is costly, and which others would wish to have in imitation. It is useless to urge that your subjects should not allow themselves a display which is seemly only for you. The princes near you wish to do almost what you do, the great nobles pride themselves on imitating the princes, the gentlemen desire to be like the nobles, and all the middle-class wish to follow in the footsteps of the financiers whom they have seen rise from the ranks. . . . Send your courtiers home to pass a few years on their estates, to look after their affairs; teach them to live frugally; show them that you only respect those who live a regular life and look after their business properly; show disdain of those who ruin themselves foolishly."[1]

Admirable as is this homily, it is obvious that a man of Fénelon's penetration could not have written it if he had still been dwelling at Versailles; human nature and the power of tradition is omitted from his calculation, and the Puritan Court which he was attempting to prepare for a future generation would not have been likely to attract the descendants of de Conti or de Rochefaucauld. Truly he was no courtier; but it is not so much for its candour (a quality to be found in all his letters to the Prince) as for the manner in which, under one head or another, he sketches the condition of the people, that the "Examination of Conscience" is of such importance. Then, indeed, human life and the human nature that finds expression in the struggle for existence rather than in the search for novelty, inspire his pen and give his words the vividness of passionate feeling. A few lines suggest the picture, the reality of which was sickeningly familiar to every Frenchman who did not deliberately turn away from contact with the great majority of his fellow-subjects. If war was the pleasure of the King, it was needful to find men to make an army, and because the soldier in the ranks suffered even more sharply and continuously than the peasant on a great nobleman's estate, it was found necessary to resort to coercion, and claim all who had not means or interest to buy immunity, in the King's name. It was a system that had become familiar

[1] *Œuvres de Fénelon*, vol. xxii., *Examen de Conscience*.

enough, but, nevertheless, Fénelon was constrained to make his protest. "To allow men to be taken without selection and against their will; to cause the distress and often the destruction of a whole family deserted by its head; to tear the labourer from his plough, and keep him to ten or fifteen years' service, during which he often perishes of misery in a hospital without the relief or tending he requires, and if he deserts, to break his head or cut off his nose—nothing can excuse such a system before either God or man." If the peasant had brought himself under the arm of the law, he was no less an object for compassion. A capital sentence seems merciful compared to the horrors to which a convict was condemned; he became, in fact, the slave of the State, and because labour was scarce, it was desirable to obtain as many convicts for as long a time as possible. The abuse of such an arrangement was inevitable, the suffering that ensued upon it indescribable; and the king of Fénelon's ideal must not rest easy till it had in some measure been reformed. One point in his examination lifts the veil a moment that hid one of the plague-spots in the condition of the people: "Are you particular to have every galley-slave relieved at the end of the time of punishment appointed by the law? Do not say that if this justice is observed there will be a lack of men for convict-labour."[1]

Nothing could be more significant of the spirit of the time than the final suggestion deprecating an argument which was probably accepted as complete justification for disregard of the law. By such glimpses it is possible to estimate the task awaiting

[1] *Examen de Conscience.*

the king of Fénelon's imagination, the king who was to have trained himself by private self-discipline, who was to have acquired knowledge of the laws, the habits, the customs of his kingdom; of the numbers, the employment and comparative conditions of *all* his subjects; who was to be the supreme judge and watchful overseer of the administration; who was to be, in short, the friend and yet the father and leader of his subjects, having made it his business to "see, hear, and speak to many people, learning by experience to study mankind, and knowing them by free and constant intercourse."[1] No wonder that the Dauphin, sharing the ideal and living more closely in touch with the reality than did his master, was made depressed and melancholy by their overpowering contrast and by the immensity of the enterprise required of him; for, in fact, the weight of responsibility which Fénelon would have had him take upon his shoulders was calculated to crush the most ardent of optimists, and optimism was a quality entirely denied to him. But on one point obedience would have been easier, and it may be that that was the most important point of all. Louis XIV. himself might have found glory in caring for his people if the insatiable greed of conquest had not filled every chamber of his mind. A warning against the love of war is the refrain that runs through *Télémaque*, and *Télémaque* was written amid the influences of Versailles, at the very elbow of the King; afterwards, when the glories which were the result of war were no longer present with the writer, that refrain was never silenced if he wrote of politics.

[1] *Examen de Conscience.*

In the case of his "Examination," the two contrasting aspects of his life are evident. Much of it could only be the work of a man familiar with the innermost secrets of the Court, with all the hidden jobbery and corruption which was sweeping away the prosperity of the realm: and Fénelon, who knew the Court so well, knew the lives of the peasants also—the crying need of the labourer fighting with the barren soil to win subsistence, of the convict doomed to perpetual suffering, often against all law of justice and humanity, and of the soldier, whose case appealed the most to his sympathy.

In youth as well as in his later life he made himself the servant of such as these, and his figure was as familiar as it was welcome in cottages and hospitals and prisons; no sin was so black, no disease so repellent as to place the sufferer beyond the reach of the comfort and inspiration that Fénelon could give if his presence was desired. Thus, from the point of view of the people, he was competent to speak with authority; he knew that war could bring them no advantage that would compensate for its inevitable evils; but, when his exile had removed him from all the influences of the Court, it must be admitted that he approached the question too much in the spirit of the partisan. To spare the lives of the French subjects, he would have employed foreign mercenaries to fight their battles for them, forgetful that the scarcity of money made the support of alien troops almost impossible, and that the pillage and violence for which these free-lance companies were always noteworthy increased the horrors of war a hundred-fold.

Careful student though he was of history, and close observer of the events of which he had any cognisance, his priestly training and environment made him incapable of forming a general estimate with justice on military subjects. In an individual case, such as that of the Duke of Burgundy, however, it was otherwise. He foresaw the risk to the Prince's reputation when, in 1702, the command was placed in his inexperienced hands; but his perpetual warnings had weakened any power he might ever have possessed, and he was forced to watch the melancholy fulfilment of his prophecies in silence. His impotence to help her gave additional bitterness to his sorrow for the misfortunes of his country. Among his papers is a plan of government of extraordinary elaboration, which deals with reforms political, military, and domestic, as sweeping and more practical than in the "Examination." It displays an astounding knowledge of the past affairs and present condition of Church and State, and would have proved invaluable to a king whose standard corresponded with the writer's; but the date of its compilation is significant of the tragedy of his life. It is headed November 1711, when the Duke was already Dauphin, and only one precarious life kept him from the throne.[1] The next political pamphlet that Fénelon drew up was written in the March following, and referred to the measures to provide for a regency which the Prince's death necessitated.

There have been notable instances in history of priests who wielded greater power than the kings themselves, but never one to whom religion was the rule of life. Had the

[1] *Œuvres de Fénelon*, xxii., *Tables de Chaulnes*.

Dauphin lived, the history of France must have contained that phenomenon, and the result in national development would have been a curious study. The Prince had not the grace and majesty of his grandfather, or the reckless gaiety of Henri IV. His very virtues were repellent to his associates, and he clung to the minute observance of religious ceremonial as the King did to the smallest detail of etiquette. But perhaps, with Fénelon beside him, with his view of life and duty widened by his prerogative, and his scruples modified by experience, he, who had early learnt to realise and deplore the sufferings of the people, might have won their love, and gradually put his theories into practice and brought justice within the reach of the poorest of his subjects. Such had been Fénelon's ideal. "In the name of God, Monseigneur," he had written when the Prince was just entering upon manhood, "do not let yourself be cast down by the evils that you see around you; the world is full of them. As for me, I thank God from the bottom of my heart in that He has granted sufficient courage to so great a prince as you are, to learn experience as a simple individual, to be a man among other men. In sooth, Monseigneur, the more you tell me that you see of evil the more you give me pleasure, not that the evil should exist, but that it should be made known to one who, by the grace of God, may have power to remedy it."

Fénelon was hopeful when he wrote those words; but then the story of the Prince's life had not yet unrolled itself before him. It proved a melancholy story; but in relation not only to Fénelon, but to the King himself, it is of great importance.

The stormy childhood of the Duc de Bourgogne has been described already. It was merged in a youth of spasmodic but pronounced austerity, although the gloom of his natural temperament was brightened by the charms of the girl-wife to whom he was united, first for political expediency, and afterwards by every tie of sincere affection. He had learnt to regard Fénelon as his spiritual leader, giving him a responsibility differing from that which he gave to his confessor, but in reality leaning on him more than on any other adviser. The distance that divided them did not alter their relations; but their correspondence (maintained fitfully, and only with great precaution) is at first devoted to purely religious subjects, from which Fénelon only departs to urge his pupil to cultivate the appearance of sociability and good-humour, which were so essential to his position, and in which rumour reported him to be so grievously lacking, even when he was engrossed by the amusements of the Court. He had the spirit of a gallant race, however, for all his melancholy; and if he drank in Fénelon's theories regarding the advantages of peace, he was none the less eager to take his share of danger and excitement on the battlefield. He was nineteen when his wish was granted, and he was sent to lead the army in Flanders; and in addition to his pleasure at the glorious opening before him, was the delight with which he anticipated a visit to Cambrai, which was found to lie upon his line of route. He wrote from Peronne (April 25, 1702) an eager, boyish letter announcing his arrival at Cambrai, and that the King had given him permission to meet the archbishop, although it must be in the presence of a witness. The interview took place, in fact, in the presence of many witnesses while the young soldier dined, and Fénelon and his little prince had not a moment for intimate and confidential intercourse. "To-day, after five years of separation," Fénelon wrote sadly on the same afternoon, "I have seen my lord Duke of Burgundy, but God has seasoned this blessing with very great bitterness."[1]

But rumour spoke well of him, and Fénelon rejoiced. The King's grandson was an inexperienced boy, and necessarily incompetent to command an army, but in his first assay he had the Marshal de Boufflers at his elbow, an experienced veteran who was content to guide while the Prince seemed to hold the reins, and for the time he was gracious and had caught the trick of popularity. It was an unfruitful campaign for the interests of the nation, but of benefit to the new commander; and when he returned to Versailles Fénelon wrote a vigorous appeal to M. de Chevreuse to help him to make a fresh start at the Court, and not lose by two days' gloom and awkwardness all that he had won in his weeks of absence.

The Prince's second campaign was of equal service to his reputation, but there, for a time, his military service, begun so auspiciously, came to an end, and five years at Court ensued which proved to be full of difficulty. The Prince's natural temperament was not pliable; he was austere in manner, and appeared to be constantly in judgment on the frivolities of the Court. This in itself was enough to arouse the antagonism of his contemporaries, but the unpopularity which was gradually attached to him had a yet more serious cause. He was the most

[1] *Correspondance de Fénelon*, vi. 307.

prominent figure before the eyes of the nation after the King, but when the King died it was not he, but Monseigneur the Dauphin, who would wear the crown. The pupil of Bossuet had developed very differently from the pupil of Fénelon; he would have made as weak and unprincipled a king as ever sat on any throne, and even as heir-apparent he was a puppet in the hands of a few favourites as dissolute but far more competent than himself. These noted the importance of the Duke, who was favoured by his grandfather, and made it their business to injure him in public opinion as far as might be. Prominent in the cabal was Vendôme, a man of extraordinary power, one of those freaks of nature who possess genius of the highest order and are yet dominated by abominable vices; he was in every way repugnant to the Duke, and it may be believed that the aversion was mutual. The heir-presumptive had no more dangerous enemy than the foremost general in his grandfather's army, who feared the Puritan influences which might be introduced at Versailles at the death of the King if the Dauphin were not strenuously supported; and, being himself a man without religion, mocked at the power held by the Archbishop of Cambrai even while he dreaded it.

All the Court knew of Vendôme's opposition to the Duke and of the reasons for it; Fénelon knew it at Cambrai; doubtless the tonsured gossips whispered and laughed over it in Rome; but the King was completely unconscious. Never had there been a more curious instance of his impenetrability nor one more ruinous in its results. It was no wonder that Fénelon, seeking to fashion the model of a king, would have him know his subjects by free and constant intercourse. It was inevitable that the shortcomings of the King he knew should suggest his exhortations to the King he hoped some day to see, and, had Louis XIV. attempted to attain to that intimate knowledge of mankind instead of vigorously shutting his ears to every whisper that could enlighten him, he might have avoided a humiliating and disastrous blunder. At the beginning of 1708 he was resolved upon a new movement in Flanders to recover the prestige lost by his unsuccessful support of the Pretender, and, that it might be begun under the most favourable auspices, he gave the command to the Duke of Burgundy. There is something sublime in his unflinching confidence in the prerogative of royalty. The Prince was twenty-six, and had borne a part in two campaigns; but though he displayed the courage and spirit which befitted him, there was no reason to believe that he possessed conspicuous military genius, and the task with which he was entrusted was one of extreme difficulty. The allied armies commanded by Marlborough and Eugène were centred in Flanders, and it was the King's command that his troops should no longer be content with maintaining the defence of the frontier, but should become the aggressors and endeavour to regain his possessions in Brabant. He was not, it is true, guilty of the folly of sending the Prince to conduct these precarious operations unaided, but with inexplicable perversity he selected Vendôme for his coadjutor. The scheme was kept secret till all arrangements were concluded, but when it was announced it carried

FÉNELON THE POLITICIAN 269

dismay to the heart of every friend of the young commander.

The two thus strangely associated were opposed to each other by every natural instinct and every influence of development. Vendôme possessed a commanding presence, combined with an easy bearing which caught the fancy of the troops; he was daring, unprincipled, confident. The Prince had none of those graces of manner and appearance that smooth the way to popularity; he was scrupulous, over-anxious, and consequently dilatory. Vendôme despised him, and he loathed the personal character of his adviser. The result of the campaign was easy to foresee, and every circumstance seemed to proclaim that disaster was inevitable. "Fire and water are not more different, nor more incompatible than Monseigneur de Bourgogne and M. de Vendôme," wrote Saint-Simon. "After so many losses and misfortunes, in a dearth of everything, with troops accustomed to doubt the capacity of their generals, and who, by reason of misconduct, have got into the habit of never confronting the enemy and of forestalling defeat, this sad and unpromising moment does not seem to me suitable for placing Monseigneur de Bourgogne at the head of an army which thinks it very creditable if it does not run away or be overtaken by any disgraceful disaster."[1]

Assuredly there were no good omens attendant on the enterprise. The only consolation that Fénelon or his friends could evolve from it was the influence which the Prince might be able to exercise in the army, which, under Vendôme, was abandoned to the most deplorable

[1] *Saint-Simon,* xi. p. 106.

licence. It is significant of the prejudices which dominated Louis XIV. that, *dévot* though he professed to be, he feared the association of such a man as Vendôme with his grandson less than he feared the Archbishop of Cambrai; once again the Prince passed by the doors of his friend and tutor, and once again he was forbidden to have that moment of confidential intercourse with him which both coveted so ardently. Nevertheless, the Prince made the most of their public interview. "As he sat at dinner in the inn he said aloud that he would never forget how very much he owed him. Without ever whispering to him, he hardly spoke to any one else, and the eagerness of his glances riveted on the eyes of the archbishop—glances appealing for all that the King forbade him—were so eloquent, combined with his first words to the archbishop, that all who saw were carried away, so that the court of the archbishop, despite his disgrace, was swelled by the presence of the most exalted persons from that time forward, who hurried—on various excuses of travel or proximity—to win his present good graces and future protection." [1]

It was a critical moment in the life of the young Prince, and he and Fénelon were fully alive to its importance. Then, if ever, he needed the direction and encouragement of a wise counsellor, and Fénelon was yearning to deliver himself of such advice and warning as might avert impending dangers. But the King's will was law, and the King's infatuation would not permit his grandson to derive help from such a source. It was necessary for both the Duke and the archbishop to be

[1] *Saint-Simon*, xi. 179.

obedient to the letter of the royal order, but both seem to have felt that the royal perversity absolved them from adherence to the spirit of it. Fénelon, having been denied adequate opportunity of speech, lost no time in writing to his "little Prince," but his letter has not been preserved, and we can only judge of its purport from the reply:—

"VALENCIENNES, *May* 21, 1708.

". . . I am enchanted with the counsels that you give me in the second part of your letter, and I implore you to renew them whenever you are so inclined. It seems to me, thank God, that I have some part of those sentiments to which you exhort me, and that, in showing me my deficiencies, God will give me the strength to overcome and to use those means of grace that you recommend to me. It seems to me that, considering you never see me, you have no slight knowledge of me. Regarding Jansenism, I hope, by the grace of God—not as they understand it, but as it is understood by the Catholic Church—that I shall never fall into the snares that they would set for me. I know the heart of their doctrine, and I know that it is more Calvinist than Catholic. I know that they write with cleverness and reason. I know that they profess the severest morality, that they attack all relapses fiercely; but I know at the same time that they do not always practise it. You know the examples which are only too frequent. I shall give special attention to all that concerns churches and the houses of the clergy; this is essential, and I shall maintain absolute strictness thereon. I implore you to continue your prayers; I have more need of them than ever. Unite them with mine, or rather I will join mine to yours, for I know that herein a bishop is above a prince. You do wisely not to come here, and you may see that it is so because I did not sleep at Cambrai. You may be sure I should have done so but for the decisive reasons that prevented me. Otherwise I should have been overjoyed to see you during my stay here and to consult you on many matters wherein you would have been more competent to advise me than any one. You know the friendship for you I have always had, and that I have upheld you through all unjust accusations. Be assured that nothing could lessen it, and that it will last my life." [1]

This letter has been given fully because it is especially characteristic of the Prince and of his relations with Fénelon. He was on the eve of a campaign which might make or mar his own career and was of extreme importance to the position of France. He held a position calculated to turn the head of so young a man, and his brain might well have been filled with dazzling visions of military glories, to the exclusion of all other reflections or anxieties. As we read the letter it is not hard to understand why the Prince was not popular with his contemporaries. The young men of the day were bred to arms, and the traditions of the army pointed to gaiety, to gallantry, to an irresponsible pursuit of pleasure, which, by its very recklessness, appeals to the imagination; there was no possibility of sympathy and fellowship between them and one who could sit, surrounded by the glitter and pageantry of battle, and write to an archbishop of the

[1] *Correspondance de Fénelon*, i. 76.

condition of his soul and the shortcomings of the Jansenists!

The story of that disastrous episode is briefly this. The Prince from the first was conspicuous for personal bravery, had he held a subordinate position he might have distinguished himself honourably, but Vendôme consistently opposed his commands and undermined his attempts at strategy, being apparently more desirous that the future Dauphin should be dishonoured in the eyes of the nation than that the French forces should be victorious over their foes. He did not even disguise his antagonism, but had the effrontery on one occasion to tell the Prince in public "that he was only there on condition of obedience,"[1] notwithstanding which assertion he did not hesitate to assign all possible blame to him. Defeat followed defeat. Vendôme and the Prince were at cross purposes continually, and hampered the movements of the army at every turn by their disputes. After the overwhelming disaster of Oudenarde the condition of the latter became desperate; the Marshal, not content with counteracting all his efforts in the field, had effectually obtained his disgrace with the King, and forsaking that prudence which distinguished his personal conduct early in the campaign, the Prince gave way to a frivolity and childishness in the pursuit of relaxation which, combined with a scrupulous adherence to the most puerile conventions of his religion, destroyed the remaining fragments of his reputation and of his popularity.

Fénelon was sufficiently in touch with the sentiments of the Court and near enough to the actual seat of war to

[1] *Saint-Simon*, x. p. 212.

be kept fully informed of the ebb of popular opinion, and he watched with a breaking heart. It had been far easier to accept failure as a necessary discipline for himself than to see it inflicted on one whom he loved as he loved his little Prince; nevertheless his affection and his interest did not blind him, and never did he prove the sincerity of his friendship more strongly than at this decisive moment.

There are many letters from him which all testify to his singleness of heart and purpose, letters containing exhortations to energy, to tolerance, to self-forgetfulness, to self-control—to all the virtues, in fact, in which the young commander was most lacking and of which he stood most in need. But there is one in especial which, with its reply, portrays the Duke and Fénelon more vividly than any second-hand description.

Fénelon wrote from Cambrai on September 24th, at a moment when the outcry against the Prince from all sorts and conditions of Frenchmen was loud enough to satisfy Vendôme himself, and would have involved indirect insult to the King, but that his own wrath was so great that he would not suffer his grandson to be referred to in his presence. And Fénelon, though he would have borne the burden if he could, though he felt the disgrace and humiliation showered on the young soldier as bitterly as if it had fallen on himself, yet had the strength to press the lesson home, that the ideal king of his dreams might still arise triumphant from the ruin of the Prince's self-confidence and pride. He tells him unflinchingly what the world is saying of him; a few days earlier he had written with diffidence, hinting that the voice of the mob may be untrustworthy, and the chance to retrieve himself with competent people, " to do to the end all that an old and experienced leader would do to put things to rights,"[1] still remained to him; but the general outcry silenced such suggestions of consolation and Fénelon dared to echo its denunciations. Under seven heads he sets forth the main points in which the Prince has failed, enlarging on them from his own old experience of the child at Versailles.

"CAMBRAI, *September* 24, 1708.

" Far from wishing to flatter you, Monseigneur, I am collecting here all the worst things that are spread about the world against you.

" I. It is said that you are too fastidious, too reserved, too limited to a few men who influence you. It must be owned that in your childhood I have always found you apt to be fastidious, and not to welcome new faces. Although I am sure that since then common sense and right-mindedness have taught you to suit yourself to the public, who have a sort of right of easy intrusion on their princes, it may chance that there still remains to you some vestige of the old habit. But further I cannot be astonished that you have shut yourself up more than usual at such a time of excitement and difficulty, where sides are difficult to choose, and you find every one at cross purposes. You are more capable of pleasing the public than any other prince by your conversation. You can be gay, sociable—very charming, if one may dare to say so; your mind is so endowed and so cultivated that you can talk to all and suit yourself to each. That is a

[1] *Correspondance de Fénelon,* i. 82.

constant attraction which depends on yourself only, and only costs you a little self-suppression and good-nature. God will give you the strength to submit yourself if you desire it. . . . It is the advantage of great princes that those who risk ruin or death for them are recompensed by an apt and gracious word. The whole army will sing your praises if they find you friendly, genial, and kind-hearted.

"II. It is said, Monseigneur, that you pay too much heed to people of small experience, of limited capacities, and feeble and timid character: they go so far as to accuse them of cowardice. I have no idea to whom these charges point; I imagine them to be very unjust. They add that, your own abilities being very superior to theirs, you defer too much to their advice, which leads you to courses very little to your honour. It is probable that these reports arise from spite and jealousy. It may be, also, that M. de Vendôme's adherents have spread them, but at any rate, they have become very general. You know best how much truth there is mingled with the slander. A prince so enlightened as you are is very well able to judge the strength and weakness of those about you. I know that it may sometimes be better to listen to men who have good sense and true hearts but are not brilliant, rather than to others who dazzle you; but a display of confidence should be accommodated in some degree to public reputation. In all this, I am only feeling my way, for in truth I neither know, nor guess, on whom these charges fall.

"III. It is said, Monseigneur, that, as you evidently distrusted the reckless counsels of M. de Vendôme, you have allowed yourself to fall in with them too easily. They add, also, that this complaisance has, in some degree, alienated the chief commanders, who had hoped you would assert your authority, and that you would call those who needed it to order. I suppose those who speak thus do not realise that you have only yielded to the counsels of M. de Vendôme in deference to the wishes of the King.

"IV. Many people hold that you might have attacked the enemy in their entrenchments (which were of no account) since the 5th of this month; that the vacillation and discord of the commanders, which reduced them to the necessity of awaiting the orders of the King, gave the enemies ten days to secure their position. They say that formerly you listened too much to M. de Vendôme, and on this occasion only, when he seems to have been in the right and to have suggested a course likely to win you honour, you would not believe in him. For my part, Monseigneur, I think you have shown great wisdom not to have risked anything on so hazardous a suggestion against the judgment of M. le Maréchal de Berwick and the most experienced officers in the army. . . . What I hope is that a certain number of wise people who understand the circumstances thoroughly will make the justification of your action thoroughly known. It is not fitting that a great prince such as you are should condescend to such explanations; but I hope that there will be persons eager to make them at the fitting moments. It is said on every side that Mme. la Duchesse de Bourgogne does marvels in this direction, and that her behaviour has been admired.

You see, Monseigneur, no rank can place men above criticism.

"V. It is said, that although you are grave and reserved you waste time which should be given to serious matters in frivolity, which is out of place and displeasing to the military men. If you need relaxation to rest your mind, try to suit it to the great position that you fill, as well as to the inclinations of your age.

"VI. It is said, Monseigneur, that your deliberations are not sufficiently secret, that you take little pains to make them so, and that even the enemy can easily discover your intentions, because they are made known in your army. I see that the disputes among the general officers, in whom you cannot avoid confiding, may be largely responsible for the exposure of your resolutions. People who are quarrelling become excited, argue, and talk one against the other at the expense of all secrecy. M. de Vendôme has his confidants, who are allowed to know everything and to talk about everything from their point of view in his defence. It is the case, also, Monseigneur, that your eagerness, in conjunction with your voice which is by nature somewhat piercing, causes you to be heard from a considerable distance when you are excited in argument, and in this, when important affairs are concerned, you cannot be too careful, for secrecy is the very foundation of everything.

"VII. It is said, Monseigneur, that there is not sufficient care taken in your army to discover what the enemy are doing. They add that no one takes pains to foresee and provide for difficulties, to gain a knowledge of the neighbouring districts and all the surrounding country. Long ago, I heard men of experience in such matters say that M. de Vendôme never attended to these details, that he provided for nothing and chanced everything, that he thought everything possible and easy, and was often taken unawares; that he would not listen to or believe in any one, and that he was just the same in Italy as in France, very brave, very daring, and incorrigibly vague."[1]

The letter is extended to far greater length, but the conclusion is the counsel of the spiritual adviser, rather than the man of the world: "I thank God, Monseigneur, that He makes you feel at such cost to yourself and by such sharp lessons that you must distrust yourself, and despair of yourself. 'I can do all in Him who strengthens me,' says St. Paul."

That is the sum, not only of this but of many another of Fénelon's exhortations, but that is merely the moral most consistent with his office and relations towards the Prince. It is as a testimony to his friendship that the foregoing is remarkable. He had realised the situation with a practical clearness of vision which proclaims that his mysticism was not incompatible with statesmanship; not only his heart and imagination, but his keen intellectual faculties had been centred on the young commander throughout the ill-fated enterprise, and he had the courage to lay the hateful truth before him plainly and without prejudice. It might have meant the severance of their friendship; the Prince was resentful and humiliated, disgusted with the malevolence which

[1] *Correspondance de Fénelon*, i. 88.

had entrapped him, and conscious, probably, that his own failings were to some degree responsible. It is in such moments that men are least masters of themselves, and the Archbishop of Cambrai had no legitimate claim to resort to such unsparing candour. Nevertheless, in his reply, the Prince showed himself worthy of the love he had inspired; he defends himself, it is true, for calumny had been at work against him, but his defence is interspersed with acknowledgment of many failures and mistakes. "You will find me not nearly so good and virtuous a man as you believe; you will see only failures and relapses, slackness, neglect, and laziness in my most important duties; changeableness, fastidiousness, pride, haughtiness, contempt of mankind; I am given up to individuals, to the world, to life, without having the true love for the Almighty above all things, and of my neighbour as myself."[1]

The letter betrays the bitter disappointment that was overwhelming its writer; and, in truth, the Duke had received a blow from which his spirits, never very elastic, did not recover; but it was an encouragement to Fénelon to persist in his efforts to help and advise him, and the counsel contained in successive letters from Cambrai is the outcome of the reflections of a thoughtful and religious man, one who knew the Court, and possessed a certain insight into the mind even of the King himself, and, moreover, combined some of the wisdom of a man of the world with the instincts of a priest.

The Prince, a prey to the self-absorption which had survived the other failings of his childhood, did not

[1] *Correspondance de Fénelon*, i. 91.

understand the gravity of his own position; he might admit as a general maxim that "no man is above criticism," but he could not seriously believe that a subject would have the audacity to attempt to injure him with his grandfather. Fénelon, on the other hand, realised that the subtle combination of truth and slander brought to bear against the Prince, was murmured in the most sacred precincts of the palace; that the King had listened and believed and allowed his anger to be nourished by apt and discreet insinuations, and that, in such a case, the King's anger might be terrible. "That which is certain, Monseigneur," he wrote, "is that you have urgent need of caution with the King, and of silencing the unreasonable exasperation of the public. You cannot show too much care, respect, attachment, and submission in anything you write or do, but it is necessary that you should set forth very strong reasons very strongly, omitting nothing that leaves an opening for suspicion on your conduct."[1]

Possibly there was a dearth of very strong reasons for the Prince's actions. He had been required to fill an office that presented enormous difficulties to Generals of double his age and of specialised capacity and experience, and he had lost his balance. A few loyal supporters might have saved him from disgrace, but these had been withheld, and he became the scapegoat of the national discontent and the King's resentment. And in this hour of peril, after ten years during which he had been little more than a memory, Fénelon became once more the guide and director of his actions. Their intercourse

[1] *Correspondance de Fénelon,* i. 94.

required the most scrupulous secrecy, for the Vendôme faction hated the Archbishop even more than the Duke himself. But Fénelon's adherents were faithful, and for the time their correspondence was maintained unbroken.

At length the only course left open to the Prince was to return to Court and justify himself before the King, and Fénelon, who suspected the weakness of his cause, and knew the failings of his character, watched the event in an agony of suspense. "Dare I suggest to you the manner in which you should address the King," he wrote, "in his interest, in that of the State, and in your own? You might begin by humbly and openly confessing certain things which are perhaps a little against you. . . . Ask with the utmost eagerness that in the next campaign you may have your revenge and retrieve your damaged reputation. You cannot show too much eagerness on this point, and this great enthusiasm will partly acquit you of the indolence of which you are accused. Ask to have a General under you who will help and teach you without wishing to govern you like a child. . . . No one ever required so much vigour and eagerness as you stand in need of at this crisis. A bearing which is strong, lively, dignified, and urgent, and yet respectful and submissive, will do you infinite good in the opinion of the King and of all Europe. If, on the other hand, you are timid and hesitating, the whole world, which awaits this decisive moment, will give up all hopes of you, and decide that, after having been feeble with the army, to the damage of your reputation, you do not even dream of retrieving yourself at Court. They will picture you shutting yourself up in your own rooms in the company of a selection of flattering women. The people still love you enough to desire to see the chance that would redeem you; but if you miss the chance you fall very heavily. The thing is in your hands. Your pardon, Monseigneur; I write madly, but my madness proceeds from too great zeal. In my most pressing needs I can only pray, and this I do unceasingly."[1]

In days when the friends of princes were required to be courtiers, such words as these were specially effectual. Fénelon's mysticism and philosophy were forced to yield before the eagerness of living hopes and anxieties; and human love, too strong to give him time to calculate effects and phrases, inspires his rapid pen. "Your pardon, Monseigneur, I write madly!" that is the hurried after-thought, when a remembrance of his little Prince's great inheritance occurred to him.

The reception which the Duke of Burgundy met with on his return might well have made him reckless. The Vendôme cabal were waiting with malignant satisfaction for the false step that should send him headlong to irremediable ruin. But though they had not scrupled to assure the King that the Prince's mind was still full of the teaching that the author of *Télémaque* had given him, and were secure of rekindling the royal anger if they breathed the name of Fénelon, they did not realise that the Prince could still appeal to the wise judgment of the exiled priest who, in his solitude, had seen how the dastardly conspiracy, more potent at Versailles than it had been in Flanders, might be confounded, and who inspired the resolute and manly candour with which the

[1] *Correspondance de Fénelon*, i. 95.

Duke of Burgundy redeemed his honour and surprised the world when he was once more brought face to face with his grandfather.

It is plain that Fénelon perceived the defect of the training he himself had given his pupil. The maxims of Saint-Sulpice had required greater modification to fit the heir of France, and they had taken deeper root than could have been predicted. Fénelon's letters to the Prince after his return to Court are in curious contrast to those intended for the young soldiers and courtiers with whom he corresponded, and prove that the Prince needed to cultivate the balance of mind which makes piety practical, rather than piety itself.

"The Little Prince reasons too much and does too little. His deepest studies end in futile resolves and vague speculations. He should see other men, study them, understand them, without revealing himself, learn to talk firmly, and have a quiet authority. Idle amusement dissipates thought, impairs the mind, degrades the whole man, and is contrary to the designs of God."[1] Such was Fénelon's unsparing criticism of one on whom he had centred the deepest sympathy and interest of his life, and it distinguishes the chief blemish of the Prince's character. His private conduct was morally irreproachable, but the puerile frivolity which had made his father, the Dauphin, contemptible, was sometimes to be traced in him, while the net result of his reading and meditation seemed to amount to very little, and tempted the world to ridicule his rigorous and somewhat theatrical habits of self-discipline. From the worldly and practical

---

[1] *Correspondance de Fénelon*, vol. i. 141, to de Chevreuse, January 1711.

point of view his life was a failure; he spent it in laborious preparation, and those who loved him predicted a great future for him, but in actual performance he accomplished very little. His lack of geniality cancelled the good effect his example might have had, his influence with the King was not strong enough to take effect in anything important, and even his intervention in the disputes among the bishops was of too temporising and tentative a nature to be decisive. Death silenced the sanguine expectations of his supporters; he lived to be Dauphin only, but even while he lived the Chevalier de Ramsai describes how popular Cambrai became as a stopping-place for gentlemen of high degree, who had suddenly perceived what pleasure and instruction might be derived from the conversation of the exiled Archbishop, who was also the friend of the future King.

Fénelon accepted such attentions with simplicity; when he held interest he had never favoured those who flattered him, and if it should be given him once more, he saw no reason to reconsider his use of it. But the King was past seventy, and the time had come when it was legitimate to hope that the exile's years of patient endurance were near their end, and better days dawning for himself and for the nation. The hope proved illusive —the new Dauphin had hardly grown accustomed to his title when the mortal illness of his young wife overwhelmed him with grief, and a few days after her death he fell ill himself. He had been summoned to Marly (it is characteristic of the discipline at Court that neither sorrow nor sickness absolved him from obedience), and he went, though he seems to have believed that the journey was destined to be his last. A similar premonition took possession of Fénelon, and with the threatened disappointment of his dearest hopes, that optimism—which was almost a part of his religion, and which he had always relied on for support when the clouds hung thickest—failed him; his love of his country was not shaken, but in mourning over her misfortunes he learned to attribute them to the shortcomings of individuals, to the cancer of greed and vice and petty tyranny that had spread through every department of the State, and to anticipate a judgment on her such as had descended on the offending nations of Holy Writ.

"For a long time I have had terrible fears for him," he wrote on the first news of the illness of the Dauphin; "if God be no longer enraged against France, he will recover, but if the wrath of God be not appeased, there is much to fear. I can ask nothing. I tremble, and I cannot pray. Send me word how he is; you know my anxiety. May the Lord have pity on us!"[1]

This is the expression of a state of mind into which Fénelon had never been betrayed by the heaviest personal misfortune. It was the darkest moment of his life, for the God who was ever in his thoughts, the loving Father to whom it was his chief desire to direct his fellow-creatures, had become a menacing and awful Deity, before whom he fell, trembling and silent. To him such a condition meant despair, and his faith delivered him from it. "I begin to hope that Monseigneur le Dauphin will not die," he wrote the day following. "I have found it easy to pray for him, which was

[1] *Correspondance de Fénelon*, iii. 270.

not the case at the beginning. Yet there is a fear in the bottom of my heart that God's anger against France is not appeased." [1]

This was written on Monday, February 16th. At midnight the following Thursday the Dauphin died, and even those who had been most ready to criticise regarded his death as a national calamity. "God thinks differently from men," was Fénelon's comment. "He destroys that which He seems to have made expressly for His glory." [2] Truly it was hard to find any consolation, save in the resignation that his religion taught, for there was nothing to mitigate the darkness that enveloped the prospects of the nation. The Dauphin's eldest son only survived his father a few days, the younger (Louis XV.), was an infant of a few months old, and, as the King had passed his seventieth year, it was inevitable that France should soon be plunged into the chaos of a long minority.

Fénelon was not destined to witness the disasters that awaited her, but he foresaw and dreaded them; his friends attempted to seize the opportunity and work upon the King in his hour of grief to summon the exile back to Court, but Fénelon himself accepted the failure of their efforts with indifference. On one point only was he still vulnerable: he knew that a long series of letters which he had written to his little Prince would now fall into other hands, and it was intolerable that they should be read by the light of over-mastering prejudice. To deliver them he was moved to do that which he had disdained to do for fifteen years—appeal to the influence

[1] *Correspondance de Fénelon*, iii. 270.   [2] *Ibid.* iii. 275.

of Mme. de Maintenon. Even in this he failed. Mme. de Maintenon, indeed, incited by M. de Beauvilliers, seems to have done her utmost, but the ban of the King's displeasure was as comprehensive as it was inexorable.

"I wished to return to you all that has been found of yours and of Monseigneur de Cambrai," she wrote to the Duke; "but the King desired to burn them himself. I confess that I regretted it deeply, for nothing finer or more excellent was ever written. If the prince we are mourning had any faults, they were not due to flattery or over-diffidence. One may rest assured that those who walk uprightly are never confounded."[1]

The trite conclusion is characteristic of the writer, and it is easy to believe her testimony that the letters were worth preserving. But their value was only an additional reason for their destruction. It was not desirable that such witnesses to the honour of the man whom the King hated should be left for the enlightenment of future generations.

No system of self-suppression could kill the personal ambition which (in a pure and yet definite form) had been an abiding influence in Fénelon's character. But it did not survive the Prince's death; thenceforward his anxieties were for his country only, and his experience of the King's self-absorption and indifference to the future drove him to the borders of despair. "If human prudence can be of any avail," he wrote to M. de Chevreuse, "it requires that use should be made of every moment from the present to establish a guardian-

---

[1] *Correspondance de Fénelon*, i. 177.

ship and education for the young Prince which would be already instituted should we have the misfortune to lose the King. It is urgently demanded in the name of his honour, his renown, and his love for his people and the royal family that he should take every measure prompted by human wisdom with this intent. Not to put this matter before all else is to expose the State and the Church to the most desperate dangers. There must be an attempt to convince Mme. de Maintenon and all the Ministers of this by the right methods, that they may do their utmost with the King. The Father Confessor should enter upon it also with all possible force, as being in the obvious interest of religion. Very much might be said on this point, but you are more competent than I; I have neither time nor strength. I pray that our Lord may inspire you. We have never been in so great a need."[1]

There was no vagueness either in his forebodings or in the measures he proposed to counteract them. His grief only made his vision clearer; his independence of any personal interest gave him a power which was impossible to those who were themselves at the centre of affairs. As formerly he had realised without seeing the shameless band who gathered round the feeble figure of the Dauphin and stirred him up to jealousy and hatred of his son, who wove a net of conspiracy and slander to drag down a prince whose chief offence was hatred of the vices his persecutors loved; so now, among the throng that came and went and whispered and intrigued among the failing glories of Versailles, he could dis-

[1] *Correspondance de Fénelon*, i. 174.

tinguish those whose murmurs had the tinge of treason, whose voices, when the time came that they might dare to lift them, would call down ruin and disgrace on France.

"There is everything to be feared from the Huguenot party, the Jansenist party, the discontented of every class, from the princes left out of the regency, from creditors paid and unpaid, from numbers of undisciplined troops . . . ; one way or another there is a powerful party ready made for a prince who may be anxious to satisfy either revenge or ambition."

M. de Berri, youngest of the King's grandsons, was a dangerous factor in the general confusion. Not from his own pretensions, for he was as contemptible and fatuous a creature as his father, but because he had married the daughter of the Duke d'Orléans, the famous Regent, and was completely in his power. Fénelon's one desire was to see a Council of Regency, chosen from those wise and experienced statesmen who still remained to steady the tottering fortunes of the kingdom, firmly established while the King still lived. But the King's unconquerable dislike to contemplating his own decease and its results frustrated every attempt in this direction, a state of affairs on which Fénelon, who regarded death with more resolution, found it difficult to calculate. "It seems to me to be much to the purpose that the good Duke (M. de Beauvilliers) should see Mme. de Maintenon; that, to establish confidence between them, he should talk openly, laying all these things before her to obtain her assistance.

"It is just this that will call down the blessing of

God and the gratitude of all France upon her; it is working for the peace, the glory, and the welfare of the King. If the King fails in this confusion, she will have everything to regret. It is no true endeavour to comfort and support the King, to spare him certain painful and distressing details every day. Thorns will spring up every hour under his feet; they can only be prevented by plucking them out. It is immediate peace, the suppression of the Jansenist party, the regulation of finance, the careful reform of the army, the establishment of a wise council, authorised and recognised, as soon as possible, which can bring settled peace to the King and support the kingdom in spite of so many dangers. We shall owe everything to Mme. de Maintenon if she can so direct the King. . . .

"The good Duke should express all the gratitude due to the former good offices of Mme. de Maintenon. . . . I do not think that Mme. de Maintenon is inspired by grace, or even with pre-eminent prudence. But how can we tell what God intends? At times He makes use of the feeblest tools—at least for the prevention of misfortune. There must be an attempt to humour and still speak the truth to Mme. de Maintenon. God's will be done in all things."

The advice was good; but Fénelon's influence on politics, direct or indirect, was a thing of the past. He undervalued the difficulties of the King's temperament, aggravated by advancing years. Perhaps, in the bitterness of memory, he over-estimated the power wielded by Mme. de Maintenon. And the calamities which he would fain have warded off swept down on France. The young

King grew up degenerate, the State was almost bankrupt, every department of the Government was the prey of corrupt and unscrupulous courtiers, the Jansenists and the rebellious Cardinal became a recognised power in the Church, and the disbanded soldiery devastated the country districts. But fate spared Fénelon at length, for, when these things came to pass, he was already in his grave.

CHAPTER III

FROM CAMBRAI TO VERSAILLES

MUCH has been recorded and much imagined regarding the reign of Louis XIV., but its greatness, universally acknowledged as it is, proves on close scrutiny to be so far incomplete, that its result may be traced in the chaos of 1789 rather than in the illusive glories that amazed the world a century earlier. The halo that surrounded the Great King is rather the result of a peculiar faculty of impressiveness, that exalted him in the eyes of those immediately about him and so secured his reputation with the many who were content to accept a popular belief, than the effect of any deliberate effort of his own. It is a curious paradox; for it is the witness of these satellites which convicts him of a thousand unworthy weaknesses, and yet it is their admiration that originally set him on the pinnacle where, in defiance of all attacks, he still remains in isolated dignity. There were men among his faithful and devoted servants who are superior to any accusation of self-interest, but who were bound to him by the claim of a personality which, while it dominated them, did not blind them to his faults. Such as these were the prop and mainstay of the Court that assembled at Versailles and Fontainebleau, though they did little to enhance its gaiety, and such as these were also the links between Fénelon, the exile who had never loved the King, and the vortex of influence and power towards which he cast many a backward glance of longing, and from which he was debarred for ever.

The deprivation to which his banishment condemned him was much more, however, than the blighting of ambition; compensation for such a regret as that would have come in threefold measure if the King's grandson had lived to wear the crown. But there was no remedy for the loss of the sympathy and friendship his earlier years had brought him—the daily intercourse with minds that reflected his own thoughts and yet inspired and exhilarated him. He had, it is true, his little circle of adherents in his palace at Cambrai, and they were the solace and consolation of his life; but all their loyalty and their many high and admirable qualities could not make them his intellectual equals; they were his disciples rather than his comrades, and therefore could not give him the stimulus which he had been wont to claim from the most gifted men and women of the day. It is easy to overlook, it is impossible to over-estimate the effect of the calamity. Fénelon was in the flower of his manhood and at the zenith of his capacities; he possessed the gift of language in a degree which impresses itself on the most unlettered of his readers, and his brain was a mine of learning and imagination. What he had written when he left the Court was recognised rather as a suggestion of future achievement than as a present claim on reputation; and, had he been a man of letters only, it is indisputable that success of the most permanent and satisfying order lay within his reach. But, as the world regards it, Fénelon never grasped success; he was a splendid failure, but failure is written over every notable chapter of his life. Amid the flashing of keen wits, the conflict of eager argument, his mind must have been stirred to the effort of creation and the world have been the richer; but, either because the severance of his life cut him off from all incentive, or the fatigue of controversy had sapped his energy, or loneliness and disappointment had withered all ambition, the years at Cambrai left his literary promise unfulfilled, and not till near the end, when the treason of Cardinal de Noailles had stirred him to burning indignation, did he give proof once more of the faculty of expression which with him was a natural instinct.

His loss may be measured by the loss to those he left behind. Experience sanctions the cynical conclusion that the blank left by an individual, however indispensable he may have seemed in his own eyes and the eyes of others, is soon bridged over and forgotten in the stress and rivalry of human life; but, in the case of Fénelon, it is proved by the generous fidelity of his friends that their need of him was a need that could not be extinguished by considerations even of self-interest and expediency. To remain his friend was to risk disgrace as complete as his; nevertheless there was a definite section of those nearest to the King, and most dependent on royal favour, who were as loyal in their friendship as though the Archbishop of Cambrai was singled out by the magic smiles of royalty. The fact is as much to his credit as to theirs, for the hold which the spiritual force of his character attained over such men as de Chevreuse and de Beauvilliers made it inevitable. The latter had come very near to paying the penalty which was required of so many others for his opposition to the opinions of the King; he was a natural object of suspicion, because it was primarily due to him as Governor to the Duke of Burgundy that Fénelon had come to Court, and when the royal disapproval was pronounced against his colleague the King looked to him for a vehement disavowal of sympathy with the offending priest. He looked in vain. De Beauvilliers was prepared to deny belief in the Quietist doctrine, and to pledge himself that no whisper of such heresy should reach his charge's ears, he was ever ready to temporise; but, though the claim of his office might command his silence, he watched ceaselessly for the opportunity that might be used in Fénelon's interest, and periodically made sincere though fruitless efforts to obtain the remission of his sentence. The King gave evidence of his sagacity in overlooking de Beauvilliers' offence in this matter; for the Duke was worthy of his reputation for honour and integrity, and his moral character had earned the especial regard of Mme. de Maintenon, whose friendship he shared with his brother-in-law, de Chevreuse. Saint-Simon records that it was her habit to dine once or twice weekly at the house of one or other of these two, in an intimacy that would not admit of the presence of servants at the meal. Before his banishment Fénelon was the most welcome guest at these austere festivities. It was a privilege which Mme. de Maintenon seldom extended to any but the chosen four on whose friendship she relied; but the presence of Fénelon proved rather an inspiration than a check to their confidential intercourse, and when his place knew him no more, and it was vain to hope that he would ever again break in on the limitations of that small circle, the bonds that held them together broke, and the resentment of those who had been true to the exile raised a barrier that divided them from the King's wife.

De Beauvilliers was strong enough to be independent of her good graces. Having weathered the storm of Quietism, his position might have been invulnerable, but he was so far possessed by the spirit of moderation that his most cherished opinions never betrayed him into rash expression. It has been seen that this prudence earned him a certain measure of contempt from Fénelon; but an earnest wish to serve the King was incompatible with recklessness of speech or action, and it is possible that if de Beauvilliers had not condescended to practise the personal discretion which his friend disdained, the nation would have been the poorer by the loss of his wise influence, and Fénelon himself have suffered by the severance of his strongest link to the Duke of Burgundy. It seems to have been accepted that the judgment of the tutor was more valuable than that of the governor in all that affected their common charge. From Cambrai Fénelon gave constant and detailed counsel regarding the best methods of training a prince whose nominal period of training had elapsed, with a confidence which seems to indicate that de Beauvilliers recognised the master-influence in him. Nevertheless, their friendship reflected the character of the Duke rather than that of Fénelon, and it is expressed in their correspondence, which was voluminous. The vanity of human wishes, the necessity of resignation, and the expediency of teaching the young Prince to consider the needs of others more than the grandeur of his own position—these are the topics which occupy the thoughts of Fénelon. Those flashes of wit, of sentiment, of passionate regret, that give so many of his letters the human living touch, are absent when he writes to his former colleague. For the most part he is as wise, as even-tempered, as judicious as de Beauvilliers himself. There is a flaw of sympathy somewhere, and it may be traced to the chief defect in the Duke's character. De Chevreuse, who knew him best, recognised and deplored it with a candour of which Fénelon (who never spared his friends when criticism might invoke amendment) was never guilty.

"You know the good Duke thoroughly," wrote de Chevreuse; "he overcomes his natural timidity so far as he can, and I could give instances of courage and resolution which in him mean heroism. If they could be habitual, and he did not despair so easily and give up his attempts to overcome a prejudice against him, he would reach, or rather would have reached, an ascendancy which no one could have disputed, and which would have been of infinite service to the State."[1]

But the good Duke, in spite of his many strong and admirable qualities, never did master the failing which those who loved him best admitted, and therefore missed the ascendancy that might have been of infinite service not only to the State, but to the friend whom fate had made the victim of royal prejudice. That there were reservations in Fénelon's confidence towards him is evident, and in this lies the explanation.

With de Chevreuse it was otherwise. There was not

[1] *Correspondance de Fénelon*, i. 101, April 1709.

one of those whom Fénelon left behind him at the Court who meant so much to him, or one more worthy of his friendship. His name is inseparably linked with that of de Beauvilliers in all the memoirs of the time. Family ties strengthened the deep affection that united them, and whether for criticism or praise they are coupled as though they had every thought and sentiment in common; but, in fact, de Chevreuse, in his relations with Fénelon at any rate, has very definite individuality.

Their connection had no official basis, for de Chevreuse held no recognised position in the household of the Prince, and as his home was in Picardie, within easy reach of the diocese of Cambrai, Fénelon's disgrace did not completely separate them.

If it could be said with truth that Fénelon knew de Beauvilliers thoroughly, the same assertion might be made with even greater emphasis regarding de Chevreuse. The charm, the gentleness, and the great intellectual attainments of the latter, which Saint-Simon describes, appealed especially to Fénelon when he was smarting from Bossuet's violent hostility; but he recognised in these very attainments a subtle danger against which he did not hesitate to warn their possessor. Perhaps because he was himself in constant conflict with a like temptation, he is as eager to deprecate independent investigation of religious dogma as St. John or Thomas à Kempis. " Let me impress on you that, without knowing it, you very often yield to your natural inclination towards argument and curiosity. It is a life-long habit, which influences you unconsciously and almost perpetually.[1] . . . Our philosophy must give

---

[1] *Correspondance de Fénelon*, i. 22.

place to the simplicity of the Gospels. Blessed are the poor in spirit—from which I infer: Woe to the gifted, to the wiseacres who absorb so much knowledge, and to the philosophers who are confident in themselves, to the minds who would probe everything and gloat over their powers as a miser on his wealth. 'I thank Thee, O Father, that Thou hast hidden these secrets from the wise and prudent, and hast revealed them unto babes.'[1] . . . Self-willed and anxious search after a certainty which is not possible is manifestly an instinct of nature, not of grace; you cannot be too much on your guard against it."[2]

The nature of these warnings seems to reveal the character of their object. The spiritual instincts of de Chevreuse were predominant, and developed year by year, but he had too keen and penetrating a brain to submit easily to the passive acceptance of dogma which the Roman Church demanded; in his youth he had touched on the perilous borders of Jansenism, he shared eagerly in the speculations of Mme. Guyon, and in later life Fénelon's influence was his chief defence against the intellectual allurement of fresh heresies. In his warnings Fénelon proved himself a true pupil of Saint-Sulpice; he had himself been schooled to obedience, and had proved his loyalty at the cost of bitter humiliation, and even when he knew that his exhortations would come directly into conflict with aspirations and endeavours that in themselves were pure and laudable, he attempted to maintain the spirit of the motto, *Scientia Inflat*.

It is difficult for those who love the memory of Fénelon not to deplore the narrow bigotry which had

[1] *Correspondance de Fénelon*, i. 23.   [2] *Ibid.*, i. 24.

power to shackle him; but for his priesthood, he might perhaps have braved the danger that is incurred by all who give free licence to their thoughts, and enriched the world with the fruit of his deep and earnest meditations. But the value of his priesthood to a priest of the Roman Church is a force wholly beyond all ordinary calculation; he is trained to the sacerdotal theory till it becomes an inherent instinct, inseparable from his faith, and to violate it is to violate the very fabric of his being. Therefore Fénelon, forbidden to explore the regions of speculation and research, was brought back to a personal striving after spirituality so intense in its concentration that it is impossible to realise it by the light of common experience; and to the few to whom he revealed himself, he could write nothing and say nothing which does not bear the hall-mark of that secret influence.

"Never man possessed his soul in peace as he did," wrote Saint-Simon of de Chevreuse. If that were a true description, it is not wonderful that he was singled out by Fénelon as the friend that was most necessary to him, for—do what he would to train himself—peace never came into the soul of Fénelon. His was not a nature to which peace was possible, life had too strong a hold upon him; and the holiness to which he did attain was won at the cost of constant warfare against worldly and ambitious instincts. Association with de Chevreuse meant calmness and refreshment, and Fénelon gave in return a sympathy which the Duke and Duchess knew how to value; for he had the power of understanding sorrows he had not experienced, and of giving comfort that bore the touch of comprehension. There is a special instance of it at the death of the Chevalier d'Albert, a promising young son of M. de Chevreuse, who was personally dear to Fénelon: even in the first rush of grief he distinguishes between that which will be felt by father and mother. "I am sure that you will carry this cross in peace, and that you have already made your sacrifice to God of this dear child which it has pleased Him to take back. But I grieve for the tender heart of Mme. la Duchesse, although I do not doubt that she yields to the will of God; yet I fear that her heart must suffer much, and I pray our Lord to comfort her."[1] That was his first greeting to them, and when another and more bitter, although secret phase of sorrow, succeeded, they turned again to him. It was a dissipated age, and the young man, who had died gallantly in battle, had lived as recklessly as his contemporaries, thus leaving a hidden wound in the hearts of those who mourned him. Fénelon, in spite of the austerity with which it was his custom to confront the vices of the age, in spite of the sternness with which he repudiated the easy confidence in God's mercy that ensnares so many, brought healing even to such pain as this in a spirit of large-hearted tolerance that is as unexpected as it is welcome. "You must not give way too much to distressing thoughts. The frailty of such early youth in a life so full of diversion is not so poisonous as some sensual vices which are refined into the disguise of virtues in later life. God sees the clay of which He has moulded us, and has pity on His poor children. Besides, although the force of nature and example may lead a young man in some degree astray,

[1] *Correspondance de Fénelon*, i. 30.

we can, notwithstanding, say what the Church says in the prayers of the dying, 'Nevertheless, O God, his hope and trust was in Thee.' A foundation of faith and religious principles which has been overwhelmed by the excitement of passions is stirred in a moment by imminent danger. Such an extremity as this routs all life's illusions, lifts a sort of veil, reveals Eternity, and recalls the realities that have become shrouded. However little God may seem to be working in that moment, the first instinct of a heart that has ever been accustomed to Him is to throw itself on His mercy. Neither time nor exhortations are needed for Him to be felt and heard. To Magdalene He said but the one word, 'Mary,' and she replied to Him but that other word, 'Master'; and no more was needed. He called His child by her name, and she was already returned to Him. That ineffable appeal is all-powerful: a new heart and a new soul are born in the inmost being. Weak men who can only see the surface desire preparation, definite ritual, spoken resolves. God needs only a moment wherein He can do all and see that it is done."[1]

In no passage of his writings does the infinite tenderness of Fénelon's nature find such pure expression as in this: the lad who had gone forth full of the joy of living, careless of danger alike to soul or body, had vanished out of sight without a word to reassure those whom he left behind that the religion which to them was everything had been anything to him, without a moment for those priestly ministrations which to the Roman Catholic are of such limitless importance. Yet Fénelon the priest,

[1] *Correspondance de Fénelon*, i. 31.

strong in his belief in the sacerdotal power, showed that he could go beyond and above it to the stronger truth of God's infinite love and mercy, and give assurance of a hope which the mourners had not dared to cherish for themselves.

Saint-Simon, who was a staunch admirer of de Beauvilliers, recorded and deplored that to him and to de Chevreuse Fénelon was to the last "the soul of their soul, the mind of their mind." This again was especially the case with de Chevreuse: no subject was too intimate or domestic for the advice of the Archbishop; the matrimonial affairs of his numerous family are discussed with a curious amount of detail, and Fénelon, in replying on these and other matters of the Duke's personal business, shows conspicuous discretion in concerns that are purely worldly, even when he exhorts him to put such cares aside and give more of his thoughts to spiritual things. In fact, Fénelon's practical interest in the lives of his friends is second only to his eagerness in politics; in both he was keen and far-seeing, and all his natural aptitudes fitted him to steer his way amid the stir of rivalry and whisperings of rumour. These were the chief dangers in the life of court and city, and that Fénelon did not come to port in safety is due—in so far as he is himself responsible for shipwreck—to the power that Mysticism exercises over her votaries, a power unknown to the vast majority who never hear the summons, but illimitable in its dominion where it has once attained ascendancy. Fénelon, it must be remembered, had his way to make; he could not hold aloof from all discussion and competition as did de Chevreuse. The latter stood high among the peers of France and was enriched by his marriage, and, being so endowed, his character and talents made him pre-eminent at Court, and left him free to ignore its inconsistencies. Fénelon, on the other hand, was forced by circumstances to be definite; there were many proceedings customary at Court which were not, to say the least, compatible with the constant spiritual communion that he had taken as his ideal, and his attitude towards these things was one of unmitigated censure—in this connection, at least, he had no tolerance for human nature's weakness. Others saw and deplored the same abuses, and were silent. Racine was, by nature, hardly less religious, but he stifled his instincts because he loved both King and Court. He described himself as "a man who spent his life thinking of the King, studying the great actions of the King, imparting to others his own feeling of love and admiration for the King,"[1] and here unconsciously he unveiled a truth, for thus and thus only was it possible for a man of pure morality to share the life of Versailles and Marly without perpetually doing violence to his better nature. To love the King was to be magically blinded, and Fénelon's eyes remained clear and observant, though he held that open denunciation of the evil was not within his province.

The silence of de Beauvilliers was only a compromise, and de Chevreuse, when Fénelon was gone for ever, paid little heed to the allurement of a society whose corruption he had already realised. None of the

[1] *Correspondance de Racine*, Appendix, lett. 6.

three made open effort to reform it. They were outwardly far less strenuous, far less sanguine in the cause than Mme. de Maintenon; yet their presence, it may be, did more to induce a spirit of purity and self-restraint than could be effected by the most vehement crusade. The isolation in which each one, by the power of his personality, was placed amid the throng of dissipated triflers was in itself a rebuke, and there is something in the position that, even now, lays hold on the imagination, as it must have arrested observation at the time. It is difficult to realise the reaction that would have supervened on the succession of the younger Dauphin, save by a study of the conditions of Whitehall when Cromwell reigned there, and such reforms as could satisfy the friends of Fénelon would seem to have required the outward and visible signs of revolution to prepare their way. The Court of France as it might have been remains only a fruitful topic for speculation; what it was at its most favourable period affords illimitable scope for wonder.

"The regret at never hearing reasonable conversation is almost enough to kill me," wrote Mme. de Maintenon to de Noailles; "for eight days I have had no relief. The pea-chapter still lasts; the longing to eat them, the pleasure of having eaten them, and the delight of eating them again, are the three points that have engaged our princes for four days. There are ladies who, having supped with the King, and supped well, have peas to eat at home in defiance of indigestion: it is a fashion, a rage—and one thing follows another. You have some strange lambs, Monseigneur." And Mme. de Maintenon wrote from Marly, where only those whom the King esteemed most highly were admitted. It was well for the young prince—deprived of Fénelon's counsel, and confronted by the rigidity of de Beauvilliers—that he could turn to the friendship of de Chevreuse instead of being thrown on such society as this, and it was well that the friendship of the two dukes allowed no rivalry between them, for de Chevreuse, having none of that official authority which de Beauvilliers never relinquished, possessed a closer influence over the real inclinations of the Prince. It is to him rather than to the established governor that Fénelon pours forth his yearning anxiety concerning his pupil's welfare—his high ideal for him, his misgivings as to its attainment. "If the little prince does not see the necessity of becoming firm and vigorous, he will make no real advance; the time has come to be a man. The life of the country where he is, is a life of weakness, of indolence, of cowardice and relaxation. Let him become more and more humble beneath the Hand of God; but strong before the eyes of men. It is for him to win love and fear and respect for a goodness that is one with power."[1]

Such is the oft-repeated burden of Fénelon's letters in the darkest days of the Prince's life, when the great cabal against him was most potent and most threatening. And de Chevreuse, who was endowed with infinite tact and personal charm, was eminently fitted to be the channel for such exhortations and rebuke. The interest of local dangers, of general politics, and of new and

[1] *Correspondance de Fénelon*, i. 130, July 1710.

audacious heresies—keen as was Fénelon's participation in them all—pales before the pre-eminent interest of the Prince's mental and spiritual development; and there is little opportunity of judging what the correspondence of de Chevreuse with the archbishop would have been without that absorbing topic, for the death of the Duke followed closely on that of the Dauphin, and Fénelon and de Beauvilliers were left to face the ruin of their hopes and labours, without the unconquerable optimism of de Chevreuse to support them.

The great distinction of the correspondence between the two dukes and Fénelon is the purity of thought and expression that never fails on either side. It is difficult to turn from the pages of Saint-Simon (or many another of his contemporaries) and realise that he lived in the same world as de Beauvilliers and de Chevreuse; that the incidents that figured so largely in his thoughts must have come equally beneath their notice; that they breathed the same heavy air and heard the same eternal chatter, and yet remained untainted by its poisonous influence. And Fénelon himself, though he was eating out his heart in banishment, had no room in his reflections for petty malice. "I do not know if I deceive myself, but it seems to me that I have no fear for myself or for my personal interest; but I love France, and I am faithful, as is my duty, to the King and to the royal family."[1] Those words were written to his most intimate friend in the freedom of confidential intercourse, and may be accepted as the true expression of his sentiments. He had other correspondents at the

[1] *Correspondance de Fénelon*, i. 110, December 1709.

Court, but with them it is likely that he would have retained a certain measure of reserve, as much from regard for their safety as from fear of exposure, and his personal loss must have been felt the more heavily where it involved the withdrawal of his confidence.

No one deplored his absence with greater vehemence than Mme. de Noailles, a lady of a gayer and more enterprising character than most of those whom he counted as his friends. She held a prominent and distinctive place among the ladies of the Court, and was as virtuous as she was lively, but the name she bore was one that had earned the distrust of Fénelon. Her husband, M. le Duc (afterwards Marshal of France), was false to him, and the vacillations of her uncle, the cardinal, had cost him dear; consequently, his letters to Mme. la Maréchale became few and far between, and though her efforts to resume their former intimacy were untiring, they were all in vain. It was obvious to Fénelon, and probably to all whom it concerned except herself, that her close alliance with Mme. de Maintenon forbade intimate correspondence with Cambrai; but she was a favourite with fortune, and could not brook denial of her wishes with equanimity. Another reason for their severance may lie in the natural melancholy which his misfortunes brought to Fénelon. Mme. de Noailles was more of a kindred spirit to the Abbé de Langeron, and at Versailles, when all went well, her merriment may have been a welcome diversion; but de Langeron, with all his love of laughter, was well aware that mirth could only find occasional season at Cambrai, and it was his graver side that riveted the affection of his superior. He kept his gaiety for the entertainment of the lady whose friendship he insisted on retaining.

Mme. de Noailles was the mother of twenty-one children, and possessed abnormal skill in selecting eligible husbands for her daughters (a faculty which subjected her to the banter of the abbé). She must have been a woman of very unusual force of character and intellect, but, fortunately for her, she was not of the fibre to which Mysticism readily appeals. She lived in the world, and (though she accepted the exhortations of Fénelon with meekness, and ardently desired their repetition) she was distinctly of the world; indeed, even his strongest claim upon her gratitude was due to the assistance he had rendered to effect the marriage of her son with Mdlle. D'Aubigny,[1] when the Abbé de Fénelon stood highest in favour with Mme. de Maintenon.

In those days the de Noailles family were close allies of his, and if they introduced a worldly vein into the higher intercourse which existed between himself and the families of his more serious-minded friends, the relaxation may not have been unwelcome. In any case, her loyal love for the exile is a fine and worthy trait in the character of Mme. la Maréchale, and their necessary separation had its bitterness for Fénelon. "Every day, Madame," he wrote to her in 1698, "I deplore the necessity I am under of displeasing people for whom I shall preserve the deepest attachment all my life."[2] And Mme. la Maréchale, for

---

[1] Niece to Mme. de Maintenon.
[2] *Correspondance de Fénelon*, xi., Appendix.

all her unrestrained vivacity, had as sober an estimate of the worth of Fénelon's attachment as Mme. de Chevreuse or Mme. de Beauvilliers. It was not necessary to be *dévot* to feel the charm of his society or confide in his judgment, but it was only those to whom his religion made stronger appeal than his great mental abilities and social brilliancy, who retained the perilous outward tokens of his friendship after his disgrace.

He had great comprehension of the spiritual side of a woman's character, but a Roman priest who is at one with the fundamental theory of his order can hardly escape a certain contempt for a sex which is entirely shut out from the mystic privilege and dignity he receives at his ordination, and the knowledge of women which Fénelon did obtain was so intimate as to be disenchanting. With one only he seems to have allowed himself to stand in some measure on an equal footing. This was Mme. de Laval, a cousin by blood, and afterwards, by her second marriage, his sister-in-law, and we owe to her a glimpse of the light-hearted youthfulness which the rigid restraints of Saint-Sulpice had disguised into the semblance of a natural gravity.

Fénelon had been presented to the Priory of Carenac in 1681, when he was in his thirtieth year, by his uncle, the Bishop of Sarlat, and was received by the townspeople on his first arrival with a pomp and ceremony that afforded him intense amusement. He approached the priory by river, attended by an immense escort, and was received on the bank by the monks and a numerous crowd of spectators. The absurdity of these proceedings appealed to him, and enabled him not only to find enjoyment in them himself, but to impart it to his cousin. "The vast concourse divided to make a path for me," he writes in mock heroics, "each one with watchful eyes, seeking to read his fate in mine: thus I ascended to the castle with slow and measured steps, that I might give a little more indulgence to the general curiosity. Meanwhile a thousand mingling voices awoke the echoes with shouts of glee, and on every side was heard these words, 'He will be the delight of the people.' Behold me having reached the entrance, and the address of the consuls being conveyed by the mouth of the royal speech-maker! Who can describe the beauties of that harangue? He compared me to the sun: soon after I was the moon: all the brightest of the other stars had the honour of resembling me; from thence we got to the elements and the meteors, and finished satisfactorily with the beginning of the world. By that time the sun had already gone to bed, and to complete the similitude between him and me, I went to my room to prepare to do likewise."[1]

There is much that is painful in the after correspondence of these two; it is well that it should begin with laughter. While both were young, their relationship gave a freedom to their alliance that made it especially valuable to Fénelon, whom circumstances had so divided from his own family that his sisters never seem to have claimed any share in his confidence. Mme. de Laval was the daughter of the Marquis Antoine de Fénelon, and had married very young; in 1686 she was already a widow with one son, Gui-André, the M. de Laval to whom some

[1] *Correspondance de Fénelon*, ii. 3.

of Fénelon's letters of spiritual counsel are addressed. Her solitary condition developed her natural force of character, and it is evident that she was a woman of marked individuality. Fénelon was a member of a large family, many of whom must have been competent men of business, but it was to his widowed cousin that he confided the superintendence of his monetary affairs, with which, in the pressure of his duties, he felt himself incompetent to cope. He gave her unrestricted power: " In all matters that call for a decision, decide, and forget that I am in the world to be consulted on my own business. I should be only too glad to help you in any of your own concerns; but I am of no use except to give trouble."[1]

The post of business adviser to so unworldly a principal was, in fact, no sinecure. Fénelon would ask for nothing, even while he was at Versailles, and his salary was always in arrears. It was impossible to live at Court without submitting to the monstrous system of fees required by the Court officials, and for these ready money was constantly required. Fénelon appears to have had no private fortune, and even with the most scrupulous economy the revenues of Carenac were insufficient to supply his need; evidently he resorted to the plan of borrowing on the security of his appointment, and Mme. de Laval was his chief creditor. There are references also to loans of plate which the royal tutor required at Versailles, but was wholly unable to provide, and all such obligations began at last to weigh heavily upon him. " Do not imagine that this is any lack of confidence," he pleads; " I would rather be indebted to you than to any

[1] *Correspondance de Fénelon,* ii. 5.

one. I owe you too much to have any false delicacy about it; but a final reckoning is absolutely necessary to obtain a clear view of my little savings and to deal fairly. Do not put yourself about to make an exact reckoning or to give me items. So long as the sum is fixed, it does not matter to me what you fix it at."[1]

Such arrangements as these testify to a deep and confiding friendship, and Mme. de Laval seems to have felt herself honoured by the call made upon her purse and faculty of management. But her son's interests were prior even to those of Fénelon; she resisted his appeal that she herself should accept a post at Court, because she believed it derogatory to the young marquis, and she, who prided herself on heaping every sort of obligation on her friend, condescended to sue for his influence to place her son in the household of the little prince. Considering their mutual relations at that time, how deeply he was in her debt, and dependent on her help, it is a great proof of Fénelon's unflinching adherence to a principle that he refused her request. At a later period a second opposition to her wishes divided them for ever, but in those early days her affection for him survived the rebuff undamaged, and the letters spread themselves over many years, varying the discussion of family events with the explanation of small disagreements, confidences on domestic and financial difficulties, and all those graphic details of personal thought and action which are the witnesses of a confiding intimacy. Mme. de Laval married the Comte de Fénelon, an officer of the King's Guard, in 1693; but the marriage was not announced to the world

[1] *Correspondance de Fénelon*, ii., 13 July 1692.

till two years later, and was not a fortunate one for the lady, for M. de Fénelon (although he seems to have had no very strong convictions) was included in the disgrace that the question of Quietism brought upon his brother, and dismissed from the Court.

It is a matter for question whether the candour which alienated Mme. de Laval from Fénelon was an error in judgment on his part. She was a devoted and adoring mother, and because her friend seemed to her to stand above the level of human nature, she turned eagerly to him for the benefit of his wisdom on the subject that was nearest to her heart. He was well disposed towards her son; his letters generally include some message to him, and he had won an influence and hold upon him; but he was perfectly competent to see his faults. The young marquis was for some time an inmate of the palace at Cambrai, but Fénelon did not urge that his sojourn there should be prolonged. "His brain is quick and developed," he wrote of him; "he understands outward things with ease and is very inquisitive about everything that goes on around him; but he is still very light-minded. He takes no pleasure or interest in any study, or labour, or course of reasoning. All his tastes are turned to bodily exercise and boyish amusements. He is big already; his frame grows stronger, and all exercise does him good. He is horribly bored at Cambrai, and in spite of all that can be said to him, he always imagines that when he goes to Paris or to your estates he will be a very dashing nobleman. Such feeble-mindedness is natural enough at fourteen."[1]

[1] *Correspondance de Fénelon*, ii. 48.

The report was not likely to find favour with his fond mother, and may have counteracted the effect of the very sage advice Fénelon offers in the remainder of the letter. M. de Laval was probably very difficult to manage, and possessed exalted rank and deeply impoverished estates, a combination especially disastrous to a careless and light-minded temperament. Fénelon was placed in a most difficult position with regard to this young man; he seems to have studied his character almost as he had studied that of M. de Bourgogne, and to have felt that the responsibility of his training rested in a great degree upon himself, and consequently that candour was incumbent on him. Mme. de Laval seems to have reproached him, and his attempts at softening his verdict are not happy. "I greet him with all my heart, I love him dearly," he writes a year later, when the object of their mutual anxiety was no longer under his care. "If he will work, study, reflect seriously, listen to the advice of persons of experience who are well disposed towards him, behave simply and naturally in everything, avoid evil companions and endeavour to make himself worthy of good ones, choosing only those who possess good sense and virtue, without pretending to copy them in detail, he will prove a real consolation to you and to me." The reservation is so comprehensive that the writer can hardly have thought it probable that M. de Laval would comply with its conditions and prove himself a consolation to his kinsfolk, and in a postscript he allows his zeal once more to get the better of any tendency to conciliation. "One of the things I would impress most strongly on M. votre fils is never to speak lightly. It is thus that one falls unconsciously into the weakness of saying what is not completely true." [1]

Mme. de Laval loved her son better than any living being, and her friend, with the best intentions, strained her toleration to the utmost; nor was it any compensation for his strictures when he urged the lad to be completely subservient to her—few mothers would welcome the implication that their sons were not competent to stand alone or regulate their conduct in the smallest details. "Tell her everything for and against yourself without reservation," he wrote to M. de Laval. "You will only find peace in this complete abandonment. I seem to myself to be always with you two, and that God is with us both." [2]

His remedy for the weakness of character he had detected was impracticable as well as repugnant to those concerned, and Mme. de Laval resented the detection itself; a rupture was inevitable, and at length it came. Its immediate cause is curious and characteristic. Every Frenchman of position who did not take orders joined the army when he was an age to do so, as the natural duty of a loyal subject of a warlike king; but Gui-André de Laval was the sole hope of a woman who held to her desires with the tenacity of a strong and narrow nature. She could allege a certain delicacy in his constitution as her excuse, and she combated the custom of a chivalrous age with desperate resolution. Fénelon was more deeply imbued with the gallant traditions of his race; priest though he was, he knew that manhood makes a claim which may not be denied, and though his heart went out

[1] *Correspondance de Fénelon*, ii. 49.   [2] *Ibid.*, ii. 67.

in ardent sympathy for the mother, he cherished and applauded the warlike instincts of the son.

The letter that brings the correspondence of five-and-twenty years to a conclusion sets the situation graphically before us.

"CAMBRAI, *February* 12, 1706.

"When I arrived here from Brussels I found your letter of January 27. I confess, my dear sister, that it has greatly surprised and troubled me. I hoped that you would not take it amiss that I should truly represent my thoughts to you in a letter that was for you only, without interfering in the direction of your son's conduct. It seemed to me that there was a wide difference between directing and eagerly suggesting what seems clear to oneself, and thus I was very far from imagining that my letter could bring upon me that which you have written to me. But I suppose I was mistaken, since you regard it thus. At least my mistake shall be a limited one; because, since you desire it, I will refrain from declaring my opinions to you. Nevertheless, I shall always accept with an open mind anything you may care to tell me of your motives. No one would be more rejoiced than I to be convinced that they are good ones, just as no one could regret it more than I shall if they are insufficient. But, allowing them to be as weighty as you believe them, I consider your son is greatly to be pitied, for in that case he will find himself confronted on the one hand by a mother who has excellent reasons for preventing him from entering the service, on the other by the world which, oblivious of his secret reasons, will regard him as irremediably disgraced if he does not serve. Already he is in his twentieth year; other men of position take care not to be so old as that before entering the service: they serve from the age of fourteen or fifteen. France will afford no instance of a man of well-known family who has not taken part in some campaigns by his twentieth year. The world will never understand the reasons for such an eccentricity, which is utterly against all the prejudices of the whole country. I infer that your son finds himself in a most difficult position. He is reduced to one or other of these extremities, either to disobey his mother, who has good reasons for forbidding him to serve, or to let himself be branded by Society because those good reasons will never be understood. For my part, I have no choice but to be silent, to be deeply distressed, and to pray that God may give the spirit of wisdom to mother and son. The one thing certain is that I shall never show that I disapprove of your conduct in anything, and that I would rather never speak again than allow a word against you to escape me. From the depths of my heart, my dear sister, I am always yours." [1]

If these letters be compared to those which Fénelon wrote to the many other women to whom he offered consolation and advice, it becomes evident that his friendship with Mme. de Laval had in it a personal note; that he distinguished her from the throng of those who craved his help and kindness, and gave her, it may be, that love which is so much a part of human nature that even his lifelong and rigorous training in self-suppression could not completely crush it. If this

[1] *Correspondance de Fénelon*, ii. 69.

were so, the weakness brought its own retribution. In his effort to bring the instincts of her motherhood to reason, and save her and her son from inevitable dishonour, he won his point indeed, for Gui de Laval took his natural place in the army of the King, but he forfeited the confidence in which he had delighted for five-and-twenty years, and Mme. de Laval never sought his friendship or advice again. This loss came to him with many others, but it may be that among them all there was not one more bitter.

CHAPTER IV

FÉNELON THE ARCHBISHOP

IT is evident that Fénelon felt the most ardent interest in the development of such affairs as were directed from Versailles. The internecine warfare of the Church, the claim of a French prince upon the crown of Spain, the most intimate details that concerned the Duke of Burgundy—all these things were of vital importance to him. Nevertheless, though he might strain his eyes regretfully when he gazed in the direction of the Court, it should not be concluded that all his interest in life was absorbed in the vain endeavour to span the leagues that separated him from Paris, or that he spent his days in impatient expectation of despatches from de Chevreuse or de Beauvilliers, or even from the little prince himself. He awaited them eagerly enough, no doubt, for nothing could ever supersede the interest that his years of tutorship had made a portion of his very life; but the waiting was only a half-conscious mental attitude, his duties and his position at Cambrai were a prominent reality, and every hour brought its appointed task to be fulfilled.

The state and dignity of the princes of the Church of Rome in the seventeenth century has no parallel at the present day. Cambrai became French territory in 1678,[1] and previous to that date her archbishops had

[1] By the Treaty of Nimèguen.

taken rank as princes of the Holy Roman Empire, with almost sovereign rights over the diocese. Under French rule the position was hardly less exalted. The nominal revenue was 200,000 livres, although the difficulty of collecting it reduced its actual value to a lower and fluctuating sum; and, had he chosen to assert himself, Fénelon might have established a despotic jurisdiction over the Flemish people, whose brooding discontent at being cut off from Germany furnished innumerable pretexts for oppression. The palace of Cambrai was in keeping with the royal dignities assumed by its archbishops. A portion of it was burnt down soon after Fénelon's appointment, but was rebuilt on the original plan, and, as it stood during his residence, was as magnificent a castle as any feudal chief could have desired. The careful investigations of Ledieu have left details of its construction, as well as of the life of its inhabitants, but the correspondence of Fénelon and his friends gives no idea of the outward surroundings of his exile; they are always too much engrossed with other matters to refer to the impression made by vestibules or battlements.

"The old archiepiscopal building," says Ledieu, "encircling a large courtyard, was stately and magnificent. In front of it is a public square, down the length of which stretches the metropolitan church of Nôtre Dame. The entrance to the palace is to the right, at the west; the church to the left. The little door of the palace that goes straight from the carriage gate leads beneath a gallery or open portico, ornamented by pillars and paved with black and white marble, which extends the whole length of the court, and supports a high covered gallery. There are many apartments which look on to the street for gentlemen of the household here. At the end of the court is a grand staircase where the gallery ends, and the part between the staircase and this gallery is the part which was burnt, and is still in ruins. The other side of the staircase is a suite of many rooms and anterooms, with an apartment in a recess for M. l'Abbé de Chanterac, the whole running from east to west between the courtyards and the garden. To the left is the archiepiscopal chapel, the entrance to which is on the same floor with the new apartments of the archbishop. Beneath this chapel, occupying the length of the left side of the courtyard, corresponding to the grand gallery which is opposite on the right, is a little low covered gallery, very old, and very gloomy and ruinous, leading from the palace to the metropolitan church. The principal entrance to this church is in the courtyard of the palace, and is always closed, only being opened for the archbishop when he is officiating."[1] Lediau proceeds to describe with much elaboration the new offices built by Fénelon, and the upper storey where "the prelate had very convenient apartments, comprising a room (with a canopy, beneath which is the great archiepiscopal cross) with three great windows to the south, a vast bedroom with two great windows, also to the south, a passage room with one great south window, and on the other side a little bedroom with a north window, and at the end a great square study quite full of books, which has a great window in the middle towards the east, three great south windows,

[1] *Journal de l'Abbé Lediau*, vol. iii., September 1704.

and three to the north which look over the gardens that enclose the building. This makes, in the new building, four rooms on the same level and *en suite*, with two great doors and two folding-doors and windows to the south all along, which gives ample room to walk, and takes the place of a gallery; and, indeed, we walked there after supper *tête-à-tête* with great convenience, and afterwards with his nephews and other friends of the house."

The furniture also engaged the attention of Ledieu. He noted the magnificence of the state bedchamber and the four portraits after the manner of Rigaud of the King of Spain, the King, the Dauphin, and the Duke of Burgundy, which hung above the mantelpiece, and from thence passed to a little north room where the hangings were of dull grey woollen stuff and the bed was small and narrow. "This is where I sleep," the archbishop said to me; "the grand bedchamber is only for show, this is for use."

Very little attention seems to have been spared for the garden, which was enclosed by high walls and intersected by rows of trees that there might always be shade; but the mass of building, old and new, dominating the little town of Cambrai, must have been very impressive to the stranger approaching from the southern side, to whom Cambrai was but a name connected with the perpetual frontier warfare in which the King delighted. In most cases association with the archbishop seems to have obliterated all thought of the archiepiscopal dignities. Fénelon reduced the outward trappings which custom identified with his position as far as possible; but there was dignity enough in his tall spare figure in the plain purple soutane which was his habitual dress, to be independent of the pomps and ceremonies with which his predecessors hedged themselves, and the people learned to revere him more by seeing him pass by in the country walks which were his only recreation, than if he only drove along the road in state, and found no leisure to greet them and distinguish them by name. His natural gifts, his high intellectual powers, and the command over the characters of others which he possessed to such an extraordinary degree, absolved him from any necessity of posing before the world either to maintain his dignity or to claim sympathy for his misfortunes. Instead he practised the utmost simplicity in all personal matters, and when he was at home adhered to a regular routine, which Saint-Simon has recorded in the following words:—

"He awoke early, but his physical delicacy forced him to rise late. He made his bed a retreat from whence to say his offices and other prayers, to read and answer his letters, and to administer his diocese, which was quickly done owing to the great knowledge of it which he had acquired. As soon as he was dressed he said Mass, that is to say, if there was no festival at which to officiate—these he never missed—then went to his study to get through his business, and a little before dinner joined his guests, who were always numerous. He presided at rather a large table, doing the honours and carving, but eating nothing solid and little enough of anything else, afterwards talking with the same company; when they withdrew he went sometimes to pay formal visits of civility in the town and the palace precincts, sometimes to the hospitals, being always anxious to walk unless the weather were too wet. He was curiously fond of walking, and made long circuits in the country, always with his *grand-vicaire* or other priests in his household, that he might discourse on the business of the diocese. He seldom entertained any one at supper on his return, except those who lived with him. For a little while afterwards he amused himself watching the games of *tric-trac* or *ombre*, not taking part himself, and withdrew early." [1]

When Fénelon's disgrace was fresh it isolated him as the King intended it should do. Even friendship with him weakened the popularity of the de Chevreuse coterie, and it was far easier for those who lived on the Flemish frontier to ignore his presence than to profit by the pleasure of his society. But it was impossible that such conditions should endure. M. de Montberon, the Governor of Cambrai, was openly and unflinchingly faithful to the exile, and he and his wife welcomed Fénelon as one who honoured their house by entering it. The change in public opinion was gradual but persistent, and, according to Saint-Simon, to find favour at the palace at Cambrai was coveted almost as much, in the last years of the archbishop's life, as to find favour at Versailles. Saint-Simon is unfailing in exaggeration: there could not have been even a faint reflection of the intrigue and adulation that surrounded Louis XIV. in Fénelon's household; but it is probably true that the reserve of power in the man, the possibility of strength and domination should some public crisis call for it, did

---

[1] Saint-Simon, *Écrits Inedits*, iv., p. 461.

FÉNELON THE ARCHBISHOP 327

impress itself upon the younger generation and break through the clouds of calumny that had obscured him in his prime.

The reminiscences of the Chevalier de Ramsai commemorate the position of Fénelon in his later years, although the writer is too much disposed towards eulogy to be completely trustworthy. His connection with Fénelon began in 1710. He was a scion of an old Scotch family, exiled for his sympathy with the Stuarts, a man who had read and travelled much and prided himself on his independence of thought. But having passed by rapid transitions from one form of faith to another, and discovered the manifest defects of each, he found himself approaching the scepticism that is an almost necessary result of such experiments. In this condition he came to Cambrai, being anxious to see a man who was reported to be a thoughtful and accomplished scholar and at the same time a sincere Roman Catholic. He stayed at the palace for several months, and was never weary of talking with his host, who was ready to listen patiently to all his arguments and speculations. If the record of these conversations, which de Ramsai professed to set down while they were fresh in his memory, be trustworthy, it is a valuable testimony to the tolerance of Fénelon. The shortcomings of the priesthood would seem a difficult topic for discussion between a Roman Catholic archbishop and a layman, but de Ramsai entered unflinchingly upon it.

"What, Monseigneur," I said to him impetuously, "you would have me regard any earthly society as infallible! I have observed most sects. Let me tell you, with all respect, that the priests of every religion are often more ignorant and more corrupt than other men. I suspect them all equally."

Fénelon's reply is the clue to his method of reconciling the difficulties of the Roman doctrine. "If we do not raise ourselves above what is human in the conclaves of the Church, we shall see nothing that does not shock and revolt us and foster unbelief; we shall see only passions, prejudices, human weakness, considerations of policy, intrigues, cabals. But we should rather worship the wisdom and power of God, who reaches His ends by means which would seem destructive to them. It is here that the Holy Spirit shows itself master of the human heart. It uses the apparent frailties of individual priests to accomplish His promises, and with wondrous providence directs them in the moment of decision, and conforms them to His will. It is thus that God works in all things, and by all things. Civil and ecclesiastical authorities alike obey His laws. All fulfil His designs, whether freely or by coercion. It is not the sanctity of our superiors, or their personal capabilities, which makes our obedience a divine virtue, but inward submission to the Spirit and Will of God." [1]

Fénelon had deep and painful experience of the failings of the priesthood. All his powers of administration being concentrated on his diocese, he allowed nothing to escape him, and there are strange revelations of the practices of the country curés in his correspondence with M. de Bernières, Intendant of Hainault.[2] He erred on the

[1] De Ramsai, *Vie de Fénelon*, p. 117.
[2] *Lettres Inedits de Fénelon.*

side of toleration, though the scandalous living of the clergy was as abhorrent to him as to the most ardent of the Reformers; but he seems to have been incredulous of many of the charges brought against them, and could only be convinced by the most conclusive evidence and the open defiance of the culprits. It was no wonder that it seemed to him that the most pressing and important duty for a lover of the Church was to train and prepare a worthier type of servant for her. "Give me kind hearts and common sense," he wrote, "and I will undertake to set them on the right road. I will be like a brother to them. I do not ask for polish or astounding talent; I only desire ordinary capabilities and real devotion to God."[1] He did not spare himself in the endeavour to mould such material into the country priest of his ideal. Nothing ever clouded his affectionate memories of M. Tronson and Saint-Sulpice, and it was his ambition to reconstitute the seminary of the diocese on the same lines, entrusting the supervision of the students to priests who were members of the Congregation. Formerly the seminary had been at Valenciennes; but Fénelon desired to have it under his own eye, and removed it to Cambrai. His disgrace and the timidity of M. Tronson were the obstacles to his scheme, for the superior of Saint-Sulpice would not risk the possible danger of direct connection with Cambrai, and on his death-bed Fénelon refers to the business as not being entirely accomplished; but he allowed no drawbacks to daunt him in his endeavour to make the priests of his Flemish diocese an example to their degenerate colleagues.

[1] *Correspondance de Fénelon*, v. 39.

De Chanterac was his chief assistant in this work; but Fénelon devoted personal care and reflection to the students, examining them himself, and endeavouring to estimate their individual capabilities. The Chevalier de Ramsai was especially impressed by his system in this matter, and was present at some of the gatherings of the students. "Besides the instruction he gave them during periods of retreat and at the chief festivals," he writes, "he conducted conferences once a week on the origins of religion. He desired that any one should tell him of their difficulties. He listened with infinite patience, and replied with the kindness of a father. Often the objections that they made were quite beside the mark. Far from impressing this upon them, he put himself upon the level of each one, suiting himself to their capacities, and giving weight to the feeblest dispute by some turn which made it possible to go to the root of it. I have often heard him hold these conferences, and have admired the apostolic humility with which he made himself all things to all men, as much as the grandeur of his discourse." [1]

The combination of spiritual religion and practical wisdom which de Ramsai found in Fénelon made so deep an impression on him that he became a convert to the Roman Church, and even when he was permitted to return to England he remained faithful to the doctrines which he had learnt at Cambrai. Thenceforth to him the memory of Fénelon was sacred, and in after years his literary powers proved of inestimable value in arranging the writings of his master, and defending him from calumny. The characteristic that especially arrested the attention

[1] De Ramsai, *Vie de Fénelon*.

of the young Scotchman was indeed a prominent trait in the complex personality of Fénelon; his sense of duty was so high that no consideration of individual interest would cause him to violate it. All that he did, he did for the glory of God; and though in his letters it is often evident that he found the pressure of small claims to be almost overpowering, he neglected none of them on the plea that his capabilities fitted him for more productive labour, but accepted each as a part of his appointed training in self-discipline and patience. This adherence to the routine which his position seemed to require of him enhanced the monotony of his life at Cambrai; as the years passed, and the limitations that arose from his disgrace were gradually removed, he would have been the most honoured guest at any house where he might chance to seek a welcome, and the society which had once been his chief enjoyment was often within his reach again. But he turned from such allurements to read and answer letters, to interview the raw uncultured youths who had aspirations towards the priesthood, to calm the squabbles of a country curé and his congregation, and drive here and there throughout the length and breadth of the diocese to see for himself that his agents fulfilled their trust, and that nothing he might do for the welfare of his people was left undone. If the development of the man can be gathered from his writings, it seems as if the system of constant self-suppression, which was his rule of life during his years of exile, had deepened and enlarged his powers of thought, and formed in him a character above the reach of a successful cardinal and courtier. Neither disgrace nor personal bereavement had power to embitter him, and the spare figure in the purple soutane, who reigned in the palace with quiet but absolute authority, for whose coming Mme. de Montberon, the great lady of the district, waited with constant and feverish impatience, while the country people stood bare-headed as he passed, was, in fact, a greater power in the country than if the young and courtly abbé of twenty years before had fulfilled the popular predictions, and won every dignity that King or Pope can give.

The religious atmosphere of the Court was a vitiated atmosphere, and even Fénelon was more likely to be infected by its corruption than to purify it by individual effort. A sensational doctrine was secure of popularity among people who desired relief from ennui at almost any cost, but the personal religion which was Fénelon's message to the world was as far from them as from the light-minded generation which had passed away. The King and Mme. de Maintenon favoured outward observances, but to Fénelon, in his later years, these seemed only the shell of the reality: "Sacraments, ceremonies, sacerdotalism, are but useful aids for the support of our frailty."[1] That was his maxim, and he could even remonstrate with the Duke of Burgundy because it was said that he kept Lent and attended the services of the Church in so marked a manner as to be a reproach to his easy-going relatives. Fénelon had no illusions as to the effect of outward forms in the essentials of religion; no man could have obeyed the dictates of the Church more scrupulously than he had done from his childhood up. Yet when his course was nearly run, when others

[1] De Ramsai, *Vie de Fénelon*.

looked up to him as an example of piety, and it would have been hard to find the smallest detail of his outward conduct susceptible of criticism, he could reveal his true self with passionate sincerity in such words as the following: "As for me, I spend my life in ill-timed anger, in vain talking, in fretting over intrusions that disturb me. I shrink from the world, and despise it; nevertheless, it pleases me a little. I feel old age creeping on gradually, and grow used to it without loosening my hold on life. There is no reality about me, neither inwardly nor in outward things. When I try to realise myself, I seem to be dreaming; I see myself only as a figure in a dream."[1]

This is a return to the old effort at self-analysis against which he constantly warned others; but it shows that no amount of adulation could take from him the humility learnt in the solitary years that followed his disgrace, and that he knew the need of beginning again and again, as though no step in the upward path had yet been made, because his own soul convicted him of sins unsuspected by those who knew him best. The death of de Langeron revealed to him how closely he had held to the happiness of an earthly friendship; but even after that bereavement and the other sorrows that followed close upon it, he still made some attempt to maintain a spirit of cheerfulness in his surroundings at Cambrai. He was never without the presence of children there; the suite of rooms above his own were reserved for them, and not only his nephews and great-nephews, but the sons of his intimate friends, were placed beneath his care, that he might train them to be good and chivalrous gentlemen. Very few of these

[1] *Correspondance de Fénelon*, i. 156, to Mme. de Mortemart, July 1711.

boys were intended for the priesthood, but the confidence that Fénelon inspired was so great that it was believed the child reared under his eye would be better fitted to bear his part in Court or camp than if he spent his earliest years in the company of princes at St. Germain or Versailles. The children were a special feature in the life at Cambrai, and Fénelon loved them. "*Mes vénérables marmots*" was his name for them, suggestive of the half-familiar terms on which they stood with him.

The brothers of Gabriel, Marquis de Fénelon (who was one of a family of thirteen), became inmates of Cambrai as soon as their age permitted, and when they passed into the world they were succeeded by others of a still later generation. The last of his little guests were the grandchildren of his friend de Chevreuse, and, harassed though he was by national disasters, he could spare time to study and report upon them and express his pleasure in their company. The eldest, Paul de Montfort, was eleven years old, and of him Fénelon wrote with whimsical gravity that he was "wise, reasonable, and disposed towards piety, although a little light-minded and indolent from love of amusement. . . . I hope that God will form him for the Church. If he was a little older and I were a little less old, I should have many schemes for him; I love him dearly."[1] The two brothers, sons of the Duc de Chaulnes, who were the playfellows of Paul de Montfort, received even more detailed criticism. The younger, M. le Comte de Picquigny, at seven years old appears to have been almost as desperate a character as the Duke of Burgundy at the same age. "M. le

---

[1] *Correspondance de Fénelon*, i. 191, July 1714.

Comte de Picquigny is clever, impudent, and sharp of tongue," wrote Fénelon to his anxious father, " but his temper is violent, and he has not yet enough sense to control it. He gets into a passion, and does not overcome his caprices easily; but he has a foundation of strength and reason from which one may expect much. He must be managed with gentleness, firmness, persistent patience. It is impossible to avoid punishing him a little, otherwise he would behave very badly even towards M. son frère, whom he wishes to hit until he hurts him very much. Nor does it seem easy to make him see his faults; he becomes coldly defiant, and disdains punishment. But provided he is taught by degrees to control himself, the child has excellent qualities. He has a very decided character, and only requires softening. Time which brings reason, teaching, example, discipline, will moderate his childish impulsiveness; it must be restrained."

If the little count did awake memories of Fénelon's first pupil, it made him the more welcome. " I delight in having them here," he wrote of the children ; " I love them dearly, they cheer me up, they do not trouble me in any way. Even when I go for my visitations they will be just as well here as at Chaulnes. Naturally the household goes on as usual, they cost nothing extra. I cannot be away for long ; I shall be charmed to find them here on my return." They were with him still during the autumn which was the last of his life, so that from the day that he entered on his duties at Versailles until his death he may be said to have given a definite proportion of his time and energy to practical demonstration of his theories on education. Even before there had been public acknowledgment of his genius for this particular duty, and before his judgment was weighted by the responsibility of office, he wrote a book, to which some reference has been made in an earlier chapter, and which is conclusive evidence of his competence to undertake the training of the young.

His treatise, *Sur l'Éducation des Filles*, taken in conjunction with *Télémaque*, reveals in him a knowledge of child-nature that is most remarkable. There is hardly a page of it which might not afford profitable study to parents in the present day, and although two centuries of experience have so fortified the arguments on which he insisted that the cause of women's education no longer needs a champion, his picture of the result of ignorance still finds its prototype in modern life : the vacant minds requiring perpetual diversion, the hungry faculties wasting themselves on poisonous plays and novels, which he depicts, are not unknown to a more enlightened age than his.

In this little book Fénelon boldly approached the subject of education in its most comprehensive aspect. He ventures on advice as to the food and management of young children, believing that their training should begin before they could speak. The fashion of leaving them with uneducated persons is one which he utterly repudiated, for he regarded the earliest years as of unspeakable importance in the formation of character. "Never let them show themselves off," he says, "but do not be worried by their questions, rather encourage questions; they are the most natural opportunities of teaching."

He spared no pains to provide easy, pleasure-loving parents with food for reflection; his deep love for children sharpened his keen observation of all that concerned them. He was, probably, admitted to the most intimate relations with the families he numbered among his friends, and thus saw family life under every aspect. He discovered that children are always watching others—even as he did himself—but that with them imitation ensued on observation, and all their future welfare might depend on the example given by those about them, so that it was impossible to over-estimate the responsibility of their first guardians. The reader of *Télémaque* would be disposed to label the author as a stern disciplinarian, and the records of Fénelon's dealings with the Prince sustain the impression of his severity; but in the earlier treatise he shows another side, he enters into the mind of a child until it is difficult to remember that we are listening to a priest who had been reared in ecclesiastical seminaries and had hardly known a home. He recognises the necessity of discipline; but if the child has merited disgrace, he pleads that there should be some one to whom she can turn for sympathy, thus showing that he had fathomed that overwhelming sense of loneliness which is one of childhood's chiefest terrors.

Truly the child who trod the path of learning under his guidance need never have realised it was steep. "Make study pleasant," says he; "hide it under a show of liberty and amusement. Let the children interrupt their lessons sometimes with little jokes; they need such distraction to rest their brain. . . . Never fear to give them reasons for everything. Never give extra lessons as a punishment."

In short, it was Fénelon's method to treat children as reasonable beings instead of unruly animals whom it was necessary to coerce against their will, and his object to make them regard learning as a privilege and a delight, not as a penance forced upon them by the tyranny of their elders. His power over children is a charming trait in his character; but it was one of the factors of his downfall. Without it he would not have won the heart and soul of the Duke of Burgundy and the consequent jealousy of his compeers; without it his career might have run more smoothly and successfully, but he would, nevertheless, have missed the strong human love and sorrow which made his sympathies so intense and universal. Necessarily it was only among boys that he could prove the wisdom of his reflections, and it is to be regretted that the daughters of his friends could not profit by his schemes for their welfare, for he seems by some strange faculty to have read the heart of a girl-child. "Give them something to manage on condition that they give you an account of it," he pleads; "they will be delighted with this confidence, for it gives an incredible pleasure to the young when one begins to rely upon them and admit them to serious concerns." The words will awaken memories in the minds of most women, but through what power did that knowledge come to the young priest of Saint-Sulpice? How could he tell that the days and hours of girlhood are more apt to be blank and heavy with lack of fit employment or amusement than full of the traditional innocence and sunshine? If his contemporaries had listened to him, the level of thought in Court society would have been raised, and as the ideals of the richer classes became higher, their treatment of the poor must have reformed. An endless vista of possibility opens before such speculations. But the gay folk did not listen; they loved him, and were ready to defend him, if it did not damage their own interests; but they considered him a visionary, and continued to regard their babies as incumbrances, and their boys and girls as rebellious beings to be controlled by iron traditions of repression.

Yet, in Fénelon's schemes to make the children good and happy there was nothing sensational or revolutionary. "Observe," says he, "that to carry out this plan of education it is not needful to do anything that requires great powers, only to avoid great faults, such as have been pointed out here in detail. Very often it is only a question of not pressing the children, of being devoted to them, of watching them, of winning their confidence, of replying sensibly and clearly to their little questions, of letting their brains work out things for themselves, of reproving them patiently when they blunder and do wrong." In short, it is very often only a question of loving them, and it was by loving that Fénelon must have learned to know and understand the children. Therefore these thoughts and plans of his for their happiness brighten his record with a light that all the squalid scandal of the Quietism controversy cannot shadow, and are of as much value to those who love his memory as the deepest of his studies in theology.

It was his mission also to interpose sometimes between the young and old when conflicting interests were destroying all hope of quiet family life. In such cases his appeal would be made to the older generation in favour of the younger. His sympathy was always with the latter, and he possessed an extraordinary power of projecting himself into the position of the thoughtless soldier or the young bride who rebelled against the traditions of her husband's family, representing their temptations and difficulties, and praying on their behalf for patience and tolerant kindliness from their elders.

There seem to have been no human conditions in which his advice was not regarded as the best solution of a difficulty, and instances of the versatility of his influence recur perpetually in the records of his latter years. The English prince known as the Old Pretender was an officer in the French army in the year 1709, and his duty took him near to Cambrai. The account of his interview with Fénelon given by de Ramsai is a curious one. Fénelon assumed once more the position of Mentor towards Télémaque, and gave his counsel to the unlucky son of the exiled king. He recommended him above all things never to force his subjects to change their religion. "No human power can force the impregnable defences of freedom of thought. Force never convinces people; it only makes hypocrites. When kings mix in religious controversy they enslave religion instead of protecting it. Give civil toleration to all then, not as if approving all, as if it did not matter, but as if patiently enduring all that God endures, in the desire to lead men back by gentle persuasion."[1]

[1] De Ramsai, *Vie de Fénelon*.

The Prince had no opportunity of attempting to put these counsels into practice, but Fénelon in giving them betrayed his ignorance of the temperament of Englishmen, and of the fact that at that period they were dominated by hatred of the Roman Church. In his own mind he conceived an ideal of the whole world as a republic over which God presided, and of each nation as a great family. The nations might be divided, yet, as sharing a common human nature, their interest for the development and happiness of the race must be in common, and, therefore, wars must cease. The misery of warfare had come so close to him that this was a necessary part of every project of his for national or international welfare, and stamped each as chimerical, even to thoughtful men.

The older Fénelon grew the more the necessity of warfare outraged his reason, and the more fiercely he endeavoured to obviate it; but in this matter the flaw in all his arguments is obvious, and even the celebrated Tables of Chaulnes, which he compiled deliberately, and in conjunction with M. de Chevreuse, are not exempt from a blemish that destroyed their practical utility. Their interest is due, in fact, rather to their connection with Fénelon than to their political value. They were the first-fruits of the sudden revulsion of feeling produced by the death of the elder Dauphin and the unlooked-for promotion of the Duke of Burgundy to the honours of the heir-apparent. It was confidently believed that Fénelon himself would soon be at the helm, and the contemptible conspiracies which had made the life of the young prince a misery, and prepared concerted opposition to the influence of the archbishop, vanished as completely as though they had never been. It was a moment when a man might well give rein to his imagination, and the ideal constitution drawn up, in a week they passed together at Chaulnes, by Fénelon and de Chevreuse, could not have been imposed upon the country as the Great King had left it; it could only have served as profitable study for the Dauphin in leisure hours, and, perhaps, suggested projects of possible reform.

Fénelon's politics are most convincing when he finds himself in definite opposition to the existing system. If he originates a theory of his own he is apt to become visionary, although, had he been called upon to put his theories into practice, the wisdom which characterised his administration of his diocese would unfailingly have modified his idealism. Not in principle only, but in actual fact, the misfortunes of the nation affected him more deeply than any personal sorrow; distrust of the King was at the root of his anxieties, and he was moved sometimes by his foreboding to passionate and forcible expressions which no private calamity could wring from him. It seemed to him that the King had ruined the nation, and not exalted it as his flatterers maintained, and he scoffed at the veneer of sanctity which he assumed in his old age. "Will God be satisfied with devotion which is expressed in gilding a chapel, in telling of beads, in listening to music, in being easily shocked, and in expelling a few Jansenists? . . . They praise the devotion of the King, because he does not rebel against the Providence that is humbling him. It is enough that we should think he has made no serious mistake, that he should regard himself as a pious king whom God is testing, or at the most as a king who has sinned in his youth, like David, from the weakness of the flesh. But do they tell him that he must realise that he has plunged himself into a chaos from which all escape seems hopeless by the destruction of all order? . . . When despotism is obviously bankrupt and overwhelmed, would you look to the venal folk who have fattened on the blood of the people to ruin themselves to uphold it?"[1]

Such words as these breathe the spirit of revolution, and are the expression of Fénelon's inmost thought. The Duc de Chevreuse was always the recipient of such outpourings. De Beauvilliers stood too near the King to listen to them, for it would have needed very little straining to twist an accusation of treason out of the letters that were despatched from Cambrai to Versailles. Perhaps the King's inveterate dislike to Fénelon was only another indication of that discriminating insight into character which was so strong a factor of his greatness; for, while the old régime continued, the priest, in spite of his nominal love of peace, must have proved more and more a disturbing element as he himself developed and his influence increased; and it is conceivable that there were men about the Court who revered and secretly applauded the archbishop, and yet were glad that so many leagues divided him from the centre of affairs.

There was one method by which the King might have evaded the stigma of persecuting a subject whose reputation stood so high. He might have silenced Fénelon the politician by a pledge of honour as binding

[1] *Correspondance de Fénelon*, i. 132, to M. de Chevreuse, August 1710.

as the fiat of the Pope upon his mystic speculations, and left him free to find his place in the world of letters and delight the lovers of literature, present and to come. The people of Cambrai would have been the losers, but there are sufficient indications that Fénelon, either as a literary critic or a historian, would have ranked among the masters of the craft. His appointment as tutor to the princes made him a member of the Académie Française, but his talents were in themselves sufficient to secure the honour, and had he remained within reach of Paris he might have been a moving spirit there. Even in his exile he watched the proceedings of the representatives of national scholarship with eager interest, and in the last year of his life a letter from the President of the Académie Française called forth a striking manifestation of his literary genius. His *Lettre à l'Académie Française* is worthy of its celebrity. It contains within the compass of a pamphlet his deliberate judgment on subjects whose interest does not lessen with the passage of the centuries. It betrays that he was capable of theories for the world of letters, as startling as those with which he threatened to revolutionise the world of politics; and it displays the depth and extent of erudition he had acquired in spite of the many labours and distractions of his official life.

One of the needs for which, had circumstances permitted, he would have attempted to provide, is equally a need of the present day—that of authorised and reliable criticism. It was his suggestion that the Académie should devote itself to a detailed examination of the standard works in the French language, and prepare popular editions with notes on the author's style, aim, and general scheme.¹ He had lived too much alone to fully understand the difficulties attendant on literary criticism conducted by a species of committee; for the amount of deliberation required to put this idea in practice must have necessitated a very strict limit on the number of authors chosen for such distinction. The poverty of the language was another opportunity for the efforts of the Académie; and it is interesting to see that Fénelon—whose style is so unlaboured that every thought seems to have been born in his brain ready clothed for exposure to the world—should have recognised the need of words that would be comprehensive in themselves and require no enlargement. It is evident that he had studied poetry from the craftsman's point of view, and it is especially in poetry that words conveying the fine gradations of expression are essential. Classical scholarship made him impatient of the love for rhyme, in opposition to the taste prevalent at Court. "If I am not mistaken, our poetry loses more than it gains by rhyming," he said. "It loses a great deal of its variety, its ease, and harmony. The rhyme being far to seek, the poet is often reduced to spinning out and weakening his meaning; he makes use of two or three supernumerary lines to lead up to the one that he requires." ²

It may be inferred that Racine found no favour with Fénelon. He was the favourite of Mme. de Maintenon, and the fashion at the Court during Fénelon's term of office there; but the flowery elegance of his diction was

[1] *Œuvres de Fénelon,* xxii., *Memoire sur les Occupations de l'Académie Française,* part ii.
[2] *Ibid., Lettre sur les Occupations, &c.,* part v.

so much at variance with the subjects that he selected for his dramas that Fénelon regarded them as a travesty on the classic writers. For Molière Fénelon had unstinted praise; his intimate acquaintance with the works of the great playwright is made evident by frequent references to him in his correspondence, and his own knowledge of the literary art taught him to recognise a master. But he is not an unbiassed judge of Molière, for here again he deplores the frequent effort after rhyme, and, moreover, the spirit of comedy is necessarily antagonistic to the real traditions of priesthood.

It is the subject of oratory to which he brings the practical experience of a lifetime. There was little scope for the exercise of that art among the laity, for the government was in the hands of a few prominent men who, if they ever listened to each other's efforts at eloquence, did so with closed doors, and deprecated any attempt to sway or illuminate the mind of the people by public speeches. The judicial system also was so corrupt that the most eloquent of advocates made but a slight impression, and it was from the pulpit only that a man could secure a hearing. The abuse of such a state of things was patent; raw youths, eager for notoriety, and with no other qualifications, were admitted to the priesthood. "Young men of no reputation hasten to preach," moaned Fénelon. "God knows how I reverence the ministers of His Word; but I am making no personal reflection when I say that they are not all equally humble and diffident. People fancy they see them seeking the glory of God less than their own, and that they are more anxious about their own career than about the salvation of souls. What can one hope from the sermons of young men without deep learning, without experience, without having won any reputation, who play with words, and desire, possibly, to make their fortune in the ministry, when it is a question rather of sharing the poverty of Christ, of bearing His Cross by self-renunciation, of overcoming the passions of mankind that we may convert them. The man who is worthy of a hearing is he who only uses words as the expression of thought. There is nothing more contemptible than the professional speaker who uses words as a charlatan uses his remedies."[1]

Fénelon's views on oratory were indeed a counsel of perfection; but they contain suggestion as much for the present time as for his own, and if tradition may be trusted, he did not fall far short of his ideal. "*Il pense, il sent, et la parole suit.*"[2] Thus, with epigrammatic terseness, he summarised his notion of a true orator's experience.

There remained another field of thought which presented special attractions for him, although in his later years his duties interfered with his investigations. Historical research was an art which he believed to have been neglected and to require the encouragement of a recognised body such as the Académie to be worthily prosecuted, but here once more his ideals are a little above the range of human attainment.

"The good historian is of no period and no country," says he; "although he loves his country, he must not be

[1] *Lettre à l'Académie*, part iv.
[2] *Œuvres de Fénelon*, vol. xxii., *Dialogues sur l'Eloquence*.

partial towards it. The French historian must be neutral towards France and England: he must praise Talbot as freely as Duguesclin. . . . There are many isolated facts which teach us nothing but names and dry dates: it does not matter whether one knows these names or not. I do not know a man if I only know his name. I prefer a less exact and less judicious historian, who mutilates names and yet gives the details simply like Froissart, to those who say that Charlemagne held his parliament at Ingelheim, that then he left and went to fight the Saxons, and that he returned to Aix-la-Chapelle; all of which teaches me nothing useful. The chief perfection of a history lies in its order and arrangement. To arrive at this order the historian must take in all his history and make it his own; he must see it all as in one view; he must turn it round and round to every side until he has found the true point of view. He must show the unity, and thus derive, so to speak, every event from the same origin: thus he instructs his reader to good purpose, he gives him the pleasure of predicting, he interests him, he places the plan of events in each period before his eyes, he unravels what had to happen before him, he makes him reason without reasoning with him, he spares him infinite repetition, he never lets him grow weary, and also he makes his narrative easy to remember by the continuity of the facts. A well-chosen incident, a well-remembered saying, a gesture which portrays the humour or the genius of an individual, is an original and precious light on history, and brings the whole man before one's eyes.

"If a really enlightened man set to work to write on

FÉNELON THE ARCHBISHOP

the rules of history he might unite examples with his principles; he might criticise the historians of all ages; he might remark that a really good historian is perhaps even more rare than a great poet."[1]

Fénelon attacks these questions with all the fire of the young reformer rebelling at the established canons that sap the human interest from his favourite study; and it is strange to find the date of his letter to be but a few months before his death, and remember that he could not hope to see the fulfilment of any of the schemes he might propound. So strong was his interest in education that it is much to be regretted that he did not write a more comprehensive work upon the subject; but on one point his judgment could not be accepted by a more enlightened generation. The question that so frequently disturbs the peace of the Roman Church, that of permitting the reading of the Bible to the laity, was one of those on which he was consulted, and it must be acknowledged that he took the old and narrow view. He considered that there was great danger of heresy and rebellion against the Church if the Bible were read by the ignorant. The freedom of early days was only suited to purer conditions. It should be the great aim of the Church to fit the people to read Scripture, but before they were ready it was casting pearls before swine, and very likely to harm them.[2]

This was his method of upholding one of the faultiest contentions of the Roman Church, and the weakness of the argument breathes the very spirit of priestcraft. Primarily he was a priest of the Roman Church. If we are

[1] *Lettre à l'Académie.*   [2] *Œuvres de Fénelon*, vol. iii.

tempted to forget it because his tolerance was so much wider than his creed, the reminder comes, as it must have come inevitably if one of his guests ever forgot that the courteous gentleman and man of letters who presided at Cambrai was vested with the dignity of an archbishop. The power of the Church, if once admitted, was without limit, and the humblest-minded of her servants felt himself bound in honour to assert her claim on deference. Fénelon was called upon to formulate his conception of ecclesiastical dignity, when he had borne the weight of it himself for many years, in his address at the consecration of the Elector of Cologne, who, having been deposed in the course of the War of the Spanish Succession, became Bishop of Cologne and Ratisbonne in the spring of 1707. The Elector received his consecration at the hands of Fénelon, and the exhortation that preceded it is of the deepest interest as containing the mature expression of Fénelon's estimation of the Church. His thoughts had centred on that subject. He had sacrificed much to save his loyalty, and in his later years he taught himself to believe that his ideal was a reflection of reality. Historically, it is easy to prove the extent of his delusion, but his isolation made its acceptance easy, and many opportunities were given him of raising the traditions of individual priests. The possibilities of advancement, social and financial, which the Church offered to the ambitious was one of the abuses which he desired to abolish. "Listen to Jesus Christ," he cried from the pulpit of the great church at Lille. "He came not to be ministered unto, but to minister. You see Him, the Son of God whom you are about to represent, in the midst of His people. He did not come to enjoy riches, to receive honour, to taste of pleasure, to wield worldly power. Rather He came that He might humble Himself, that He might suffer, that He might support the weak, heal the sick, win the hard-hearted and rebellious, diffuse His blessings among those who injured Him the most, extend His arms continually towards a people who denied Him. Do you believe that the disciple is above His Master?

"If your people only see you at a distance, only see you in state, only see you surrounded by all that will dry up their confidence, how can they dare to break from the crowd to appeal to you, to tell you their troubles and find their help in you? How can you teach them to regard you as a father if you always claim to be their ruler?"[1]

The people of Cambrai could witness that these were no empty precepts, and Fénelon's friends were forced to realise that personal enjoyment and private interest must give way before the duties of his ministry. "I must confer with the chapter on a lawsuit; I must write and despatch letters; I must examine accounts. How dreary would be life made up of these perplexing details but for the will of God which glorifies all He has given us to do."[2]

That is the note to which Fénelon toned his life at Cambrai, making himself the servant of all, and glorying in the honour of such service, fearful of the outward pomps the Church conferred upon him, yet accepting them in all simplicity because he faithfully believed the Church to be directed by his Master.

[1] *Sacre de l'Electeur*, point iii., *Œuvres de Fénelon*.
[2] *Correspondance de Fénelon*, vi. 328.

CHAPTER V

THE SPIRITUAL LETTERS

It is to be deplored that a man of such ability as Fénelon should have expended his powers on the ephemeral subjects involved by religious controversy. He did not pause to consider how brief and passing the questions which to him appeared momentous might prove to be, and lavished the whole force of his intellect on obscure details of belief and ritual that, after two centuries, have completely lost all interest or importance. On the other hand, the work which still keeps him in the front rank among religious writers was never intended for general reading. The Spiritual Letters of Fénelon have never, and probably can never be superseded; but some part of their enduring power is due to the fact that they were intended to meet the individual needs of the persons to whom they were addressed—that his mind, as he wrote, was concentrated in the effort to realise the special character that he endeavoured to strengthen, with its chief temptations, its failings, and its possibilities. Those who received his letters knew that they were intended for themselves alone, and the personal touch adds greatly to their value to readers of the present day; for, while his most thoughtful exhortations are not free from the prejudices and delusions of the period if intended for a multitude, the counsel he destined for a single troubled soul has in it an insight and directness that will find its mark and bear its message in endless repetition, while the years pass and human nature remains unchanged.

There is a part of the collection of Fénelon's correspondence distinguished from the rest by the name of Spiritual. The classification is, however, somewhat arbitrary, for the spiritual side of his letters is as impossible to separate from the general bulk of correspondence as are his spiritual aspirations from his general character. In his later years there was no one to whom he wrote with such freedom and enjoyment as to his nephew, the young Marquis of Fénelon, and again and again, almost unwittingly as it would seem, he strays from the review of local incidents and comments on family affairs to questions that concern the conscience and the soul alone. This is characteristic, for, in fact, Fénelon would not have recognised any division, and the youth to whom he imparted all his anxieties on temporal subjects seemed to him the natural recipient for his religious speculations. Among all the letters written at Cambrai, those addressed to his favourite nephew are therefore the most descriptive both of his individual and spiritual life.

Gabriel de Salignac, Marquis de Fénelon, who became the great and unfailing interest and consolation of his uncle's declining years, seems to have been worthy of his privileges. He was only nine years old at the time of Fénelon's banishment from Court, and had been placed under his care four years earlier. At Cambrai he had the companionship of his brother (a second Abbé de Fénelon) and of the young Marquis de Laval, besides that of the three friends of the archbishop, who were all young enough to sympathise in the pursuits of an intelligent boy; and he made himself at home in his ecclesiastical surroundings with a philosophy which his kinsman, Gui de Laval, would have done well to emulate. It was said of him in later life that he was a man with two great ideas—the glory of God and the glory of his uncle. The description was, doubtless, intended to be flippant; nevertheless, it represents the man. The atmosphere of religious thought in which he spent his early years influenced all his conduct, and when he made his plunge into the chaos of temptation and delight which Fénelon termed the world, he never had a period of reaction, but remained faithful to God and to the memory of his uncle while his life lasted. His training and education seem to have been undertaken with some misgiving; but Fénelon found it difficult to refuse a service to his family that depended on himself, because he had so repeatedly to deny them the benefit of his interest at the Court. "I cannot, and I do not wish to do less by my family than to take charge of the education of a child who is their hope. I must, at least, show this goodwill towards my kindred."[1] Such was his method of accepting the responsibility, with no prevision of the blessing that he was preparing for himself.

The young marquis was the grandson of Fénelon's step-brother. The tie of blood was, therefore, not so

---

[1] *Correspondance de Fénelon*, ii. 16, Sep. 1693.

close as to necessitate intimacy, but the two regarded each other as father and son, and there is infinite pathos in Fénelon's endeavour to restrain his anxiety for Gabriel's safety when he came to man's estate, realising fully that it was fitting he should desire a post of danger, and yet shrinking in terror from the result. He can allow for the claims of ambition, of pure daring and gallantry, and of self-interest, for his own priesthood had never dimmed his eyes to the considerations that sway the lives of other men; but he had one unfailing maxim with which he summed up every question: "The chief thing, if I mistake not, is simply to follow the instincts of your heart, listening only to God and renouncing all regard for the world."[1]

The way of godliness was not the way to popularity, and this was, therefore, a hard saying for a man who had to hold his own in the army and at Court; yet Fénelon was far from ignoring the advantages of popularity. He urged them on the Dauphin from his childhood onwards, and he had similar solicitude for his nephew. Sometimes, indeed, his exposition of the deference that should be paid to the great seems to foreshadow the counsels of Lord Chesterfield. "I cannot refrain from scolding you a little because you do not see more of the people you should cultivate. It is quite true that the chief point is to improve yourself, and to be devoted to your duty, but you must also win some consideration for yourself, and set yourself on the way to promotion. Now you will never succeed, but will always be left without a suitable appointment,

[1] *Correspondance de Fénelon*, ii. 70.

unless you acquire some capacity for winning those who are in power, or on the road to it. . . . Very often there is only sloth and timidity and indolent self-indulgence in this semblance of modesty which avoids commerce with people of distinction. By reason of self-conceit, one likes to spend one's life in the society one is accustomed to, in which one is at ease, where one is sure to get on. One's self-conceit is disturbed when there seems to be a chance of not getting on, and of bowing before others who are all the fashion. In the name of God, my dear son, never neglect affairs without which you cannot fulfil the requirements of your position. One may scorn the world and none the less realise the necessity of humouring it. Religion should detach us from it; we must not forsake it from carelessness or eccentricity."[1]

The foregoing may seem to indicate a worldly wisdom not consistent with the point of view from which Fénelon professed to regard the affairs of life. That, indeed, would be no reason for suppressing it in an endeavour to realise his true character; but on closer consideration the advice he gives is rather the obvious testimony of common sense than evidence of an undeveloped faculty for pandering to the great. His own disgrace was an obstacle to the advancement of all who bore his name, and he felt it incumbent on him to do all that appeal and admonition could do to stir his nephew to consider his own interests. The fact that the young man required an incentive in such a matter, when his contemporaries were pushing and struggling to win the interest that was of far more

[1] *Correspondance de Fénelon*, ii. 81.

marketable value than the highest natural capabilities, testifies to the influence that had surrounded him in boyhood. But he had not chosen the life of the recluse; he was the head of a family whose honour had remained untarnished through many generations, and it was his uncle's chief desire for him that he should not only prove himself unworldly, but hit the mean between the self-suppression of the monk and the self-indulgence of the courtier, that he should bear his part in the world with glory to himself and benefit to others, and yet never loosen his hold on the religion to which he had come so near in the quiet years at Cambrai. There is no connection in which Fénelon shows his true manliness as he does in these letters; his nephew came very near to his heart, his later years were full of sorrow, and every fresh bereavement made him cling more and more desperately to the few on whose attachment he could absolutely depend. He knew to the full the dangers attendant on a soldier's life, and when his fears get the better of him, and he implores the young commander not to run unnecessary risk, there is, almost invariably, an afterthought that cancels his momentary timidity. If Gabriel was remiss in his duty to society, he seems to have been only too zealous in his military duties; but Fénelon does not ask that for his sake he should set some value on his life. Mme. de Laval herself had hardly more temptation or a greater claim to plead for caution; but Fénelon, waiting at Cambrai in hourly apprehension of news that would have snatched the last possibility of personal happiness from him, will only allow himself to urge that his nephew should curb his eagerness as God directs him. "Listen in quietness and silence for what God asks of you, and then do that only. You will see that all that is excessive will restrain itself, and that what is insufficient will appear to be so, so that the gift of grace will teach you the right medium unerringly. That is all that I desire; I care a thousand times more for your fidelity than for your life." [1]

To a soldier surrounded by the excitement of constant danger, while his blood ran quick with the enthusiasm of chivalrous warfare, and daring pure and simple loomed larger in his view than all the virtues, such an exhortation may have seemed strange and impracticable, but it was only the obvious application of the creed by which Fénelon ruled his own life and had trained his nephew. To him there was no condition of life not unworthy in itself which was outside the scope of the direct influence of God. Divine Omniscience was to him as practical a truth as Divine Omnipotence, and the necessary result of belief in the infinite wisdom of the Father was a constant demand for its direction.

His anxiety for the safety of the life that was so precious to him was not, however, in accordance with his old theories of passive acquiescence; but he was spared the overwhelming blow which he never ceased to anticipate while Gabriel commanded his regiment at the front. The young marquis was wounded in the leg, and though he struggled to fulfil his duties at headquarters for more than a year, the hurt (which lamed him for life) at length obliged him to take leave of absence, and in the period of suffering and depression that ensued Fénelon

[1] *Correspondance de Fénelon*, ii. 97, August 1712.

was untiring in his efforts to encourage him to resignation and endurance.

Both welcomed the opportunity afforded by his enforced idleness of meeting at Cambrai. No shadow of distrust or disillusion seems ever to have fallen across their mutual affection, and Fénelon's chief fear for the young man was lest he should let his religion be bound so closely to the surroundings of his home as to injure its individual claim, and also lest he should display a disdain of the world's attractions unfitting to one of his years and position, a temptation which seems to have been constantly present with him. Certainly Gabriel de Fénelon was not in any way a type of the nobleman of the period. In his case, as in that of the Dauphin, the strength of Fénelon's personality was overwhelming; the lives of both bore the impress of the one character—the character of a mystic and a priest—and their contact with the world, though it confronted them both in its most frivolous and most alluring aspect, could not eradicate or even soften the hall-mark he had set upon them. If Gabriel had been a prey to the slack morality that was the fashion, it must have destroyed the value of their intimacy, for when Fénelon came face to face with his nephew it would not have been possible to hoodwink such penetration and experience as his, and it is significant that after one of these meetings their alliance seems invariably to have renewed its strength. Gabriel is still addressed by the childish and untranslateable nickname "Mon Fanfan," and Fénelon speaks his mind with the confidence of a true friendship. "I desire that you should make yourself beloved, but God only can make you lovable, for by your nature you are too stiff and harsh to be so. The hand of God must mould you till you are tractable and yielding; He must make you gentle, attentive to the judgment of others, distrustful of your own, and as humble as a child."[1]

It is not evident whether Fénelon was his nephew's sole confessor, but on one occasion he petitions for two separate letters, under the same cover, one of general news and the other confined to the affairs of the soul, while his own replies, being intended for one reader only, have no such division. The faults that he detected were evidently not of the gravest kind, and it is probable that Gabriel erred chiefly in externals, and was as reserved and churlish as the Dauphin, so that tolerance for others and a more absorbing faith are Fénelon's chief desires for him. "O mon Fanfan, how happy you would be if you would give yourself to meditation, and if you would accustom yourself to act with simple and intimate dependence on the divine spirit in every detail of life. It will never fail you unless you fail it first."[2]

Those words come from the depths of Fénelon's heart. The ties of affection and of blood alike brought Gabriel very near to him, and they represent the appeal he longed to make to all who had learnt the grammar of his own belief. But there were some who had not learned even its rudiments, and yet were able to recognise in him something above the limits of the life with which they had been hitherto content. Among the friends of Gabriel de Fénelon was one who did not

---

[1] *Correspondance de Fénelon*, ii. 112.
[2] *Ibid.*, ii. 115.

belong in any way to the section of society which had claimed the archbishop as a leader in his period of favour. The Chevalier Destouches won a high reputation with the army, but in Paris he was chiefly known as a *bon vivant*, addicted to the most reckless self-indulgence, and he died in the prime of life, his end being hastened by intemperance. Nevertheless, he was always a welcome guest at Cambrai, and Fénelon's letters to him are full of a very real affection. Perhaps if their connection had begun a few years earlier it might have had a different sequel; their correspondence extends over a period of three years, the last of Fénelon's letters being dated only a few weeks before his death, and proves that there must have been some qualities in the character of the chevalier which might, by the influence of sympathetic friendship, have been developed into a desire for self-control and self-respect. The letters are a curious instance of Fénelon's power of projecting himself into the lives of others. They are written at his saddest period, but there are few of them that have not a vein of liveliness; and though he never misses an opportunity of urging the young soldier to overcome his faults—faults that must have been especially repugnant to his nature—his counsels are given in a bantering tone that was far more likely to find a hearing with the light-hearted culprit than severe and sober exhortations. The chevalier valued his friendship, and was so far impressed by his reproofs as sometimes to resent them; but Fénelon clung to his object, and while he has his pen in hand and the thought of the young soldier and his wasting opportunities in his mind, forgets himself and his own pressing and overwhelming sorrows in the hope of vanquishing the lower nature and calling out the high and noble capabilities whose existence he had recognised.

At that time those whom he needed most were being taken from him one by one, until it seemed, as he once said himself, that all whom he loved were doomed to die before him. There were fears that Gabriel's wound would prove incurable, all his hopes had turned to disappointment, and Fénelon might have justified himself, in his old age and failing health, if he had made no further effort to turn the hearts of the disobedient to the wisdom of the just; but he proved by those letters, full of a kindly comradeship with one whose way of life was utterly antagonistic to his own, that his ideal was not founded on any theory of what the world expected of him, but on the rule of love, unselfish and untiring, that was his Master's.

It is in this rule of love that we must seek the explanation of Fénelon's extraordinary influence; life had been a hard and difficult school to him, but it had taught him to conquer himself, and in learning his lesson he learnt also how to teach. The names and circumstances of many of those who appealed to him are unrecorded, but they were almost innumerable, and his replies are evidence of their widely differing experience; for in his counsels there is nothing stereotyped, the needs of each were different, and to each he gave his best.

There were some who came to him who found it hard to face all that he asked of them, and to these the strong severity that underlay his gentleness was manifest. "You fear to feel the yoke, and therein lies the real root of a certain unbelief that you urge upon yourself. You wish to persuade yourself that you are not yet sufficiently convinced, and that, in this condition of doubt, you can make no advance towards religion without doing it rashly, and with the risk of speedily relapsing. You persuade yourself that you doubt, to avoid having to yield yourself and to sacrifice a miserable freedom which self-love cherishes. Honestly, what have you that is real and substantial to urge against the truths of religion? Nothing but the fear of being made uncomfortable and of leading a life that is laborious and sad; nothing but the fear of being led further towards perfection than you desire. It is only because you grasp religion, because you feel its sovereign power, because you see all the sacrifices that it inspires, that you fear it and will not yield yourself to it. But let me tell you that you do not yet know how sweet and pleasant it is. You see what it takes from you, but you do not see what it gives. You exaggerate the sacrifice without picturing the consolation. God teaches you, waits for you, prepares you, makes you willing before He commands you. If He thwarts your evil desires, He gives you, by His love, a longing for truth and goodness which will be stronger than all your other disordered longings. What are you waiting for? That He should work miracles to convince you? No miracle would rid you of the vacillations of a self-esteem that dreads exposure. What do you desire? Unending arguments: when all the while you realise in the bottom of your heart that which God has the right to claim of you? . . . You deserve that God should abandon you as a punishment for such prolonged resistance, but He loves you more than you know how to love yourself. In His mercy He pursues you, and troubles your heart that He may win it. . . . Is it to be wondered at that the Infinite is beyond our comprehension, which is so feeble and limited? Would you measure God and His mysteries by your standards? . . . Instead of judging God, leave yourself to be judged by Him, and acknowledge that you need that He should set you in the right way." [1]

The force of conviction is the inspiration of this passage. Fénelon needed no platitudes, threadbare with repetition, to cover the truths which were his guide to holy living. He would have others believe as he believed, and regarded reform of thought and conduct as the logical and necessary sequel of belief; but he was watchful and discriminating, and well knew how to distinguish between the profession of conversion (which Mme. de Maintenon had made fashionable) and its reality. He could applaud an evident inclination towards the ways of virtue, and at the same time single out the secret failing that was the obstacle to definite reform—whether it were vanity or sloth, or any darker form of sin. The letters intended for one person in each instance seem to lead forward by gradual steps, which show that each one had found its due response, and if we contrast the way of life habitual to the gentlemen about the Court or with the army, with the standards Fénelon required, it is extraordinary that any were found to adhere to his directions.

[1] *Correspondance de Fénelon*, v. 33.

To appeal to him when under the influence of sudden reaction was, considering the reputation of the Archbishop of Cambrai, no more than the natural instinct with which the suffering would turn to the chief physician; but when they realised the violent nature of his remedies, the unsparing detail of his criticisms, the perpetual struggle against self which was the régime that he enforced, it must have required a strength of character and power of perseverance worthy of high development to keep the rules that he laid down so ruthlessly.

Not that he could ever be accused of overlooking or undervaluing the difficulties. He knew them all, and foresaw that to some they would prove insurmountable; but he desired that they should be faced, and that the life lived in God's sight should in its outward form remain the same as when it was under the acknowledged dominion of the devil. The other method, that of retirement and complete renunciation, would have been easier, but in his view it was not God's method. "You would like a kind of repose wherein you might occupy yourself freely with what interests you, and spare yourself anything that might reopen your wounds; but that is not what God requires. He requires that that which affected and absorbed you too much formerly should present itself incessantly and be a part of your punishment."[1] This thought goes to the root of a question which was constantly appearing: whether the repentant should set the seal on their new resolutions by fleeing from the world and its temptations to the safety of the cloister, and the tendency of Fénelon's mind was, evidently, to dissuade

[1] *Correspondance de Fénelon*, v. 36.

those who consulted him from such a step, for in many instances he recognised in it a subtle form of cowardice, and desired more that the worthless bulk of society should be leavened by earnest men and women than that the monasteries and convents should be crowded. In the case of La Chanoinesse he took another line, but Mme. de la Maisonfort stood by herself, and could not be conformed to general theories, nor did her career afford an example to be singled out for imitation.

Many of Fénelon's correspondents, nevertheless, were members of one or other of the religious orders. One there was—a woman—whose connection with him seems to have extended over many years (until her death at an advanced age, in fact), and to have begun while she was still living at the Court. She was a single woman, and, judging by his letters, extremely emotional, and the failings attendant on that order of temperament were always treated by Fénelon with exceptional severity, probably because he knew by his own experience the danger of unreality induced by a religion that rested mainly upon feelings. He was not her confessor, and she does not appear to have had any definite claim upon him, but, though their intercourse was maintained entirely by letter, she depended on him and confided in him as the chief support and inspiration of her life. She seems to have had many difficulties to contend with. Those of her own household opposed her in the outward observances that she believed essential, and opposition made her the more determined; her experiences in this respect recalling those of Mme. Guyon. Fénelon does not spare her. He formed his estimate of her character; he saw that she loved applause as much in her religious professions as formerly in society, that she was in constant danger of hypocrisy, and that even her confidence in him might in its earlier stage be only a longing for sensation. He tests her by the bluntness of rebuke; he recommends her to practise the patient humility which gave most trouble to her pride; he is inclined to deprecate rather than encourage the freedom with which she lays bare her secret thoughts before him, and only a sincere and deeply-rooted conviction that his help was essential could have survived the coldness with which her advances were received. She persevered, however, and possibly learnt by perseverance the sincerity in which he thought her lacking. As the years pass there is an obvious difference in his letters; illness and sorrow had overtaken her, and, while he urges her to recognise in them the hand of God, his attitude has not the same severity. " I sympathise with you, but one must endure. We are in this world only to be purified by sacrificing our inclinations and all natural desire. Sacrifice yourself then; you have excellent opportunities; what a pity it would be to waste them!"[1]

Finally, being freed from family obligations, she took the veil. She was old, and the discipline of conventual rule bore hardly on her physical condition, and Fénelon, though he was an advocate of asceticism, would have her avail herself of every indulgence that was offered her, rebuking the zeal that welcomed bodily afflictions. With the approach of death she became fearful, and then he permits his natural tenderness to find free expression.

[1] *Correspondance de Fénelon*, vi. 85.

For those who—whether as priest or nun—made outward profession of religion, it might be customary to talk of death as desirable. A few might do so with sincerity, and with St. Francis of Assisi cry, "Welcome, good sister Death!" But Fénelon knew that such phrases were generally fictitious, and that a lonely woman would find no comfort in conventional fictions, however admirable they might be in theory. Instead, he gave her sympathy. "I can well understand that age and infirmity has made you see death close at hand with much more solemnity than when you used to regard it from a distance. . . . It is not a question of feeling delight in dying; such a sensation of joy in nowise depends upon ourselves. How many of the great saints have been lacking in this joy. Let us be content with what is given us by grace and by our own free-will. That is to say, not to listen to human nature, but to resign ourselves honestly to that which we are not privileged to welcome. Albeit human nature spurns this bitter cup, the inner being can say with Jesus Christ, 'Nevertheless, not as I will, but as Thou wilt.' St. Francis de Sales separates consent from feeling. One is not master of inclination, but one is of acceptance by the grace of God.

"Await death without regarding it so sadly as to injure yourself and weaken your health. It is sufficient preparation for death to try to relinquish all things, to be quietly repentant for the smallest faults, with the desire to overcome them, to walk in the presence of God, to be gentle, yielding, and patient in suffering, finally, to endeavour that self should die before bodily death has come."[1]

[1] *Correspondance de Fénelon*, vi. 100.

That is the fitting end of the series. Fénelon did all that man could do to calm the fears of the troubled soul, but he knew that the only efficient remedy for her disquietude rested with Another. "Feel after Him, and thou shalt surely find Him; wait for Him, and He will come," therein lay the only reassurance for the terrors of the dying, and to his view no repetition could dull its efficacy.

The influence he exercised over the men who made him the guardian of their conscience and the censor of their conduct appears to modern criticism to be further-reaching in effect and healthier in tone than his close intercourse with women; but it should be remembered that a man who held such views as inspired the letters of some of his women correspondents would not have remained among the difficulties and distractions of the world. It was not an unusual occurrence for a man of high position, who had joined in all the frivolity and wickedness of the society surrounding him, to break down every barrier that impeded him and take refuge in the silence and obscurity of La Trappe or some other religious institution, where he could devote himself to meditation and repentance undisturbed. Having done so, his need for Fénelon's guidance would cease to be imperative; but there was a claim of duty and obedience upon women who were wives and mothers which could not be set aside on any plea connected with religion, and therefore the intensity of their aspirations and the violence of self-examination found its only outlet in the system of confession. To modern criticism, again, the mental condition of these pious ladies of the Court may seem morbid and artificial; but there is probably no parallel in modern life to the violence of contrast between the dissipation that was fashionable and the purity of life and self-renunciation to which the exponents of the Roman faith exhorted their disciples. The two were almost incompatible, and Fénelon, at least, believed in the practice of confession as the only possibility of reconciling them. "You are never truly humbled before God when you are not ready to humble yourself before the man whom you consult as His minister. It is pride that gives you so much dislike to speaking. You must confess everything with simplicity, however much it costs you."[1]

That was his argument for confession, and from his point of view it was completely logical.

There were two ladies of the Court who were especially the objects of Fénelon's friendship and direction, Mme. de Grammont and Mme. de Montbéron. The sole claim of the latter on the remembrance of posterity rests in the letters he addressed to her; but these are the fruit of a deeply religious nature expanding for the help of others, and his own development may be traced in following the series. His connection with Mme. de Grammont ceased when he was banished from the Court, and the first letter to Mme. de Montbéron is dated in January 1700. His friendship for Mme. de Montbéron and for her husband was of long standing, but his apprehension of involving those he loved in his own disgrace made him reticent in expressions of regard, and he would have made no voluntary advances towards them after the condemnation of his book. M. de Montbéron was Governor of Cambrai, however, and was not disposed to waste the

[1] *Correspondance de Fénelon*, vi. 68.

THE SPIRITUAL LETTERS 371

opportunity of intercourse with the archbishop which his appointment gave him. It is possible that the facilities for intimacy with Fénelon fostered the natural inclinations of Mme. de Montbéron; she had "made profession of piety," according to the phrase current at the time, and she claimed all the assistance that a man of his character and wisdom could give her.

In 1702 he consented to become her confessor, rather against his will, for he probably foresaw the infinite difficulty of dealing with a woman of her temperament, and the result fulfilled every foreboding. But difficulty was in itself an inspiration to him, and he gave her counsel, which, if his reputation rested upon that only, and no other production from his pen had been preserved, would justify the admiration of his contemporaries and make his name immortal among religious teachers. Every rule for the life of faith may be found among those letters, and every incentive to lead a man or woman to embrace that life. He grudged no labour and spared no pains to tranquillise the morbid terror and anxieties that oppressed Mme. de Montbéron, and gradually the hints and suggestions of her personality that are interspersed in his letters form themselves into a definite and distinctive figure. She was already past middle age when she came to Cambrai, and had lived her life among her equals, surrounded by the dignified traditions of high official place and noble birth. She was a proud woman evidently, and possessed of considerable mental ability, which had, however, been undermined by the subtleties of excessive introspection. The only condition which would have satisfied her aspirations appears to have been one of perpetual religious ecstacy, enervating in itself and incompatible with practical daily life. Fénelon's own words in his letters to her give a graphic description of her temperament.

"Let me show you, my dear daughter, that which it seems to me that God desires I should lay before you. The mainstay that you have unconsciously cherished in your heart since childhood is immoderate self-esteem hidden beneath the semblance of sensibility and heroic generosity—a love of the fantastic, the fallacy of which no one has ever revealed to you. You had it in the world, and it is with you even in the most sacred undertakings. I always find in you a taste for intellectual and pleasant things which alarms me; your fastidiousness causes you to find thorns in every condition. You are an excellent counsellor for others, but you yourself are overwhelmed by the merest trifles. Everything wrings your heart; you are completely taken up with the fear of doing wrong, or with regret for having done it. You exaggerate your faults by the excessive vividness of your imagination, and it is always some triviality which has driven you to despair. There are two things which you foster in yourself, Madame, which cause you infinite suffering. One is the scrupulousness which has been rooted in your heart since your childhood, and which has developed to the highest degree during so many years; the other is your custom of always desiring to touch and feel a blessing. Your scruples prevent the realisation of love by the distress they cause you. On the other hand, the stoppage of this realisation reawakens and increases your doubts, for you believe yourself helpless, that you have lost God, and are deluded from the moment that you cease to taste and feel a transport of love. You have spent your life in the belief that you are always given up to others, without regard for yourself. Nothing encourages self-esteem so much as this tribute that one pays to oneself as being never influenced by self-esteem, but always by generosity towards one's neighbours. But all this care which seems to be for others is in truth for yourself. You love yourself so much that you wish to be always satisfied that you do not love yourself. All your care proceeds from the fear of not being sufficiently pleased with yourself; this is the secret of your scruples. You wish that God as well as men should be pleased with you, and that you should always be pleased with yourself in all that you do in God's service. . . ."[1] "There is a very subtle misconception in your troubles, for you seem to yourself to be entirely engrossed by the claims of God and of His glory, while in reality you are troubled on your own account. You truly desire that God should be glorified, but you desire that it should be by your own perfection. . . ."[2] Ah, what delight it would be to see you calm, simple, freed from self-study and vain imaginations about yourself. Now you make your sufferings and sorrows for yourself, then your peace and consolation would be in God. You turn perpetually from Him to discourse with yourself upon your sins."[3]

There is something antagonistic to the instincts of those who hold a different faith in this intimate analysis of a soul—laid bare, as it were, for the criticism of an expert; and the letters to Mme. de Montbéron are

[1] *Correspondance de Fénelon*, vi. 327.
[2] *Ibid.*, vi. 332.   [3] *Ibid.*, vi. 330.

painful reading. Fénelon gave himself to the study of her difficulties and the attempt to guide her, with a patient diligence which was completely self-forgetful; but it is more than questionable whether his power of insight and extraordinary sympathy was an advantage to her. A director of less discrimination might have succeeded where he, with all his devotion, must be acknowledged to have failed. For in spite of the sincerity of his submission, he was at heart a mystic, and Mme. de Montbéron being of the same type as Mme. Guyon, the purest and most elevated Mysticism was more destructive to her than obvious heresy. Fénelon had the most perfect comprehension of her difficulties, because, in fact, her faults were his temptations. " I am covered with mire, and I feel that I sin perpetually because I am not guided by the Spirit. The sense of my own eminence excites me. In one way I cling to everything, and that seems incredible; in another way I hold everything lightly, for I could easily renounce most of the things that foster my vanity. I am, none the less, fundamentally devoted to myself. Finally, I cannot understand my real self. It eludes me; it seems to me to change every moment; I hardly know how to say anything which does not seem to be untrue a moment later."[1]

This passage, occurring in a letter of counsel to another, reveals the same fatal habit of introspection which darkened the inner life of Mme. de Montbéron, and explains the eagerness of his efforts to exorcise a temptation of which he understood the danger. In spite of the constant occupations which his position entailed

[1] *Correspondance de Fénelon*, vi. 194.

and the public and private anxieties that filled the later years of his life, Fénelon devoted himself to her as though her peace of mind was his main object of ambition, and she, by the persistence of her self-inflicted torments, made perpetual demands on his compassion. Once having undertaken his office towards her he found his position to be one of infinite difficulty, and his sincere desire for her welfare—a desire evidently supported by personal regard as well as by the instinct of his calling—prevented him from severing the connection on any of the frequent opportunities that offered. Again and again, at a crisis of her morbid self-analysis, she accuses him of indifference, of contempt, of deliberate deception, and though his patience never fails him, his replies betray that he was not invulnerable, that her reckless charges made him doubtful of himself. " God is my witness that I have never meant to fail you in anything. I do not say so from courtesy or in the wish to comfort you. He knows that nothing would make me say that which I do not believe precisely true. But, putting aside what is past, and considering the present only, allowing that I did fail you, is that a good reason for treating God as I have treated you, and failing towards Him as I have failed towards you? Would you make God as displeased with you as you are with me? You believe it to be God's will that I should help you to serve Him and do His will; I am ready to do so. I offer myself with all my heart. Take me as I am, dull, discouraging, irregular, neglectful, lacking in attention and in tact. For your sake I will reform, and the desire to do well on your account will uphold me. Nevertheless, seek through me the will of God, of whom I am the vile and unworthy instrument, rather than my personal failings."[1]

"God, of whom I am the unworthy instrument," that is at once his defence and his support amid the many difficulties of his calling. He did not require a belief from others which he did not hold himself, but the sense of the presence of God, which is the fundamental conviction of the true mystic, involved direct and perpetual divine guidance. "Put aside all pride of intellect and soaring speculations; open your heart to Him and tell Him everything. Then, having done so, listen for His voice. You should have so prepared yourself that your whole being waits silent for His utterance, that your heart lies open to the impress of His wishes. This silence of our being, suspending our earthly passions, our human thoughts, is absolutely essential if we would hear the Voice which summons us to the entire sacrifice of self, to worship God in spirit and in truth."[2] Such was his conception of the mystic's prayer, an ideal which is reiterated with no essential difference in his sermons and published works as well as in his private letters. It interprets his view of the position of the priests, and by it he believed that they attained to the sublime condition of quiescence which he describes, and did indeed become God's agents, so that the faithful might have relied as confidently in the divine inspiration of their counsels as in the divine transformation of the worthless bread at the celebration of Mass.[3]

But Mme. de Montbéron was incapable of accept-

---

[1] *Correspondance de Fénelon*, vi. 301.
[2] *Ibid.*, v. 36.
[3] See letter to Mme. de Montbéron, *Ibid.*, vi. 369.

ing so plain a doctrine; Fénelon did not misjudge her when he told her that she failed completely in escaping from herself. "The system of direction is an intercourse which should have nothing human in it," he wrote to her. But the personal element was never banished in their relations to each other, and her self-consciousness neutralised his endeavours to raise her meditations to that celestial level to which the mystics constantly aspired. She was as sensitive to his shortcomings in his dealings with her as she was to her own lapses from her ideal of sanctity, and again and again she seems to have overwhelmed him with indignation and reproach, and desired to seek another director. Fénelon refused to resign his office, however, being well aware that she was only yielding to a passing impulse, and that it would be hard to find the patience that her moods required from any other helper. The strength and dignity of his self-control appear in his replies to these outbreaks. "It is not a question either of me or of any other person, my dear daughter; we are concerned with God only. I forgive you for the most outrageous fancies about me. I do not regard myself, thank God! But in spite of this insult, which I have not deserved at your hands, your true interests are so dear to me that I would gladly give my life to prevent you from ruining the work of God in you. . . . Allowing that all the wild imaginations of your fancy were true, resign yourself freely to them, setting no limit on their duration. Submit yourself to me, simply by faith in God, without regarding me."[1]

Absorbed in his labour for the woman's soul, Fénelon

---

[1] *Correspondance de Fénelon*, vi. 360.

may well have forgotten to be mindful of her vanity. But the position was a strange one. She had been one of the clever women of the society that included Mme. de Sevigné, and her admiration for Fénelon evidently had reference to the intellectual and literary as well as to the spiritual side of his personality. She was ready at one moment to expose every detail of her inmost thoughts, and the next, convinced that his knowledge of her folly must lower his opinion of her, to charge him with betraying a contempt of which he was incapable. To the last he never realised the true obstacle to a durable understanding between them, or that he—the Fénelon of Paris and Versailles, the author of *Télémaque*, and the chosen friend of his little prince—was too much a part of the principles he inculcated to be separated from them in the mind of a woman such as Mme. de Montbéron. She was morbid and introspective in the last degree. With every step she leaned more heavily on the supports that were intended to strengthen her at starting only, and though she seems to have been sincere in her aspirations, and the tortures she inflicted on herself far exceeded any suffering she caused to others, her development remains as a striking instance of the enervating tendency of the system of confession.

Nevertheless, if she could have been self-forgetful, if she could have abandoned the lurking desire to impress him with the intense refinement of her spiritual sensibility, and simply told him of her vain gropings after holiness and her misgivings that she was destined always to grope in darkness, she could have found no surer helper than Fénelon. For the crown and glory of his belief was also the sovereign remedy for such difficulties as hers, the knowledge of the indwelling of God, the perception of Him as love, surrounding, penetrating, and enfolding, until human pride and human wishes were overwhelmed, and the submission of "man's nothing-perfect to God's all-complete" had laid every doubt to rest. "Anxiety and misgiving proceed solely from love of self. The love of God accomplishes all things quietly and completely: it is not anxious or uncertain. The spirit of God rests continually in quietness. 'Perfect love casteth out fear.' It is in forgetfulness of self that we find peace. Wheresoever *self* comes in it inflames our hearts, and for its subtle poison there is no antidote. Happy is he who yields himself, completely, finally, and unconsciously.

"I pray that God Himself will speak to you, and that you will follow faithfully what He says to you. Listen to the inward whisper of His Spirit, and follow it—that is enough; but to listen one must be silent, and to follow one must yield."[1]

With these words the series of Fénelon's letters to Mme. de Montbéron concludes. The letter is undated, and we do not know if his death or hers, or some unlooked-for development of outward circumstances, broke off their intercourse. But such a conclusion does not leave them incomplete; and if at the end Mme. de Montbéron remained the same hysterical and impracticable enthusiast that she was at the beginning, she did at least, by her demands on Fénelon's compassion, draw out from him the testimony of his inmost soul, the revelation of him-

[1] *Correspondance de Fénelon*, vi. 466.

self, that make his letters to her as a whole the most valuable among his writings. Their number and definite sequence give them a strength which is necessarily wanting to correspondence undertaken only at some special crisis in an individual life, yet there are also passages written for the succour of others in distress that contain the very essence of religion and the true spirit of sympathy. A long procession of dim figures seems to pass before him on the road to oblivion, pausing, as the winding of the way brought them within touch of him, to "stretch lame hands of faith" towards him, to meet his reassuring grasp, if only for a moment, and hear his message, which, suited though it might be to the needs of each, was yet the same for all. "Learn to seek God within yourself; it is there you will find His kingdom. You must confide your weakness and your wants to Him: you cannot do it too simply. Prayer is but love, and love tells all to God, for we need only speak to our well-beloved to tell Him all our love. And having spoken, we must listen. What may He not tell us if we do?"[1]

[1] *Correspondance de Fénelon*, v., part ii., lett. i.

CHAPTER VI

THE LAST YEARS OF EXILE

"THE best things become the most polluted, because abuse of them is worse than abuse of that which is less good;"[1] such was Fénelon's reply to those who urged the evil of the system of direction prevailing in the Roman Church, and it may be claimed for him that he gave practical evidence that in good hands the system did good work. "I ask nothing better than to help you." That—his own phrase—is the keynote of his position. He knew how to encourage the doubters, to bring hope to the sorrowful and the sinner, to set a counsel of perfection before those who had found God. The absolute sacrifice of self—the silence of the soul; this was the ideal towards which he strove himself and pointed others.

He did not think that he had reached it, or had come near to reaching it. He knew the difficulties of others because he knew himself so well. The outcry of his own sorrows and his own failure at times breaks through the expression of his sympathy. "I only ask of you what I desire for myself. I should esteem myself more of a devil than a priest if I did not aspire to that humility, simplicity, and gentleness to which I am exhorting you . . ."[2] "I have prided myself on being wise. I have

---

[1] *Œuvres de Fénelon, Lettre sur la Direction*, vol. xvii.
[2] *Correspondance de Fénelon*, v. 29.

taken delight in the creations of my brain. I have feared that the world had not a sufficiently high estimate of my capacity."[1] These were his own confessions, written when the trials of his life were nearly over; and, because he never learnt to take his stand aloof from the struggles and difficulties of the human race, he continued to the end to maintain an influence which those whose piety was more self-conscious and more confident could never reach.

Custom and thought must change in two centuries, and two centuries are nearly gone since Fénelon wrote his Spiritual Letters. Even the phraseology of the religious teachers of the past sounds strange and unfamiliar to modern ears; nor is it possible to form a judgment of his literary style from the study of such work. It seems as if he wrote them as he would have spoken, suiting himself to his knowledge of his hearers, aiming at simplicity rather than ornament, and not disdaining homely similes if they will make his meaning forcible. But if such study leave us unenlightened touching his power as an author, it cannot fail to bring us into some measure of intimacy with him as a man, for time has hardly lessened the charm and power of those thoughtful self-revealing words. The individual touch is lost, perhaps; the readers of to-day are not privileged to feel that, as he wrote, their special needs engrossed his thoughts. Yet if they need his help he will not fail them, for his letters are the reflection of himself, a storehouse of practical religion, a treasure for the humble.

[2] De Ramsai, *Vie de Fénelon*, p. 99.

THE LAST YEARS OF EXILE 383

The charge of harshness may be brought against him. He could be very rigid in his requirements, for his ideal was high; he believed that the first step towards it was renunciation, and his rule was as strict as the rule of stoicism. "The glory of man and his perfection is to emerge from himself, to forget himself, to lose himself, to be merged in the pure love of infinite beauty."[1] The condition that such words depict was not to him an extravagance of Mysticism but a vision of possible perfection, and though it echoed Molinos and Mme. Guyon, it found a counterpart yet further back in Marcus Aurelius and in Seneca. Between Fénelon and Seneca there is indeed a curious parallel; the pagan writer had evolved many of the thoughts of the Spiritual Letters, and embodied them in a form that has many points of similarity. And herein lies the strongest proof of the sureness of the goal reached by such differing roads, a proof that may be found repeated endlessly through all vicissitudes of the world's history. "The spiritual life arising from the union betwixt God and the soul"[2] recur again and again as the ideal that a man arrives at after a life spent in meditation and study of the mystery of being. It may be expressed by various phrases and shrouded with the jargon of Quietists and visionaries, but it remains a truth that to some "this union is not more mystical than certain;" "wherever self dwelleth not, there love has her dwelling,"[3] so that the conclusion of St. John, " he that dwelleth in love dwelleth

---

[1] Joseph Hall, "Christ Mystical."
[2] *Ibid.*
[3] Jacob Boehme, *Steifel*, xi. 527.

in God and God in him," is, in fact, the foundation of all Mysticism.

Fénelon himself would not have grounded his claim to be regarded as a religious teacher on his Spiritual Letters. They were intended to meet special needs, but the needs were in their nature evanescent, and the work which he intended to be the expression of his doctrine was the treatise, *Sur l'Existence de Dieu*, which he began before he left the Nouvelles Catholiques, and never found leisure to develop to the proportions of his original scheme. Even the first part did not see the light till 1712, and the second was reserved till three years after his death. At the present time the Spiritual Letters are far more widely read, owing partly to the fact that a foundation of belief that pays no heed to the discoveries of modern science must necessarily be incomplete in relation to modern thought. But on the metaphysical philosophers of the eighteenth century the book made a profound impression; the speculations of Descartes had aroused a host of critics and opposers, and Fénelon based his arguments on the system of the French philosopher. Thomas Reid, in his criticism on the various schools of philosophic thought prevalent in his day, can turn from Locke and Hume and Shaftesbury to recognise the logical faculty of Fénelon: "I remark in passing that his interpretation of the *criterium* of Descartes is the most intelligible and the most favourable that I ever came across."[1]

Fénelon's method is an endeavour to trace back the instincts and inclinations of man to their first causes,

[1] Works of T. Reid, vol. v., p. 37, "The Intellectual Faculties of Man."

THE LAST YEARS OF EXILE 385

to attempt to account for the unaccountable, and by reducing each attempt to an absurdity, to evolve evidence of divine origin, of soul and conscience, of the something within ourselves, "the Eternal not-ourselves that makes for righteousness," and cannot be completely disregarded.

"Whence comes this wondrous impression of the Infinite which is derived from infinitude itself and has nothing that suggests the finite in it. It is in myself; it is more than myself; it appears to be everything, and myself nothing. I cannot eradicate it, or cloud it, or lessen it, or contradict it. It is in me; I did not put it there, and I only found it there because it was already there before I sought it. It remains the same even when I do not think of it, and am thinking of other things. I find it again whenever I seek it, and it often suggests itself although I do not seek it. It does not depend on me; I depend on it. If I wander away it recalls me; it corrects me, it revises my opinion."[1]

The development of his argument is not flawless, because Fénelon was so imbued with the dogma of his faith that unconsciously he accepts as postulates what could not be so regarded by men of absolutely unbiassed mind; yet the truth he finally arrives at is practically the same as the conclusion of Matthew Arnold: "The only real happiness is a kind of impersonal higher life; he that loves his life does really turn out to lose it." If that can be established, it needs no sophistry to trace the self-effacing instinct to its source in a God-given personality, an inner being, that may be hidden, but

[1] Œuvres de Fénelon, i., Sur l'Existence de Dieu, part ii., ch. ii., proof 2.

cannot be eliminated by the claims of the conscious self. Fénelon's own words will give the clearest impression of the faith without which he would have no claim to live in the memories of men, and it will be seen by his own testimony that his faith went far deeper than any of the dogmas dictated from the Vatican, so that a share in it cannot be limited to those who acknowledge the supremacy of Rome. Such a passage as the following goes beyond sectarian trammels, and belongs to all who claim it for their own, whatever be their nation or their creed : " I find in my nature a something instinctive which is absolutely real, something which is within me, yet not of me ; which is above me, yet which is in me even when I do not know it ; something with which I am alone even as though it were myself, which is truly nearer to me than myself. This something, so near, so wonderful, yet impossible to understand, must needs be God. This it is which shows me, little by little, as my limitations will permit, such things as it is needful I should know.

" The same God who gave me being gave me thought, for my being is in thought. The same God who gave me thought is not only the creator, but the object of it, at the same time infinitely comprehending and infinitely comprehensible. Thus all proceeds from Him, all comprehension, all comprehensibility, all being; there is nothing that is not of Him; we cannot understand or be understood save through Him." [1]

It is seldom that the introspective efforts of the mystics have found such definite expression, and here

[1] *Sur l'Existence de Dieu.*

Fénelon, the convinced and loyal Romanist, stands upon equal ground with Gordon, who yielded no allegiance to any Church, for both believed that a knowledge of the indwelling of God was the deepest truth in all religions. Fénelon has developed the thought enough to suggest its infinite significance. Many of the mystic writers are content to reiterate the conviction that satisfied themselves, without considering the further speculations which would naturally occur to others whose minds were differently constructed; but Fénelon had never completely merged his reasoning faculty in Mysticism, and therefore was able to allow for its demands. "Shall I deny that He is everywhere?" he says, in a vain endeavour to define that which is indefinable even in thought. "I will admit it in the general and imperfect sense; but I cannot acknowledge His corporal presence anywhere, for His presence cannot conform to our conceptions. I acknowledge in Him a Presence that is boundlesss: at any moment one can say of God, 'He is,' not requiring to say 'He is to-day,' and thus in any place one may say 'He is,' not 'He is here.'

"The only way to contemplate the eternal immensity of God is to realise that He is above time and place, that all question of time and place is irreverent towards Him. The knowledge of greatness and eternity are in close connection; they are, indeed, the same, for they represent Being without limit. Banish all thought of limit, and vain questions will no longer trouble you. God is: whatever you may add to those two words, on whatever pretext, can only confuse them, and cannot make them plainer."[1]

[1] *Œuvres de Fénelon*, i., *Sur l'Existence de Dieu*.

It is strange to find Fénelon, who spent the best years of his life in fruitless controversy, reverting to the simplest expression of all faith, and acknowledging its infinite comprehensiveness; yet he would have failed as a practical teacher, he would have failed in sympathy and wisdom, and left undone the life-work that was set him, if the abstract truth of his belief had not possessed him with such profound conviction. For this reason, our knowledge of his inner life (which meant far more in his experience than any of the great events which find a place in history) would be incomplete without the unfinished book whose proofs and arguments are now grown obsolete; and yet, if he had lived the student's life which must have had so much attraction for him, and left a literary achievement that satisfied himself, it would not bring him closer to us. The chief failing of the book as it exists is its inevitable obscurity, and the more such a theme is elaborated the deeper does its obscurity become.

The Letters on Metaphysics and Religion are placed in the standard edition of Fénelon's works as a sort of sequel to the treatise *Sur l'Existence de Dieu*, but at the present day they are less worthy of attention, and at the time of writing were the result of a definite demand for his opinion on one or other of the difficult questions that disturbed the thoughtful, and not the spontaneous expression of his own convictions. Two of them, however, derive a special interest from the fact that they were written in answer to the Duc d'Orleans, afterwards the Regent, whose reputation does not suggest that abstruse theological enigmas would have disturbed him very seriously. But it has been already pointed out that there

THE LAST YEARS OF EXILE   389

was a fashion for such intricate topics in the later years of Louis XIV. M. d'Orleans may have been influenced by it, and the particular theory that he seems to have desired Fénelon to corroborate was in keeping with his character and way of life. If his moral sense was not completely petrified, the assurance that man had no power of free-will, but was predestined to the career of virtue or of vice which he pursued, would have acted as a salve to any discomfort his conscience may have caused him, and it is, moreover, an acknowledged attribute of the Roman Church that those who have been brought up within her fold are especially susceptible to the recurrence of the claims, supernatural rather than religious, of powers whose existence cannot be forgotten. So much reliance is placed by the Roman Catholics on the supernatural, that it is to her priests rather than to any other Christian ministers that the sinner troubled by misgivings would turn instinctively.

The question suggested by the terms, grace, predestination, and free-will, were much discussed at that period. Malebranche the Oratorian wrote his great work, *La Recherche de la Verité*, when Fénelon was at the Nouvelles Catholiques, and for many years afterwards his works as they appeared were a fruitful topic of dispute among theologians of every school. The *Traité de la Nature et de la Grace*,[1] which was published when the friendship of Fénelon and Bossuet was at its zenith, inspired Fénelon to a refutation corresponding in its main points with his subsequent letters to M. d'Orleans. The subtleties of the theory propounded by Père Malebranche are difficult to

[1] Condemned by the Pope, May 1690.

follow; he desired to prove that God limits Himself to a simplicity of method, which he terms "order," in the direction of His creatures, and in his eagerness to deny free-will to man, denies it even to God Himself. His manner of proving it is, briefly, this:—

"Anything which is not included in God's design is against natural order.

"That which is against natural order is contrary to the Spirit of God.

"That which is contrary to the Spirit of God is evil, and therefore impossible.

"But that which is impossible cannot be within the scope of God's intention in any sense.

"Therefore the future cannot be in any sense conditional, because, as part of God's perfect scheme, it can have but one development."[1]

There is a very evident flaw in the last words of the third clause of the argument, because to the finite intelligence the existence of evil is not impossible. But Fénelon refuted the whole proposition on the same ground, that of the primary impossibility of assuming a limit to the power of the Almighty. Malebranche asserted that the natural order of creation was infinitely perfect, that it was blasphemy to regard it otherwise, because it had been ordered by the will of God. St. Augustine seems to have foreseen the difficulty, and answered it in saying—that the imperfection of a part may be necessary to the perfection of the whole, perfection in humanity has been reached once only, for that which is not God Himself is necessarily imperfect. And

[1] *Œuvres de Fénelon*, iii. p. 31.

Fénelon, carrying the thought a little further, suggests the principle of evolution in predicting the boundless development not only of humanity, but of creation.

The labyrinth of speculation in which the leaders of such a controversy involved themselves is thus indicated; but Fénelon, while he sympathised with the aim of every seeker after truth, was ardent in defence of the doctrine of free-will, for he had come so near to Quietism in the days of Mme. Guyon that he realised the infinite evil resulting from its negation. To deny free-will is, of course, to assert the intolerable doctrine of predestination —a doctrine that, logically, attacks the very spirit of Christianity, for it is unthinkable that the God of the New Testament created any beings to be the slaves of sin and the sufferers of punishment without the power of escape.

It is necessary to revert once more to Fénelon's own words to realise his conception of the God to whom so many sincere and earnest men have attributed complete indifference towards the human race. "The first of His gifts," he wrote, "the foundation of all others, is that which I call Self; He gave me myself. To Him I owe not only all I have, but all I am. As far as words can go we may explain it, but the mind of man can never understand the infinity of such a gift. The God who made me, gave me myself, the self I love so much I owe to His goodness, and God should be in me and I in Him (if I may so express it), seeing I derive myself from Him. Without Him I should not be myself; without Him I should not have the self I love nor the power of loving it, neither the will to love nor the thoughts whereby I know myself. All that I have and am is given me."[1]

The Father whom these words depict could not have foreordained His children to despair. The gift of grace, which taught men to work out their own salvation, might be a separate gift of Divine Beneficence, but all men possessed the knowledge of right and wrong and the power to choose which of the two appeared to them the greater good. There could be no hesitation in the minds of those to whom God was a reality, and therefore the necessity of choosing did not come home to them; but Fénelon knew how very few there were whose private interests and ambitions were overshadowed by the thought of God; they might profess to yield themselves to Him, but the claim of the world was the rule which directed them in practice.

"One can only be doubtful of the greatest good when one sees it imperfectly," he wrote, with the toleration for the delusions of others which experience had taught him; "superficial knowledge degrades it to the level of benefits which are infinitely inferior. Then the shadows that obscure it, and the distance that divides us from it, seem to equalise it with the finite things we touch and know. It is this false equality which allows man to hesitate and choose, and exert his freedom of selection between advantages that cannot really be compared. But if the greatest good should suddenly become evident, its infinite all-powerful enchantment would overwhelm all desire of free-will, and every other attraction would disappear as the shadows of night disappear before the light of

[1] *Œuvres de Fénelon*, iii. p. 306.

day. We know that most of the delights of this life are so unsatisfactory in themselves, or so insecure, that we can easily draw comparisons. As we compare, we weigh them that we may choose, and as we weigh them our inmost consciousness tells us that we are free to choose, because the claim of those things is never so strong as to destroy all balance and absolutely force our will. It is in this balancing that free-will is exercised. Take away free-will, and you take away all vice, all virtue, and all merit." [1]

This is indeed the conclusion of the whole matter. If we could see clearly, if we could remember the Spirit of Infinite Compassion which presides over the affairs of men, there would be no further question of free-will, for we should understand that to seek and follow His guidance was so convincingly the greatest good, that every other attraction would disappear "as the shadows of night disappear before the light of day." But while yet we are constrained only "to see through a glass darkly," it rests with us to grope in the midst of obscurity and misconceptions till we have found that greatest good, or to relapse into acceptance of gifts which are easier of attainment.

The pleasures of life lay very ready to the touch of M. d'Orleans, and he was not backward in grasping at them; but he pursued his career far from the influences prevailing at Cambrai, and he proved that he had but a false idea of Fénelon when he looked to him for the assurance that his evil courses were foreordained for him, and to be regarded as the will of Heaven. The only

[1] *Œuvres de Fénelon*, iii. p. 355.

concession that Fénelon would make in favour of Malebranche was of no satisfaction to the Regent, and, in making it, he involves himself in the unending complications that must ensue on the attempt to penetrate mysteries which are in truth unthinkable; for, while maintaining that man is absolutely master of his fate, he adds that God foresaw the destiny of every individual, the choice for good or ill each one would make, before the beginning of the world—an idea which seems to negative our conception of free-will.

Fénelon's metaphysical conjectures were, in fact, less logical than his purely spiritual meditations. The "Religion of Experience" was a part of himself, and his exposition of it is, therefore, strangely luminous and convincing; but in questions of abstract thought he was on the same ground as other writers, and will not bear comparison with Bossuet. It should, however, be remembered, in any criticism of his writings, that, with a very few exceptions, what he wrote was intended to meet the need of the moment only. The first part of the work *Sur l'Existence de Dieu*, the volume containing *l'Education des Filles*, and *Le Ministère des Pasteurs*, and a few of the *Dialogues des Morts*, were published during his lifetime. Also the mandements and essays resulting from the Jansenist and Quietist controversy were made public as soon as they were written, although Fénelon himself disliked intensely the *éclat* such a system lent to the squabbles of ecclesiastics. Otherwise he wrote for a few only. He never seems to have realised the extent of his literary power, and was content to give to individuals the fruit of a brain which might have inspired and

THE LAST YEARS OF EXILE 395

directed contemporary thought. His condemnation by the Pope did not deter the loyal servants of the Church from consulting him on difficult points of faith. He had many such applications, and he brought to each his full powers of reflection and of sympathy; but the reply which seems to witness most to his wisdom in dealing with them is that addressed to Père Lami, a Benedictine monk, who engaged him in a prolonged correspondence [1] on the disputed topics of predestination and grace.

"We shall find peace—not in subtle arguments, but in the simplicity of prayer; not in abstract speculations, but in daily practical morality; not in listening to, but in silencing, ourselves; not in flattering ourselves that we fathom the designs of God, but in accepting perpetual ignorance of them, content to love Him, regardless of the uncertainty of a salvation towards which we never cease to yearn." [2]

The Benedictine gloried in "pure love," and was imbued with the doctrine of the Quietists; therefore, such a reply was the perfection of sympathy, for it combines a suggestion of the purest Mysticism with a warning against that excessive reflection upon the mystery of God's design, which was especially a snare to those who had embraced monastic rule.

The manifold occupations of Fénelon's life at Cambrai, perhaps also his separation from the more exciting influences that swayed the thoughts of others, gave him in later life a moderation and a clear grasp of the essentials of belief which he had not attained at the time of the

[1] See *Œuvres de Fénelon*, iii., *Lettres sur la Religion*, 3, 4, 5.
[2] *Ibid.*, *Lettre* 3.

Quietist controversy. He was no less a mystic, but he had fuller knowledge of the actual need of men at the crises of their experience, when bereavement or remorse has momentarily snatched away the veil that shrouds reality, and understood that he could not meet it by theories of pure love and passive acquiescence. Although his years of exile were years of self-suppression and he never relaxed his efforts after the ideal that he had set before him at Saint-Sulpice, not only did he fail to reach that sublime condition of indifference to which the Quietists aspired, but, as old age approached, the gaps that death had made in the ranks of those he loved seem to have taught him to shrink from death itself as the instrument of human suffering. He is reasoning for himself when he reasons on this point with others, and was the more efficient helper for the dying because he had personal knowledge of their fears.

"If we renounced everything every day of our lives, we should not have much to renounce when it came to the last day," he wrote, "and that which terrified us at a distance would lose its terror when close at hand if we abstained from nourishing our dread with anxious speculations. To die daily will rob our final death of all its sharpness."[1]

That was his nearest approach to insensibility towards the thought of death. There was too much vitality inherent in him for the dread uncertainty that lay before him not to seem appalling, although the faith that ruled his life contained the assurance that death was gain for such as he. The ever-recurring conflict of

[1] *Correspondance de Fénelon*, vi 175.

physical instincts warring against the law of the mind disturbed the tranquillity of his outlook on the future. He had preached that "not to desire death implies not that we have not aspired after an extreme height of virtue, but that we have never reached it."[1] He was always ready to apply his own precepts to himself, and a sense of his own shortcomings in this particular gave additional sadness to the meditations of his later years. To love, with as near an imitation of the love of Christ as man may reach, had been the goal of his endeavours; but the perfect love that casteth out fear was beyond his scope, and his failure seemed to him to be the proof of a secret faithlessness. A modern philosopher, whose reason denied him the hope of immortality, declared that "death was the surest signpost to religion." It may be also claimed that death reveals the flaws in faith that were unsuspected while life held firm dominion.

Death came on Fénelon swiftly, but the thought of it had been present with him constantly since de Langeron had left a vacant place in the intimate circle of his friends. He had not then completed his sixtieth year, but thenceforward the familiar faces that represented all his happiness in life passed from him into mystery and silence in quick succession, and each new loss weakened a physique that had been always frail. In November 1714 an accident, which he regarded lightly at the time, entailed a shock to his system from which he did not recover. His carriage, in passing over a bridge, was overturned, and he describes the incident in a letter to the Chevalier

[1] *Œuvres de Fénelon*, xvii. 359, Sermons.

Destouches, for whose benefit he was always able to muster gaiety.

"It is true, my dear fellow, that I have been in mortal danger. I cannot now understand how I escaped; but for the loss of three horses one could not have been in greater luck. All my people called out to me, '*Tout est perdu, sauvez vous!*' but the windows being up I did not hear them. I was reading a book, having my spectacles on my nose, my pencil in my hand, and my legs in a bearskin bag; Archimedes was in almost like condition when he perished at the taking of Syracuse. It is a vain comparison, but it was a frightful accident. I shall be a coward regarding bridges that are near to mills. Observe, if you please, that the mill-wheel, which touches one of the edges of the bridge, that has no rail, began all at once to turn, just at the moment we were passing. One of the wheelers took fright inopportunely, and cast us to the side where it was least desirable that he should throw himself; he saved me by his death, for he stuck the pole in a hole in the bridge, which prevented my downfall."[1]

During the month that followed the friends around him recognised that his health, which was always feeble, was failing visibly. On the first day of the new year he acknowledged that he was seriously ill, and it is evident that he had no hope of recovery. On January 7, 1715, he died.

His chaplain wrote the following account of his last illness: "For the whole of the six days he permitted only the reading of the Holy Scriptures. During the

[1] *Lettres Inedits*, 84.

first days we only yielded at intervals to his desire, fearing that the attention he gave to the reading would hinder the effect of the remedies and increase his sufferings. . . . We frequently repeated to him, and he seemed to enjoy listening to, the last verses of the fourth and the first nine of the fifth chapter of St. Paul's second epistle to the Corinthians. 'Repeat that part again,' he said to me twice. . . . The two last days and the two last nights of his illness he asked eagerly that we should read to him the texts of Scripture especially suited to his condition. He said them with us so far as his strength permitted him. It could be seen by his eyes and the expression of his countenance that he entered fervently into the strong feelings of faith, of hope, of love, of resignation, of union with God and conformity with Christ, which these texts describe. . . .

"Although he had confessed on Christmas Eve before singing the midnight Mass, he confessed afresh on the second day of his illness. In the morning of the third day he desired me to have the Viaticum administered to him; an hour later he asked if I had made all arrangements for the ceremony. When I represented that his danger did not seem sufficiently urgent, he said, 'Having reached the condition of which I am conscious, nothing can be more urgent.'

"He had himself removed immediately from the little room that he generally occupied to his state room. He wished that every member of his chapter should be able to come in and be present at this act of religion. Before receiving the Viaticum he spoke a few words of exhortation to all those present, which I, finding myself at too great a distance from his bed, could only hear indistinctly.

"In the afternoon of the fourth day of his illness M. l'Abbé de Beaumont and M. le Marquis de Fénelon, his nephews, arrived in haste from Paris; he displayed keen delight at seeing them again, and asked them who had sent word to them. Distress prevented them from speaking; they confined themselves to indicating M. l'Abbé de Fénelon, who was at Cambrai when the illness declared itself. In the morning of the *jour des Rois*, having shown me that he was grieved not to say Holy Mass himself, I went, in obedience to his order, to say it in his stead. During this brief interval he seemed to have weakened considerably, and they gave him the extreme unction.

"Immediately after, he sent for me, and, having dismissed every one from his room, dictated to me the last of his letters, which he signed, commanding me to show it to four persons here, and to despatch it the instant his eyes were closed. To dictate this letter to me he summoned all his strength, because, feeling that he was ready to appear before God, he wished to prepare himself by the declaration of his true opinions. . . .

"He suffered very much during the rest of the day and in his last night. . . . The fever increased from time to time, causing delirium, of which he was conscious, and which troubled him, although nothing violent or unworthy ever escaped him. When the paroxysm ceased we saw him join his hands, at once raising his eyes to heaven, submitting and yielding himself to God in absolute peace. . . . I am still moved when I think of

THE LAST YEARS OF EXILE 401

the impressive spectacle of that last night. All the members of his godly family who were met together at Cambrai—M. l'Abbé de Fénelon, M. le Marquis de Fénelon, M. l'Abbé de Beaumont, les Chevaliers de Fénelon, M. de l'Echelle (formerly connected with the education of M. le Duc de Bourgogne), his brother, M. l'Abbé de l'Echelle, and their nephew, M. l'Abbé Devisse—all came, one after the other, in his periods of complete consciousness, to ask and receive his blessing. Some other persons from the town, whom he directed, came to receive his last blessing. Afterwards his servants came all together, and weeping, asked it of him; he gave it to them with kindliness. M. l'Abbé Le Vayer (of the Congregation of Saint-Sulpice), superior of the seminary of Cambrai, then repeated the prayers for the dying, joining to them from time to time such brief and impressive phrases from the Scriptures as were most suited to the condition of the sufferer, who remained without sign of consciousness for nearly half-an-hour, after which he died peacefully at a quarter past five in the morning."[1]

The following is the letter dictated by Fénelon on the last day of his life; it was addressed to Père Le Tellier, Confessor to the King:—

"I have just received extreme unction. It is in this condition, reverend father, when I am preparing to appear before God, that I implore you to make my true principles known to the King. I have never been anything but submissive to the Church, and in dread of the heresies imputed to me. I accepted the condemnation of my book with absolute simplicity. There was never a

---

[1] *Relation de la maladie et de la mort de Fénelon, par son aumônier.*

moment of my life when I had not the deepest gratitude and the most ardent zeal for the person of the King, the strongest respect and the most unfeigned attachment. I take the liberty of asking two boons of his Majesty, which have no reference either to me or mine. The first is that he will have the goodness to appoint as a successor one who is pious, punctual, good, and strong against Jansenism, which has great foothold on this frontier. The other boon is that he will have the goodness to conclude with my successor that which could not be concluded with me regarding Messieurs de Saint-Sulpice. The help that I have received from them I owe to his Majesty. If his Majesty would intimate to my successor that it would be best to conclude with these gentlemen what has already gone so far, the matter will be soon disposed of. I wish for his Majesty the long life whereof the Church as much as the State stand in infinite need. If I am permitted to see God, I shall constantly ask His mercies for him. You know, reverend father, with what veneration I am, &c."[1]

No more significant tribute to the personal dominion of the Great King in the hearts of his subjects was ever paid. Fénelon lay dying; the last rites of his Church had just been rendered to him, the shadows of death were drawing very near. Yet at a moment when the glories of the world must lose their fascination even for those who love them most, he roused himself, gathered his failing strength with a great effort, and mastered the weariness of suffering, that with his last breath he might justify himself before the King. For half his life he had been urging

[1] *Correspondance de Fénelon*, iv. 415.

THE LAST YEARS OF EXILE 403

the claims of the people for justice from their rulers, and none knew better than he the faults that marred the private character and public policy of Louis XIV. He had not been dazzled by the glories of the past century. He had known the misery of the people, the wickedness of the Court. For twenty years he had been persistently misjudged and persecuted. For twenty years he had not stood in the presence of the King. Nevertheless, in his last hours the thought of the King was the thought that absorbed his imagination, the fear of the King's anger troubled him when he believed he was at peace with God. Personal loyalty was the lesson the seventeenth century had taught to the French people, and the soul of Fénelon was so far imbued with it that, mystic though he was, he believed that his King would be still his foremost thought when he stood before the throne of God.

There is no record of the effect of those last words upon Louis XIV. If remorse touched him he made no sign. It had never been his policy to own himself at fault, and the disgrace that had fallen on the Archbishop of Cambrai was never publicly reversed. He could not gauge the true value of that disgrace; his conception of his own majesty destroyed his sense of proportion, and he refused to see that Fénelon's true reputation was above injury from royal disapproval, or that posterity might dare to blame him for his conduct towards any subject who had displeased him.

The last of Fénelon's letters was directed to Versailles, but the words that close the correspondence of a lifetime were written before the certainty of death had taken possession of him. They were prophetic, none the less, of what was coming. De Beauvilliers was dead, and the dread shadow had fallen on so much that was dear to him that it seemed as if its gloom had encompassed all his world. "When the heart is sick the whole body suffers," he wrote to Mme. de Beauvilliers. "I dread these business interviews for you, and everything that revives your pain. We must join in the designs of God and try to find relief for ourselves. We shall soon regain that which we have not really lost. With great strides we draw nearer to it daily. A little more and there will be no longer need for weeping. It is we who die; he whom we love lives, and will die no more. This is what we believe, but we believe it feebly. If we believed it truly we should regard those dear to us even as Christ desired that His disciples should regard Him when He ascended to heaven. 'If you loved me,' said He, 'you would rejoice.' But we are weeping for ourselves when we weep for those whom we mourn."[1] Strained nerves and physical weakness have left their impress on that farewell to his old friend. He could not conquer his own sadness even to give her comfort. The past was bitter, but it is plain he was shrinking from the future, and that the presentiment of death—strive as he might to welcome it—weighed heavily upon him. On the same day he wrote the last of the fervent personal exhortations to piety which are so especially connected with his name. It was addressed to the son of his dead friend, the Duc de Chevreuse, and is instinct with all his natural eagerness and zeal.

"Would you not be ashamed if you had broken your

[1] *Correspondance de Fénelon*, i. 199.

word to the humblest of men as often as you have to God. You say that you love Him. Is it thus that one loves one's friends who are but miserable creatures? Would you trick them perpetually with idle promises? Does God ask too much when He requires that good faith and exactitude in keeping a promise, which a footman would be justified in desiring? What will we not put before God? Some tiresome and arduous ceremony, some occupation that simply wastes your health; some use of time of which you dare not give account; something which darkens life and degrades you in the world—this is what you prefer to God. It is a terrible hallucination! Pray! Humiliate yourself to overcome its magic! Ask God to loose you from the chain of custom and inclination! Fight against yourself; make sustained and constant effort; beware of self-deception, of the tyranny of habit, of the fine pretexts whereby one can contrive to delude oneself! Pay no heed to anything. Begin a new life; it will seem hard to you at first, but God will sustain you, and you will taste of His reward. Happy is he who relies on God, and not on himself. What would I not give to see you a different man! I ask it of God in this holy season when we should be born again with Jesus Christ. You could be—you ought to be—you must answer for it to the Master. Teach yourself by means of meditation to rely upon His Spirit." [1]

This is a fitting conclusion to the long series of his letters. It was by such vigorous attacks that he forced his friends to turn from the round of pleasure and excitement that made the life of camp and Court, and

[1] *Correspondance de Fénelon*, i. 200, to M. de Chaulnes.

remember the claim of God. He did not require that courtiers should make great profession; what he urged was a personal religion. It is the spirit of personal practical religion that inspires that last letter, and it has in it the vigour of a last appeal. Ten days later he had gone down into silence, and those whose advancement he had made his special care were left to struggle upwards as best they might, unaided.

The men who had loved him best were near him when he died, but, though elaborate eulogy was the custom of the time, it was tacitly accepted that Fénelon needed none. He had desired to be known among his people, and they needed no incentive to mourn him as a friend, and even in the far-off world of Paris there were many who looked upon the future with failing hopes and saddened hearts because Fénelon, the exile who had not been a living presence there for twenty years, had passed away.

They buried him in the cathedral at Cambrai; they paid him every tribute of honour and respect while his memory was fresh. But the deepest proof of the impression he had left in the hearts of the Flemish people is the monument that now commemorates him at Cambrai, and was unveiled by those who loved his memory on January 7, 1826, as testimony that neither time nor change of thought disturb the place assigned to him.

No public tribute was paid to him. He was the last to die of the succession of great writers and great men who made the glory of France in the reign of Louis XIV. ring throughout Europe. His prophecies and warnings heralded her decline, and it may be that it was fitting

THE LAST YEARS OF EXILE 407

that his death, coming at a moment when the misfortunes of his country were falling fast upon her, and the people looked in vain for a friend or a leader on whom the mantle of the dead might fall, should not receive an outward demonstration of mourning and regret, but be accepted as a part of the national distress, in that silence which is more significant than words or weeping.

To the last he held to his ideal of the duty of a priest. All that he could do for his friends by personal effort he never failed to do; but all he possessed was the property of the Church, and after twenty years of reign at Cambrai, during which the great income belonging to his office was at his own absolute disposal, he ended a life of persistent and rigorous self-denial with no money in his coffers and no debts to any man. In spite of his ambition, in spite of the prejudices which influenced his action at more than one important crisis, in spite of the strong affections that were so firmly rooted in his heart, his public and private life were ruled by the fundamental principle which he did not fear to proclaim again and again as his conception of the truest patriotism, "J'aime mieux ma famille que moi-même, ma patrie que ma famille, le genre humain que ma patrie."

To put that maxim into practice was not an easy task. Fénelon did not shrink from difficulty, but his life is incomplete, because to the last he knew and understood his imperfections, while the vision of perfection was ever with him.

. . . . . .

It has been said that the men who make their mark indelibly on history are those who at their entrance upon life have set a goal before them, and adhere to their one object with a concentration that squanders nothing on side issues. It is thus that men attain success, and win the admiration of their fellows, and these things were not vouchsafed to Fénelon. Yet this criterion does not exclude him, for his strength was concentrated, and his purpose never faltered. Only fulfilment was not visible or comprehensible to human eyes. Neither disgrace nor disappointment daunted him. The failure of ambition only impressed on him the more that he had a message for mankind that was above all earthly influence; and though the minds of his generation were scarcely ready for it, he found no lack of listeners, for there is an inward witness in the hearts of men in every age that only needs the summons of voices such as his. We may call him pantheist or mystic; we may detect his failures and his inconsistencies; we may see how the limitations of his narrow creed confined and hampered him at every turn; but at the end his message still remains, and his voice is not yet silent. God everywhere, God immanent, "the spiritual life around the earthly life!" that is its burden. To understand the man, to see him as he stands set apart from others, we must realise this as the absorbing truth that was his inspiration.

He stumbled often, he grew weary and discouraged; the burden that humanity must bear seemed to him to be almost overwhelming; but he believed that God had guided him, that in the darkness that Presence could not leave him, because throughout his life—"closer than breathing and nearer than hands and feet"—the Spirit of Christ had been with him on his way.

APPENDIX

APPENDIX

NOTE I. TO CHAPTER I.

SAINT-SIMON ON FÉNELON.

Ce prélat étoit un grand homme maigre, bien fait, pâle, avec un grand nez, des yeux dont le feu et l'esprit sortoient comme un torrent, et une physionomie telle que je n'en ai point vu qui y ressemblât, et qui ne se pouvoit oublier, quand on ne l'auroit vu qu'une fois. Elle rassembloit tout, et les contraires ne s'y combattoient pas. Elle avoit de la gravité et de la galanterie, du sérieux et de la gaieté ; elle sentoit également le docteur, l'évêque et le grand seigneur ; ce qui y surnageoit, ainsi que dans toute sa personne, c'étoit la finesse, l'esprit, les grâces, la décence, et surtout la noblesse. Il falloit effort pour cesser de le regarder. Tous ses portraits sont parlants, sans toutefois avoir pu attraper la justice de l'harmonie qui frappoit dans l'original, et la délicatesse de chaque caractère que ce visage rassembloit. Ses manières y repondoient dans la même proportion, avec une aisance qui en donnoit aux autres, et cet air et ce bon goût qu'on ne tient que de l'usage de la meilleure compagnie et du grand monde, qui se trouvoit répandu de soi-même dans toutes ses conversations ; avec cela une éloquence naturelle, douce, fleurie ; une politesse insinuante, mais noble et proportionnée ; une élocution façile, nette, agréable ; un air de clarté et de netteté pour se faire entendre dans les matières les plus embarrassées et les plus dures ; avec cela un homme qui ne vouloit jamais avoir plus d'esprit que ceux à qui il parloit, qui se mettoit à l'aise et qui sembloit enchanter, de façon qu'on ne pouvoit le quitter, ni s'en défendre, ni ne pas chercher à le retrouver.—*Mémoires, ed. Cheruel et Regnier*, xi. p. 58, 1715.

Compare earlier description :—

"Plus coquet que toutes les femmes, mais en solide et non en misères, sa passion étoit de plaire, et il avoit autant de soin de captiver les valets que les maîtres, et les plus petites gens que les personnages."—*Ibid.*, viii. p. 420, 1711.

NOTE II. to CHAPTER II.

Provisions de Précepteur de Monseigneur le Duc de Bourgogne pour M. l'Abbé de Fénelon.

à VERSAILLES, *le* 16 *Août* 1689.

Louis, &c. À tous ceux qui ces présentes lettres verront salut.

Ayant jugé qu'il étoit temps de penser à l'éducation de notre très cher et très-amé petit-fils, le duc de Bourgogne ; nous avons voulu lui donner un Précepteur, qui puisse cultiver les bonnes dispositions qui commencent à parôitre en sa personne, en lui inspirant les sentiments de religion, et toutes les autres vertus que doit avoir un prince chrétien, et en formant son esprit aux grandes choses, par la connoissance des lettres et des sciences. Et étant informé que notre cher et bien amé, le sieur François de Salignac de La Mothe-Fénelon, doyen commandataire de Carenac, a toute la probité, les bonnes moeurs et la sagesse nécessaires pour remplir dignement cet emploi, et que toutes ces qualités, jointes à sa naissance, et aux services de plusieurs de sa famille, qui ont été honorés de grandes charges et emplois dans la guerre, de la dignité de chevalier de l'ordre de Saint-Michel et du Saint-Esprit, et de la prélature, l'exciteront à nous donner, dans l'instruction de notre dit fils, toute la satisfaction que nous en devons attendre.

Serment de la Charge de Précepteur de Monseigneur le duc de Bourgogne.

Vous jurez et promettez à Dieu, de bien et fidèlement servir le Roi, en la charge de Précepteur de Monseigneur le duc de Bourgogne, de laquelle Sa Majesté vous a honoré ; que vous vous emploierez de tout votre pouvoir, à l'élever en l'amour et en la crainte de Dieu, à règler ses moeurs selon les maximes chrétiennes, et à former son esprit, par la connoissance que vous lui donnerez des lettres et des sciences propres à un très-grand prince ; que vous ne prendrez pension ni bienfait d'autre prince que de Sa Majesté ; que vous l'avertirez soigneusement de tout ce que vous saurez importer à son service, et à la personne de mondit seigneur le duc de Bourgogne ; et généralement, que vous ferez, dans le devoir de cette charge, tout ce qu'un bon et fidèle sujet et serviteur est obligé de faire ; ainsi vous le jurez et promettez.—*Registres du Secrétariat de la Maison du Roi*, 1689, tome E.

NOTE III. TO CHAPTER IV.

FÉNELON AND THE KING.

Loin de ressentir quelque peine de ma situation présente, je me serois offert avec joie à Dieu pour mériter la sanctification du Roi. Je regardois même son zèle contre mon livre comme un effet louable de sa religion, et de sa juste horreur pour tout ce qui lui paroit nouveauté. Je le regardois comme un objet digne des grâces de Dieu. Je me rappelois son éducation sans instruction solide, les flatteries qui l'ont obsédé, les pièges qu'on lui a tendus pour exciter dans sa jeunesse toutes ses passions, les conseils profanes qu'on lui a donnés, la défiance qu'on lui a inspirée contre les excès de certains dévots et contre l'artifice des autres, enfin les périls de la grandeur, et de tant d'affaires délicates. (Au Duc de Beauvilliers, Cambrai, 26 Août 1697.)—*Correspondance de Fénelon*, i. 14.

NOTE IV. TO CHAPTER V.

BOSSUET TO HIS NEPHEW.

Ayez courage et patience ; vous travaillez *pour la cause de l'Église* : il s'agit d'exterminer une corruption et une hérésie naissante. Si le roi n'était persuadé qu'à Rome on prendra des mesures justes pour finir et pour accomplir les saintes intentions du Pape, on ne sait quelle résolution il prendrait pour mettre fin à une cabale qu'il voit sous ses yeux et qu'il supporte avec une modération digne de respect ; mais ce prince veut terminer une affaire de l'Église par des moyens ecclésiastiques.

VERSAILLES, *Mars* 10, 1698.

C'est une bête féroce qu'il faut poursuivre pour l'honneur de l'épiscopat et de la verité jusqu'à ce qu'on l'ait terrassée. Saint-Augustin n'a-t-il pas poursuivi Julien jusqu'à la mort ? (Abbé Bossuet to his uncle, Rome, November 25, 1698.)

NOTE V. TO CHAPTER V.

BOSSUET—RELATION SUR LA QUIÉTISME.

À MARLI, *Jeudi* 26, 1698.

M. l'évêque de Meaux, qui est de ce voyage, présenta au roi, le matin, un livre dans lequel il explique la conduite q'il a eue avec M. de Cambray, et ou il fait le détail des opinion de Mme. Guyon. Ce livre est une forte condamnation de tout le procédé de l'archevêque de Cambray dans cette affaire. M. de Meaux donna l'après dinée ce livre à beaucoup de courtisans que sont ici ; le roi en parla à sa promenade, et dit qu'il n'y avoit pas un mot dans ce livre qui ne fût vrai.—*Journal de Dangeau*, vol. vi.

NOTE VI. TO CHAPTER V.

LETTRE DE LOUIS XIV. AU PAPE INNOCENT XII.
(*Commencement de l'affaire de Quiétisme*).

TRÈS-SAINT PÈRE,—Le livre que l'archêveque de Cambrai a composé ayant depuis quelques mois fait beaucoup de bruit dans l'Église de mon royaume, je l'ai fait examiner par des évêques et par un grand nombre de docteurs et de savants religieux de divers ordres. Tous unanimement, tant les évêques que les docteurs, m'ont rapporté que le livre était très mauvais et très dangereux, et que l'explication donnée par le même archevêque n'était pas soutenable. Il avait déclaré dans la Préface de son livre qu'il voulait seulement expliquer et étendre la doctrine de ces mêmes évêques. Mais après avoir tenté toutes les voies de douceur, ils ont cru être obligés en conscience de faire leur Déclaration sur ce livre et de la mettre entre les mains de l'archevêque de Damas nonce de Votre Sainteté auprès de moi. Ainsi très-saint Père, pour terminer une affaire qui pourrait avoir des suites très-fâcheuses si elle n'était arrêtée dans son commencement, je supplie humblement Votre Sainteté de prononcer le plus tôt qu'il lui sera possible sur ce livre et sur la doctrine qu'il contient, assurant en même temps Votre Sainteté que j'emploierai toute mon autorité pour faire exécuter ses décisions, et que

Je suis, très-saint Père, votre très-dévot fils,
LOUIS.

à MEUDON, *ce 26 Juillet* 1697.

MEMOIRE ENVOYÉ À ROME PAR LE ROI
(*La fin de l'affaire de Quiétisme*).

Sa Majesté apprend avec etonnement et avec douleur qu'après toutes ses instances, et après tant de promesses de Sa Sainteté, réitérées par son nonce, de couper promptement jusqu'à la racine, par une décision précise, le mal que fait dans tout le royaume le livre de l'archevêque de Cambrai, lorsque tout semblait terminé, et que ce livre était réconnu rempli d'erreurs par tant de congregations des cardinaux, et par le Pape lui-même les partisans de ce livre proposaient un nouveau projet qui tendait à rendre inutiles toutes les délibérations et à renouveler toutes les disputes. Le bruit repandu dans Rome de ce projet le fait consister dans un certain nombre de canons qu'on donnerait à examiner aux cardinaux, dans lesquels l'établirait la saine doctrine sur la spiritualité, en laissant le livre en son entier.

Cette discussion, plus difficile que toutes celles qui ont précédé sur la censure des propositions, ou se ferait précipitamment et sans l'exactitude requise dans un ouvrage si délicat, ou rejetterait cette affaire dans de nouvelles longueurs dont on ne sortirait jamais ; et cependant le mal, qui demande les remèdes les plus efficaces et les plus prompts irait toujours en augmentant, comme il a fait, jusqu'à l'infini. On verrait naître tous les jours de nouvelles difficultés et de nouveaux incidents par les subtiles interprétations d'un esprit fecond en inventions captieuses ; comme il parait par tous ses écrits.

Ainsi, loin de terminer par un seul coup, en prononçant sur le livre et sur sa doctrine, comme il a été tant de fois promis, les disputes qui mettent le feu dans son royaume, Sa Majesté les verrait croître sous ses yeux, sans que le Pape, à qui il a eu recours avec une révérence et confiance filiale, daignât y apporter le remède. Ce qui étonne le plus, c'est qu'on ait ce ménagement pour un livre reconnu mauvais, et pour un auteur qui voudrait se faire craindre, encore qu'il ait contre lui tous les évêques du royaume et la Sorbonne, dont deux cent cinquante docteurs viennent encore d'expliquer leurs sentiments. Sa Majesté ne peut croire que, sous un pontificat comme celui-ci, on tombe dans un si facheux affaiblissement ; et l'on voit bien que Sa Majesté ne pourra recevoir ni autoriser dans son royaume que ce qu'elle a demandé et ce qu'on lui a promis, savoir, un jugement net et précis sur un livre qui met son royaume en combustion, et sur une doctrine qui le divise ; toute autre décision etant inutile pour finir une affaire de cette importance, et qui tient depuis si longtemps toute la chrétienté en attente. Il est visible qui proposent ce nouveau projet, à la fin d'une affaire tant examinée, ne songent pas a l'honneur du Saint-Siege dont ils ne craignent point de commettre d'autorité dans un abîme de difficultés, mais seulement à sauver un livre déjà reconnu digne de censure.

Il serait trop douleureux à Sa Majesté de voir naître parmi ses sujets un nouveau schisme, dans le temps qu'elle s'applique de toutes ses forces à éteindre celui de Calvin. Et si elle voit prolonger, par des ménagements qu'on ne comprend pas, une affaire qui paraissait être à sa fin, elle saura ce qu'elle aura à faire, et prendra des résolutions convenables ; espérant toujours néanmoins que Sa Sainteté ne voudra pas la réduire à de si facheuses extremités.

VERSAILLES, *Février* 1699.

NOTE VII. to CHAPTER VI.

Télémaque.

J'exécute avec la plus grande joie du monde, l'ordre que vous me donnez de vous parler du Livre intitulé, *Les Aventures de Télémaque*. Il est certain que c'est un Ouvrage de l'Archevêque de Cambray; et qu'il a donné pour Thême à son Disciple, le Duc de Bourgogne, les principales Reflexions qui se trouvent dans ce Livre. Je ne l'ai point lu encore. On n'en imprima d'abord qu'une petite partie: mais enfin, un Libraire de la Haie en a recouvré une Copie complète, qu'il a fait imprimer en quatre ou cinq petits Tomes. On fait grand cas de cet Écrit. On trouve que le Stile en est vif, heureux, beau; le tour des Fictions bien imaginé, &c.: mais, sans doute, ce qui a le plus contribué au grand succès de la Pièce, est que l'Auteur y parle selon le gout des Peuples, et principalement des Peuples qui, comme la France, ont le plus senti les mauvaises suites de la Puissance arbitraire, qu'il a touchées et bien exposées. (M. Bayle à Lord Ashley, Rotterdam, Novembre 23, 1699.)

NOTE VIII. to CHAPTER VII.

Saint-Simon on Le Tellier.

Sa vie étoit dure, par goût et par habitude; il ne connoissait qu'un travail assidu et sans interruption; il l'exigeoit pareil des autres, sans aucun égard, et ne comprenoit pas qu'on en dût avoir. Sa tête et sa santé étoient de fer, sa conduite en étoit aussi, son naturel cruel et farouche. Confit dans les maximes et dans la politique de la Société, autant que la dureté de son caractère s'y pouvoit ployer, il étoit profondément faux, trompeur, caché sous mille plis et replis, et quand il put se montrer et se faire craindre, exigeant tout, ne donnant rien, se moquant des paroles les plus expressément données lorsqu'il ne lui importoit plus de les tenir et poursuivant avec fureur ceux qui les avoient reçues. C'étoit un homme terrible, qui n'alloit à rien moins qu'a destruction, à couvert et à découvert, et qui parvenu a l'autorité ne s'en cacha plus. . . . Son extérieur ne promettoit rien moins, et tint exactement parole ; il eût fait peur au coin d'un bois : sa physionomie étoit ténébreuse, fausse, terrible ; les yeux ardents, méchants, extrêmement de travers : on étoit frappé en le voyant.—*Cheruel*, vol. viii.

NOTE IX. TO CHAPTER VI., PART II.

TESTAMENT DE FÉNELON.

Au Nom du Père, du Fils, et du Saint-Esprit.

Quoique ma santé soit en l'état ou elle est d'ordinaire, je dois me préparer à la mort. C'est dans cette vue que je fais et que j'écris de ma propre main le present testament, révoquant et annullant par celui-ci tout autre testament antérieur.

I.

Je déclare que je veux mourir entre les bras de l'Église catholique, apostolique et Romaine, ma mère. Dieu, qui lit dans les cœurs, et qui me jugera, sait qu'il n'y a eu aucun moment de ma vie où je n'aie conservé pour elle une soumission et une docilité de petit enfant, et que je n'ai jamais cru aucune des erreurs qu'on a voulu m'imputer. Quand j'écrivis le livre intitulé : *Explication des Maximes des Saints, &c.*, je ne songeai qu'à séparer les véritables expériences des saints approuvés de toute l'Église, d'avec les illusions des faux mystiques, pour justifier les unes et pour rejeter les autres. Je ne fis cet ouvrage que par le conseil des personnes les plus opposées à l'illusion, et je ne le fis imprimer qu'après qu'ils l'eurent examiné. Comme cet ouvrage fut imprimé à Paris en mon absence, on y mit les termes de *trouble involontaire* par rapport à Jésus-Christ, lesquels n'étoient point dans le corps de mon texte original comme certains témoins oculaires d'un très-grand mérite l'ont certifié, et qui avoient été mis à la marge seulement pour marquer une petite addition qu'on me conseilloit de faire en cet endroit-là par une plus grande précaution. D'ailleurs il me sembloit, sur l'avis des examinateurs, que les correctifs inculqués dans toutes les pages de ce petit livre écartoient avec évidence tous les sens faux ou dangereux. C'est suivant ces correctifs que j'ai voulu soutenir et justifier ce livre, pendant qu'il m'a été libre de la faire. Mais je n'ai jamais voulu favoriser aucune des erreurs en question, ni flatter aucune personne que je connusse en être prévenue. Dès que le Pape Innocent XII. a condamné cet ouvrage, j'ai adhéré à son jugement du fond de mon cœur et sans restriction, comme j'avois d'abord promis de le faire. Depuis le moment de la condamnation, je n'ai jamais dit un seul mot pour justifier ce livre : je n'ai songé à ceux qui l'avoient attaqué, que pour prier avec un zèle sincère pour eux, et que pour demeurer uni à eux dans la charité fraternelle.

II.

Je soumets à l'Église universelle et au siège apostolique tous les écrits que j'ai faits, et j'y condamne tout ce qui pourroit m'avoir échappé au-delà des véritables bornes. Mais on ne doit m'attribuer aucuns des écrits que l'on pourroit faire imprimer sous mon nom. Je ne reconnois que ceux qui auront été imprimés par mes soins, et réconnus par moi pendant ma vie. Les autres pourroient ou n'être pas de moi, et m'être attribués sans fondemont, ou être mélés avec d'autres écrits étrangers, ou être altérés par des copistes. A Dieu ne plaise que je prenne ces précautions par une vaine délicatesse pour ma personne. Je crois seulement devoir au caractère episcopal, dont Dieu a permis que je fusse honoré, qu'on ne m'impute aucune erreur contre la foi, ni aucun ouvrage suspect.

III.

Je laisse à chaque domestique, qui se trouvera actuellement à mon service au jour de ma mort, une année entière de ses gages, outre ce qui se trouvera lui être dû jusqu'à ce jour-là. De plus, je prie mon héritier çi-dessous nommé d'examiner avec mes exécuteurs testamentaires, ce qu'il seroit peut-être à propos de faire en faveur de quelques-uns d'entre eux.

IV.

Je souhaite que mon enterrement se fasse dans l'église metropolitaine de Cambrai, en la manière la plus simple, et avec le moins de dépense qu'il se pourra. Ce n'est points un discours modeste que je fasse ici pour la forme : c'est que je crois que les fonds qu'on pourroit employer à des funerailles moins simples doivent être reservés pour des usages plus utiles, et que la modestie des funérailles des évêques doit apprendres aux laiques à modérer les vaines depenses qu'on fait dans les leurs. Pour les retributions des prêtres qui diront des masses, et pour les aumones a distribuer après ma mort, j'on laisse la décision, à mon héritier et à mes exécuteurs testamentaires, ne pouvant douter ni de leur piété ni de leur amitié tendre pour moi.

V.

Je nomme et constiue mon héritier universel, Léon de Beaumont, mon neveu, fils d'une de mes sœurs, en qui j'ai réconnu dès son enfance des sentimens dignes d'une singulière amitié, et qui n'a jamais cessé, pendant tant d'années, d'être pour moi comme le meilleur fils pour son père. Je ne lui marque rien, et je laisse tout à sa discretion, parce que je suis pleinement persuadé qu'il fera, de concert avec mes deux exécuteurs testamentaires, le meilleur usage qu'il pourra de ce qu'il trouvera le liquide dans ma succession.

VI.

Je nomme pour exécuteur du présent testament M. l'Abbé de Chanterac, mon parent, qui a été mon conseil dans ce diocèse, qui m'a témoigné une amitié à toute épreuve, et pour qui j'ai une grande vénération. Je nomme aussi M. l'Abbé de Langeron, ami précieux que Dieu m'a donné dès notre jeunesse, et qui a fait une des plus grandes consolations de ma vie. J'espère que ces deux bons amis si chrétiens ne refuseront pas leurs conseils, et leur soins à mon héritier.

VII.

Quoique j'aime tendrement ma famille, et que je n'oublie pas le mauvais état de ses affaires, je ne crois pourtant pas lui devoir laisser ma succession. Les biens ecclésiastiques ne sont pas destinés aux besoins des familles, et ils ne doivent point sortir des mains des personnes attachées à l'Église. J'espère que Dieu bénira les deux neveux que j'ai élevés auprès de moi, et que j'aime avec tendresse à cause des principes de probité et de religion dans lesquels ils ne paroissent s'affermir.

Fait à Cambrai le cinquième jour de mai de l'an mil sept cent cinq.

Signé FRANÇOIS,
Archevêque-Duc de Cambrai.

INDEX

ACADÉMIE FRANÇAISE, 344-349
Aguesseau, Chancellor d', 203, 216
Albret, Hôtel d', 67
Anselm, St., 248
Aranthon, Bishop of, 99
Arnauld, Antoine, 185, 186, 187
Arnauld, Jacqueline, 180, 185
Arnold, Matthew, 385
Aubigny, François d'. *See* Mme. de Maintenon
Aubigny, Mdlle., 310
Aubouin, 159
Augustine, St., 183, 184, 193, 238, 396
Augustinus, 182, 189, 190
Austria, 246

BASTILLE, 118, 119
Beaumont, Pantaleon, Abbé de, 223, 228, 229, 230, 234, 400, 401
Beauvilliers, Duc de, and Fénelon, 9, 31, 32, 55, 56, 122, 153, 230, 295, 299, 304, 404; and Duc de Bourgogne, 32, 58, 60, 257; position with the King, 55, 343; with Mme. de Maintenon, 32, 88, 250, 288, 290; connection with Quietism, 135, 138, 176, 296; character, 56, 297, 298, 307
Beauvilliers, Duchesse de, 32, 80, 311, 404
Benedictines, 180, 395
Bernard of Clairvaux, St., 130
Bernières, M. de, 328

Berri, Duc de, 290
Berulle, Père de, 182
Berwick, Marshal de, 277
Blois, 119
Bochart de Saron, Abbé, 195
Boehme, Jacob, 6, 383
Boileau, 160, 186
Bossuet, Bishop of Meaux, favour with the King and Mme. de Maintenon, 31, 33, 68, 69, 148; friendship with Fénelon, 9, 18, 30, 31, 32, 108, 122, 173, 389; connection with Quietism, 108-117, 171, 173, 208; bitterness towards Fénelon, 123-148, 160, 168, 169, 172, 173, 174, 177, 222, 225, 227, 299; reputation, 19, 85, 108, 168, 221, 394; influence, 20, 66, 168, 243; position towards Jansenism, 189, 192
Bossuet, Abbé, 140, 142, 148, 155, 171, 175, 176, 198, 231
Boufflers, Marshal de, 266
Bouillon, Cardinal de, 155, 175, 176, 179, 208
Bourgogne, Louis, Duc de, 39-63; and Fénelon, 156, 158, 163, 166, 229, 236, 250, 252, 261, 265, 272, 355, 359; political position, 124, 267, 341; marriage, 50, 62, 63; position with the King, 59, 61, 62, 255, 268, 270, 274, 281; advisers, 32, 58, 60, 266, 297, 307; military career, 255, 263, 266, 267,

269; attitude towards the Church, 55, 197, 199, 264, 271, 332; death, 89, 202, 247, 285, 287, 288
Bourgogne, Marie Adelaide de Savoie, Duchesse de, 50, 62, 63, 277, 285
Brabant, 268
Brussels, 189

CAMBRAI, descriptions by Abbé Ledieu, 222–227, 321–324
Cantique des Cantiques, L'Explication de, 107, 114
Carenac, Priory of, 311, 313
Cas de Conscience, 190, 202, 209, 226
Catherine, St., 130
Chamillard, M. de, 242
Chantal, Mme. de, 180
Charles VI., 247
Charost, Mme. de, 80, 104
Chaulnes, Duc de, 334, 404, 405
Chaulnes, Tables de, 263, 341
Chesterfield, Lord, 355
Chevreuse, Duc de, and Fénelon, 31, 122, 230, 288, 295, 298, 304, 326, 334, 341, 343, 404; position with Mme. de Maintenon, 32, 250, 296; with Duc de Bourgogne, 60, 266, 307; connection with Quietism, 113, 138, 176, 300; character, 299, 301
Chevreuse, Duchesse de, 80, 301, 302, 311
Colbert, 31, 250
Cologne, Elector of, 350
Conti, Prince de, 186, 199, 259
Cromwell, 306

DANGEAU, Memoires de, 61
Daubenton, Père, 198
Dauphin, Louis de France, 33, 39, 46, 47, 124, 168, 267, 284, 289, 324, 341
Dauphine, La, 69
Descartes, 384

Desmarais, Godet, Bishop of Chartres, 70, 76, 81, 82, 107, 128, 133, 134, 138, 178, 191
Destouches, Chevalier, 361, 362, 398
Devisse, Abbé, 401
Dialogues des Morts, 394
Dialogues sur l'Eloquence, 347
Diziers, 118

ÉCHELLE, Abbé de l', 223, 401
Education des Filles, Traité sur l', 32, 79, 336–339, 394
Enghien, Duc d', 186, 199
England, 25, 246, 247, 330, 348
États d'Oraison, 126, 128, 129, 131, 132
Eugène, Prince, 241, 268
Eustace, Père, 190
Examen de Conscience, &c., 256, 259, 262, 263
Existence de Dieu, Sur l', 384–388, 394

Fables de Fénelon, 41
Fénelon, Abbé de, 223, 354, 400, 401
Fénelon, Antoine, Marquis de, 9, 10, 18, 312
Fénelon, Comte de, 314, 315
FÉNELON, François de Salignac de la Mothe, birth, 9; at Saint-Sulpice, 10, 14, 15, 311, 396; first appointments, 16, 17, 22; appointed to Versailles, 33; appointed to Cambrai, 50, 52; banished from Court, 138; condemnation by the Pope, 154; death, 292, 335, 397, 398, 400, 403, 406; influence of M. Tronson, 13–15, 20, 34, 38, 329; friendship with Bossuet, 18, 30, 108, 122, 128, 129, 137, 389; relations with the King, 21, 22, 30, 34, 50, 138, 242, 251, 305, 324, 402; influence among contemporaries, 8, 17, 32, 40, 70, 76, 156, 215,

INDEX

258, 334, 343, 361, 400; influence over de Bourgogne, 39–63, 158, 163, 252, 261, 273–288, 316, 324, 355; position towards the Church, 22, 128, 134, 146, 194, 207, 227, 301, 328, 344, 350, 386, 395; friendship with de Beauvilliers, 32, 56, 230, 298, 304; with de Chevreuse, 230, 299, 301, 304; relations with Jesuits, 30, 179; with Jansenists, 30, 184, 193, 201, 208, 295; with Mme. de Maisonfort, 81–86, 222, 366; with Mme. Guyon, 7, 104, 124, 132, 141, 172, 383, 391; his life at Cambrai, 219, 225, 240, 294, 322, 332, 351, 393; his political position, 241, 249, 255, 260, 290, 321, 341; his literary position, 21, 32, 41, 79, 87, 129, 158, 209, 256, 294, 336, 344, 384, 394; personal religion, 3, 71, 106, 137, 152, 248, 303, 332, 353, 358, 374, 379, 384, 391, 408

Fénelon, Gabriel, Marquis de, 223, 251, 334, 353–360, 362, 400, 401

Flanders, 265, 268, 283

Fleury, Abbé de, 9, 51

Fontainebleau, 45, 51, 60, 293

Francis of Assisi, St., 368

Francis de Sales, St., 6, 108, 130, 180, 184, 368

Franciscans, 93, 95

Frémont, 209

Fronde, the, 182, 185, 199

GABRIELLI, Cardinal, 233
Geneva, 99
Germany, 322
Germigny, 18, 33, 124, 170, 177, 222
Gobelin, Abbé, 67, 69, 70, 72, 76
Gordon, General, 387
Grammont, Mme. de, 370
Guyon, Mme., 91–121; her theory of Quietism, 7, 84, 99–101, 106, 110, 119, 127, 300, 366, 374, 383, 391; literary works, 91, 107, 114, 124; connection with Saint-Cyr, 82, 83, 108–116; with La Combe, 101–106, 143, 144, 145; persecution, 109, 110–120, 143, 144

HABERT, Père, 189, 193, 199, 217, 230
Hall, Joseph, 6, 383
Harlai, de, Archbishop of Paris, 19, 20, 31, 114, 187, 254
Hauranne, de, Abbot of Saint-Cyran, 180
Henri IV., 264
Holland, 253
Homer, 160, 161
Huguenots, the, 6, 16, 21, 31, 179, 185, 190, 290
Hume, 384

INNOCENT XII., Pope of Rome, 5, 6, 63, 130, 138, 146, 148, 152, 170, 172
Issy, Articles of, 109, 126, 129, 173
Italy, 279

JANSENISTS, the, 30, 66 (179–211), 247, 290, 292, 300, 394
Jansenius, 181, 182, 183, 191, 201, 209
Jesuits, the, and Fénelon, 30, 175, 176, 230; bigotry, 84, 179, 183, 189; position with the King, 182, 192, 196, 204; tolerance, 66, 67, 72, 74; power, 191, 195, 208
John, St., 299, 383
Joseph I., King, 246

KEMPIS, St. Thomas à, 92, 93, 299

LA CHAISE, Père, 69, 74, 180, 190, 192, 254
La Combe, Père, 101–106, 143, 144, 145

Lami, Père, 395
La Motte, Père, 105
Langeron, Abbé de, and Fénelon, 228, 238; with de Bourgogne, 58, 235, 236; life at Cambrai, 145, 174, 309; death, 237, 239, 333, 397
La Trappe, 369
Laval, Abbé de, 223
Laval, Gui-André, Marquis de, 312, 315-320, 354
Laval, Mme. de, 311, 312, 314-320, 354
Ledieu, Abbé, 168, 171-174, 178-223, 225, 230, 240, 322, 324
Lefevre, M., 223
Le Tellier, Père, 190, 192, 193, 208, 210, 289, 401
Lettres Spirituelles de Fénelon (352-380), 382, 383, 384
Lettre sur la Direction, 381
Le Vayer, Abbé, 401
Lille, 221, 350
Locke, 384
London, 247, 257
Longueville, Duchesse de, 186
Louis XIII., 182
Louis XIV., treatment of Fénelon, 7, 21, 30, 31, 50, 52, 55, 75, 123, 170, 194, 203, 231, 241, 283, 295, 315, 343, 403; in relation to heresy, 6, 15, 23, 75, 112, 123, 185; to the Church, 25, 147, 149, 155, 206, 332; to Jansenism, 186, 192, 197-203; regard for Bossuet, 33, 174, 175; relations with de Bourgogne, 255, 268, 270, 274, 281; Fénelon's letter to him, 251, 255; his failings, 67, 75, 242, 249, 250, 291, 342; reputation among contemporaries, 7, 8, 62, 68, 156, 247, 293, 305, 326, 402; his view of Télémaque, 160, 163, 169
Louis XV., 287, 292

Lourdes, 99
Louvain, 184, 185
Louville, Comte de, 45, 47, 48, 49
Louvois, Sieur de, 250
Luçon, Bishop of, 191
Luynes, Duc de, 186

MAINTENON, Mme. de, 64-90; treatment of Fénelon, 44, 76, 88, 117, 122, 136, 150, 170, 173, 176, 180, 197, 205, 220, 240, 288, 310; of Mme. Guyon, 103, 104, 111-117; position with the King, 23, 74, 88, 90, 251, 289, 291, 332; political attitude, 75, 78, 89; intimacies, 32, 67, 69, 103, 113, 133, 188, 250, 290, 306, 309, 345; faithlessness, 89, 123, 142, 186, 204
Maisonfort, Mme. de, 80-86, 222, 223, 226, 366
Malebranche, Père, 389, 390, 394
Marais, Quartier du, 65
Marcus Aurelius, 383
Marlborough, Duke of, 241, 243, 268
Marly, 60, 61, 84, 88, 142, 186, 205, 285, 305, 307
Martineau, Père, 52
Maximes des Saints, L'Explication des, 129, 131-134, 139, 140, 153, 158, 174, 175, 185, 188, 206, 217, 233
Mazarin, Cardinal, 182, 185, 199
Meaux, 116, 143, 170, 172, 226
Ministère des Pasteurs, Traité de, 21, 394
Molière, 48, 230, 346
Molina, 183
Molinos, 5, 6, 7, 84, 106, 107, 111, 123, 127, 130, 133, 179, 383
Montan, 141, 142
Montberon, Comte de, 326, 370
Montberon, Comtesse de, 332, 370-379

INDEX

Montespan, Mme. de, 67, 68, 69, 74, 258
Montfort, Paul de, 334
Moyen Court de faire Oraison, 99, 107, 114, 126, 130, 135

NANTES, Edict of, 21, 22
Netherlands, the, 25, 246
Newman, Cardinal, 86
Nicole, 185
Ninon de l'Enclos, 69
Noailles, Cardinal de, and Jansenism, 187, 189–207, 211, 230, 292, 295 ; and Quietism, 109, 123, 128, 131, 133, 144, 146, 178, 188, 217 ; friendship with Mme. de Maintenon, 74, 81, 88, 89, 170, 188, 192, 204, 206, 306
Noailles, Duc de, 24, 28, 49, 204, 309
Noailles, Duchesse de, 309, 310

OLIER, M., 10, 11, 12, 13
Oratorians, 182, 189, 389
Orleans, Duc d' (the Regent), 61, 290, 388, 389, 393
Oudenarde, 273

PARIS, 94, 102, 131, 133, 159, 172, 181, 188, 193, 196, 198, 221, 225, 241, 315, 321, 378, 400, 406
Pascal, 66, 186, 187
Paul, St., 87, 100, 279, 399
Pelagius, 183
Pérault, 209
Peronne, 265
Phélippeaux, Abbé, 171, 172, 175, 177, 178, 198
Philip V. of Spain, Duc d'Anjou, 47, 48, 247, 324
Picquigny, Comte de, 334, 335
Pirot, 231
Port Royal, 66, 180, 181, 185, 186, 187, 190, 199, 230
Pretender, the, 268, 340
Priscilla, 141, 142

QUAKERS, 92
Quesnel, Pasquier, 189, 190, 191, 192, 195, 199, 206, 211, 217
Quietism, 51, 84, 99, 105, 110–114, 118, 122, 126, 129, 137, 154, 173, 179, 187, 189, 193, 200, 205, 208, 215, 226, 230, 248, 296, 315, 339, 383, 391, 394, 396

RACINE, 89, 186, 204, 305, 345
Rambouillet, Hôtel de, 65
Ramsai, Chevalier de, 285, 327, 330, 340
Reflexions Morales de P. Quesnel, 189, 191, 211
Reid, Thomas, 384
Relation sur la Quietisme, 141, 142, 171, 208
Retz, Cardinal de, 182
Rheims, 225
Richelieu, Cardinal, 66, 181, 182
Rigaud, 324
Rochefaucauld, Duc de la, 259
Rochelle, Bishop of, 191
Roslet, Père, 198, 199
Rouen, 203
Ryswick, Peace of, 254

SAÇI, DE, 185
Saint-Cyr, 78, 79, 80, 82, 83, 108, 112, 113, 136, 204, 240
Saint-Cyran, Abbot of, 181, 182, 183
Saint-Geran, Mme. de, 70, 114
Saint-Germain, 334
Saintonge, mission to, 22, 27, 179, 235
Saint-Louis, Ladies of, 79, 80, 81, 84, 107, 113
Saint-Simon, 39, 70, 85, 156, 167, 243, 269, 296, 299, 301, 304, 308, 325, 326
Saint-Sulpice, Congregation of, receives Fénelon, 10; institution and aims, 10, 11, 12, 43, 45, 284, 300, 311, 338, 396 ; sons, 32, 70, 135, 191, 231, 329, 401

2 E

INDEX

Scarron, 65
Scarron, Mme. *See* Mme. de Maintenon
Seminary at Cambrai, 234, 329, 330, 401, 402
Seneca, 5, 383
Sevigné, Mme. de, 66, 68, 180, 378
Shaftesbury, 384
Sorbonne, College, 131, 185, 190
Souatre, Père, 189
Spain, 48, 246, 247, 255, 321
Spanish Succession, War of the, 241, 255, 350

Télémaque, 158, 159–170, 253, 257, 261, 283, 336, 337, 340, 378
Teresa, St., 130
Tillemont, 185
Torrents Spirituels, Les, 107
Tronson, M., 10, 13, 14, 15, 19, 20, 34–38, 71, 109, 122, 131, 134, 135, 138, 329

Unigenitus, Papal Bull, 206, 209
Utrecht, Peace of, 247

VALENCIENNES, 271, 329
Vallière, Louise de la, 68, 258
Vatican, the, 139, 148, 152, 155, 170, 172, 189, 193, 198, 233, 249, 386
Vaugirard, 117, 118
Vendôme, Duc de, 267, 268, 269, 273, 274, 276, 277, 282, 283
Verceil, 102, 105
Versailles, 17, 34, 42, 43, 51, 52, 57, 58, 59, 66, 70, 71, 128, 133, 137, 141, 142, 147, 148, 153, 156, 157, 158, 163, 170, 174, 188, 194, 196, 220, 222, 228, 250, 261, 267, 275, 283, 289, 293, 305, 309, 313, 321, 326, 334, 343, 378, 403
Vincennes, 117
Vincent de Paul, St., 180, 184
Virgil, 161
Voltaire, 63, 161

WHITEHALL, 306

THE END

www.ingramcontent.com/pod-product-compliance
Lightning Source LLC
Chambersburg PA
CBHW052128010526
44113CB00034B/1022